MW00582768

EPHESIANS

WISDOM COMMENTARY

Volume 50

Ephesians

Elisabeth Schüssler Fiorenza

Linda M. Maloney
Volume Editor

Barbara E. Reid, OP
General Editor

A Michael Glazier Book

LITURGICAL PRESS
Collegeville, Minnesota

www.litpress.org

A Michael Glazier Book published by Liturgical Press

1	2	3	4	5	6	7	8	9

Library of Congress Cataloging-in-Publication Data

Names: Schüssler Fiorenza, Elisabeth, 1938– author.
Title: Ephesians / Elisabeth Schüssler Fiorenza ; Linda M. Maloney, volume editor, Barbara E. Reid, OP, general editor.
Description: Collegeville, Minnesota : Liturgical Press, 2017. | Series: Wisdom commentary ; Volume 50 | "A Michael Glazier book." | Includes bibliographical references and index.
Identifiers: LCCN 2017017247 (print) | LCCN 2017027727 (ebook) | ISBN 9780814681992 (ebook) | ISBN 9780814681749
Subjects: LCSH: Bible. Ephesians—Commentaries.
Classification: LCC BS2695.53 (ebook) | LCC BS2695.53 .S38 2017 (print) | DDC 227/.507—dc23
LC record available at https://lccn.loc.gov/2017017247

To the Already and Not Yet
First Wo/man US President:
Love Trumps Hate

Contents

Abbreviations

2 Clem	2 Clement
AB	Anchor Bible
AcBib	Academia Biblica
AJSR	*Association for Jewish Studies Review*
ANRW	*Aufstieg und Niedergang der römischen Welt: Geschichte und Kultur Roms im Spiegel der neueren Forschung.* Part 2, *Principat.* Edited by Hildegard Temporini and Wolfgang Haase. Berlin: de Gruyter, 1972–
ANTC	Abingdon New Testament Commentaries
Arist. *Pol.*	Aristotle, *Politics*
Barn.	*Barnabas*
BCE	Before the Common Era
BibInt	*Biblical Interpretation*
BibInt	Biblical Interpretation Series
BibSac	*Bibliotheca Sacra*
BJS	Brown Judaic Studies
BLS	Bible and Literature Series
BNTC	Black's New Testament Commentaries
BTB	*Biblical Theology Bulletin*
BZNW	Beihefte zur Zeitschrift für die alttestamentliche Wissenschaft

CBQ	*Catholic Biblical Quarterly*
CE	Common Era
Clem. Al. *Strom.*	Clement of Alexandria, *Stromateis*
ConBNT	Coniectanea Biblica: New Testament Series
Dial.	Justin Martyr, *Dialogue with Trypho*
Did.	Didache
ExpTim	*Expository Times*
FCB	Feminist Companion to the Bible
FSR	Feminist Studies in Religion
GBS	Guides to Biblical Scholarship
Gos. Thom.	*Gospel of Thomas*
HNT	Handbuch zum Neuen Testament
HTR	*Harvard Theological Review*
HTS	Harvard Theological Studies
HUT	Hermeneutische Untersuchungen zur Theologie
ICC	International Critical Commentary
IFT	Introductions in Feminist Theology
Ign. *Poly.*	Ignatius, *To Polycarp*
JAC	*Jahrbuch für Antike und Christentum*
JBL	*Journal of Biblical Literature*
JECS	*Journal of Early Christian Studies*
JETS	*Journal of the Evangelical Theological Society*
JFSR	*Journal of Feminist Studies in Religion*
JJRS	*Japanese Journal of Religious Studies*
JJS	*Journal of Jewish Studies*
JRE	*Journal of Religious Ethics*
JSNT	*Journal for the Study of the New Testament*
JSNTSup	Journal for the Study of the New Testament Supplement Series
JSOT	*Journal for the Study of the Old Testament*
JSOTSup	Journal for the Study of the Old Testament Supplement Series

LCL	Loeb Classical Library
LTQ	*Lexington Theological Quarterly*
LXX	Septuagint
N/A[26]	*Novum Testsamentum Graece*, 26th ed.
NIV	New International Version
NovT	*Novum Testamentum*
NPR	National Public Radio
NRSV	New Revised Standard Version
N*T	New Testament
NTS	*New Testament Studies*
OBT	Overtures to Biblical Theology
Pol. Phil.	*Epistle of Polycarp to the Philippians*
PSQ	*Political Science Quarterly*
RQ	*Restoration Quarterly*
RSR	*Religious Studies Review*
RSV	Revised Standard Version
SBL	Society of Biblical Literature
SD	Studies and Documents
SJLA	Studies in Judaism in Late Antiquity
SNTSMS	Society for New Testament Studies Monograph Series
SP	Sacra Pagina
Spec. Leg.	Philo, *On the Special Laws*
STD	Doctor of Sacred Theology
SymS	Symposium Series
TDNT	*Theological Dictionary of the New Testament*
UNT	Untersuchungen zum Neuen Testament
WBC	Word Biblical Commentary
WCS	Wisdom Commentary Series
WuD	*Wort und Dienst*
WUNT	Wissenschaftliche Untersuchungen zum Neuen Testament
ZNW	*Zeitschrift für die Neutestamentliche Wissenschaft*

Preface and Acknowledgments

The dedication "To the Already and Not Yet First Woman US President" seeks to mark the social-political location of the writing of this Wisdom Commentary. This commentary on Ephesians was written during the 2016 US presidential election campaign, in which Hillary Rodham Clinton was the first wo/man to run for president as the nominee of a major political party. She won the popular but lost the Electoral College vote. As the Women's March movement demonstrated, we already have a woman president who is the "people's president." But we do not yet have a woman president! Instead we have a president who issues executive orders that ban immigrants from Muslim countries, enforces increased deportation of undocumented residents, or issues a presidential memorandum declaring that the Dakota Pipeline's (DAPL) completion is in the national interest—to mention just a few presidential decrees. It seems that hate and prejudice are trumping love every day!

Although Hillary Rodham Clinton was extremely qualified for the presidency, the vitriolic sexism she encountered was intense and palpable. Calls to "lock her up" and "burn the witch" were heard at the Republican convention and all through the land. To Trump supporters and many mainline Republicans this was an "uppity woman" who needed to be taught subordination and deference to male power. In a short essay in *Time*, Deborah Tannen, a feminist scholar of linguistics, has pointed to this "double bind" that made a woman presidential candidate like Hillary Clinton come across as inauthentic and untrustworthy. To quote her:

> A double bind means you must obey two commands, but anything you do to fulfill one violates the other. While the requirements of a good leader and a good man are similar, the requirements of a good leader and a good woman are mutually exclusive. . . . Male candidates can have it both ways but Clinton can have it no ways. . . . The most difficult aspect of the double bind is that it is invisible; we think we are just reacting to the candidates as individuals. Yet, even the words to talk about women are drenched in gender.[1]

It is important to recognize the *Sitz im Leben* (setting in life) of this feminist commentary on Ephesians, whose injunction "wives should be submissive" was once again reinforced, whereas its message on love lost out!

It is important to recognize how the rhetoric of Ephesians still shapes our religious and political discourses and imaginations. Against this backdrop the commentary examines the political understandings of marriage and household in Ephesians as well as the roles that such understandings have played in the formation of early Christian communities and that still shape such communities today. To bring notions of Scripture and politics together can have an irritating, upsetting, and disturbing effect and can jar religious imagination and sensibilities.

Moreover, insofar as Scripture is also claimed to be the liberating word of a just and loving G*d,[2] the rhetoric of liberation appears contradictory to and incongruent with a scriptural rhetoric that advocates domination and submission. And yet both the imperial language of domination and its violence and the democratic language of communal love are encoded in Christian Scriptures. They have shaped not only religious but also cultural self-understandings and ethos throughout the centuries and still do so today. Such language of subordination and control does not just belong to a forgotten historical past. Rather, as language of Scripture, it is performative language that still determines not only Christian but also political identity and praxis today. This commentary seeks to enable readers to recognize such rhetorics of struggle against and accommodation to kyriarchal[3] mind-sets and structures today.

Needless to say, like all intellectual work, the publication of a book—especially a commentary—always owes its existence to much planning, teamwork, and labor. This one is no exception but presupposes much

---

1. Deborah Tannen, "The Self-Fulfilling Prophecy of Disliking Hillary Clinton," *Time* (March 15, 2016).
2. See n. 3 on p. xlvi on the use of G*d.
3. See n. 9 on p. xlviii for an explanation of this term.

collegial work. Foremost, I want to thank the main editor, Prof. Barbara Reid, who has initiated and shepherded this Wisdom Commentary series. Without her tremendous work, organizational skills, and genius this feminist series would not have been born. Words are not able to express the importance of this series today and in the years to come. Special thanks are also due to the publisher of the academic department at Liturgical Press, Hans Christoffersen, for making this project possible, for his tireless attention to its development, and for his enthusiastic support of the project.

My colleagues and students who have contributed important commentary and reflections to this volume also deserve special thanks. Their different voices and comments enhance this work greatly. I am sorry that illness prevented womanist ethicist Dr. Katie Cannon from submitting her contribution, but I want to thank her too for the preparatory work she had already done.

I am once again grateful to my research assistants, Ms. Kelsi Morrison-Atkins and Ms. Heather McLetchie-Leader, for tirelessly supporting the research for this book. I am grateful to Kelsi, not only for researching and checking out books, copying and scanning articles, and proofreading my texts, but also for tirelessly assisting me in the work for FSR Inc. on my sabbatical leave while she very successfully passed comprehensive exams. I also owe to her the list of abbreviations. I am grateful to Heather for polishing my English, proofreading my text, and giving me critical substantive feedback. Heather also deserves special thanks for establishing the bibliography.

I am also very indebted to the Rev. Dr. Linda Maloney, the editor of this volume, for her thorough and careful reading of the manuscript and her expert suggestions to improve it. I greatly appreciate her work, her care, and her suggestions at a time when she was overburdened with other projects of her own.

I also want to thank the workers at Liturgical Press, especially Lauren L. Murphy, Deb Eisenschenk, Colleen Stiller, and Stephanie Nix, for faithfully shepherding the manuscript through the copyediting and production process. Finally, I want to thank Harvard University Divinity School for supporting my work with a research leave.

Needless to say, as ever I am grateful to Francis and Sophia Miryam for their steadfast love and support.

Contributors

María Pilar Aquino, STD, is a professor of theology and religious studies at the University of San Diego and a member of the international advisory committee of the World Forum on Theology and Liberation. She is the author and editor of more than ten books, including *Our Cry for Life: Feminist Theology from Latin America* (Maryknoll, NY: Orbis Books, 1993) and *Feminist Intercultural Theology: Latina Explorations for a Just World* (Maryknoll, NY: Orbis Books, 2007).

Carol P. Christ is an internationally renowned Goddess thealogian. She has written or edited eight books on feminist the*logy, including *Rebirth of the Goddess* (Reading, MA: Addison-Wesley, 1997), the first feminist thealogy; *She Who Changes: Re-Imagining the Divine in the World* (New York: Palgrave Macmillan, 2003), a feminist process philosophy; and, with Judith Plaskow, *Goddess and God in the World: Conversations in Embodied Theology* (Minneapolis: Fortress, 2016), which introduces embodied theological method.

Teresa Forcades i Vila is a physician, the*logian, and Benedictine nun in the mountain monastery of Sant Benet de Montserrat (Catalonia, Spain), master of divinity (Harvard, 1997), doctor in public health (Barcelona, 2004), and doctor of sacred theology (Facultat de Teologia de Catalunya, 2007). Her publications in English include *Crimes and Abuses of the Pharmaceutical Companies* (Barcelona: Cristianisme i Justícia, 2006) and *Faith and Freedom* (Malden, MA: Polity Press, 2016).

Fulata Moyo is a scholar-activist who interrogates religious resources in search of gender justice. She is the World Council of Churches programme executive and has been a visiting scholar at Harvard Divinity School. Her research-activist interests focus on how women's storytelling and the*logies inform the quest to end sexism and violence against women. She defines sexuality as embodied spirituality of interconnectedness with mother earth, and sexual intercourse as part of lovemaking helping lovers to experience the spiritual climax. See Fulata Mbano-Moyo, *A Quest for Women's Sexual Empowerment through Education in an HIV and AIDS Context*, PhD thesis (UKZN, 2009), 26, 270.

Judith Plaskow is professor emerita of religious studies at Manhattan College and a leading Jewish feminist theologian. She is author or editor of numerous books on Jewish feminism and feminist the*logy, most recently *Goddess and God in the World: Conversations in Embodied Theology*, written with Carol P. Christ (Minneapolis: Fortress, 2016).

Adele Reinhartz, PhD (McMaster University, 1983), is professor in the Department of Classics and Religious Studies at the University of Ottawa, Canada. She was the 2015–2016 Corcoran Visiting Chair in Christian-Jewish Relations at the Center for Christian-Jewish Learning at Boston College and is the general editor of the *Journal of Biblical Literature*. Her main areas of research are New Testament, early Jewish-Christian relations, and the Bible and film. She is the author of numerous articles and books, including *Befriending the Beloved Disciple: A Jewish Reading of the Gospel of John* (Continuum, 2001), *Scripture on the Silver Screen* (Westminster John Knox, 2003), *Jesus of Hollywood* (Oxford, 2007), *Caiaphas the High Priest* (University of South Carolina Press, 2011; Fortress, 2012) and *Bible and Cinema: An Introduction* (Routledge, 2013). She was elected to the Royal Society of Canada in 2005 and to the American Academy of Jewish Research in 2014.

Young Ra Rhee is a doctoral student in the Religion, Gender, and Culture program at Harvard Divinity School. She seeks to explore the problem of gender, language, and agency in Bible studies, especially in Korean Protestant churches.

Zilka Spahić-Šiljak, PhD, chairs the TPO Foundation Sarajevo and teaches at several universities in Bosnia and Herzegovina and abroad. She has published *Women, Religion and Politics* (Sarajevo: IMIC Zajedno, 2010);

Contesting Female, Feminist and Muslim Identities: Post-Socialist Contexts of Bosnia and Herzegovina and Kosovo (Sarajevo: Center for Interdisciplinary Postgraduate Studies, University of Sarajevo, 2012); *Shining Humanity: Life Stories of Women Peace Builders in Bosnia and Herzegovina* (Newcastle-upon-Tyne: Cambridge Scholarly Publishing, 2014). Her current research at Stanford University focuses on the intersection of leadership, gender, and politics.

Haruka Umetsu Cho is a doctoral student in the Religion, Gender, Culture program at Harvard University. Her work focuses on feminist theology in East Asia, especially in Korea and Japan.

Foreword

"Come Eat of My Bread . . . and Walk in the Ways of Wisdom"

Elisabeth Schüssler Fiorenza

Harvard University Divinity School

J ewish feminist writer Asphodel Long has likened the Bible to

> a magnificent garden of brilliant plants, some flowering, some fruit-
> ing, some in seed, some in bud, shaded by trees of age old, luxurious
> growth. Yet in the very soil which gives it life the poison has been
> inserted. . . . This poison is that of misogyny, the hatred of women,
> half the human race.[1]

To see Scripture as such a beautiful garden containing poisonous ivy requires that one identify and name this poison and place on all biblical texts the label "Caution! Could be dangerous to your health and survival!" As critical feminist interpretation for well-being this Wisdom Commentary seeks to elaborate the beauty and fecundity of this

---

1. Asphodel Long, *In a Chariot Drawn by Lions: The Search for the Female in the Deity* (London: Women's Press, 1992), 195.

Scripture-garden and at the same time points to the harm it can do when one submits to its world of vision. Thus, feminist biblical interpretation engages two seemingly contradictory insights: The Bible is written in kyriocentric (i.e., lord/master/father/husband-elite male) language, originated in the patri-kyriarchal cultures of antiquity, and has functioned to inculcate misogynist mind-sets and oppressive values. At the same time it also asserts that the Bible as Sacred Scripture has functioned to inspire and authorize wo/men[2] in our struggles against dehumanizing oppression. The hermeneutical lens of wisdom/Wisdom empowers the commentary writers to do so.

In biblical as well as in contemporary religious discourse the word *wisdom* has a double meaning: It can either refer to the quality of life and of people and/or it can refer to a figuration of the Divine. Wisdom in both senses of the word is not a prerogative of the biblical traditions but is found in the imagination and writings of all known religions. Wisdom is transcultural, international, and interreligious. Wisdom is practical knowledge gained through experience and daily living as well as through the study of creation and human nature. Both word meanings, that of capability (wisdom) and that of female personification (Wisdom), are crucial for this Wisdom Commentary series that seeks to enable biblical readers to become critical subjects of interpretation.

Wisdom is a state of the human mind and spirit characterized by deep understanding and profound insight. It is elaborated as a quality possessed by the sages but also treasured as folk wisdom and wit. Wisdom is the power of discernment, deeper understanding, and creativity; it is the ability to move and to dance, to make the connections, to savor life, and to learn from experience. Wisdom is intelligence shaped by experience and sharpened by critical analysis. It is the ability to make sound choices and incisive decisions. Its root meaning comes to the fore in its Latin form *sapientia*, which is derived from the verb *sapere*, to taste and to savor something. Hence, this series of commentaries invites readers to taste, to evaluate, and to imagine. In the figure of *Chokmah-Sophia-Sapientia-Wisdom*, ancient Jewish scriptures seek to hold together belief in the "one" G*d[3] of Israel with both masculine and feminine language and metaphors of the Divine.

2. I use wo/man, s/he, fe/male and not the grammatical standard "man" as inclusive terms and make this visible by adding /.

3. I use the * asterisk in order to alert readers to a problem to explore and think about.

In distinction to traditional Scripture reading, which is often individu-alistic and privatized, the practice and space of Wisdom commentary is public. Wisdom's spiraling presence (*Shekhinah*) is global, embracing all creation. Her voice is a public, radical democratic voice rather than a "feminine," privatized one. To become one of Her justice-seeking friends, one needs to imagine the work of this feminist commentary series as the spiraling circle dance of wisdom/Wisdom,[4] as a Spirit/spiritual intellec-tual movement in the open space of wisdom/Wisdom who calls readers to critically analyze, debate, and reimagine biblical texts and their com-mentaries as wisdom/Wisdom texts inspired by visions of justice and well-being for everyone and everything. Wisdom-Sophia-imagination engenders a different understanding of Jesus and the movement around him. It understands him as the child and prophet of Divine Wisdom and as Wisdom herself instead of imagining him as ruling King and Lord who has only subalterns but not friends. To approach the N*T[5] and the whole Bible as Wisdom's invitation of cosmic dimensions means to acknowl-edge its multivalence and its openness to change. As bread—not stone.

In short, this commentary series is inspired by the feminist vision of the open cosmic house of Divine Wisdom-Sophia as it is found in biblical Wisdom literatures, which include the N*T:

Wisdom has built Her house
She has set up Her seven pillars . . .
She has mixed Her wine,
She also has set Her table.
She has sent out Her wo/men ministers
to call from the highest places in the town . . .
"Come eat of my bread
and drink of the wine I have mixed.
Leave immaturity, and live,
And walk in the way of Wisdom." (Prov 9:1-3, 5-6)

---

4. I have elaborated such a Wisdom dance in terms of biblical hermeneutics in my book *Wisdom Ways: Introducing Feminist Biblical Interpretation* (Maryknoll, NY: Orbis Books, 2001). Its seven steps are a hermeneutics of experience, of domination, of suspicion, of evaluation, of remembering or historical reconstruction, of imagination, and of transformation. However, such Wisdom strategies of meaning making are not restricted to the Bible. Rather, I have used them in workshops in Brazil and Ecuador to explore the workings of power, Condomblé, Christology, imagining a the*logical wo/men's center, or engaging the national icon of Mary.

5. See the discussion about nomenclature of the two testaments in the introduc-tion, page xli.

Editor's Introduction to Wisdom Commentary

"She Is a Breath of the Power of God" (Wis 7:25)

Barbara E. Reid, OP

General Editor

Wisdom Commentary is the first series to offer detailed feminist interpretation of every book of the Bible. The fruit of collaborative work by an ecumenical and interreligious team of scholars, the volumes provide serious, scholarly engagement with the whole biblical text, not only those texts that explicitly mention women. The series is intended for clergy, teachers, ministers, and all serious students of the Bible. Designed to be both accessible and informed by the various approaches of biblical scholarship, it pays particular attention to the world in front of the text, that is, how the text is heard and appropriated. At the same time, this series aims to be faithful to the ancient text and its earliest audiences; thus the volumes also explicate the worlds behind the text and within it. While issues of gender are primary in this project, the volumes also address the intersecting issues of power, authority, ethnicity, race, class, and religious belief and practice. The fifty-eight volumes include the books regarded as canonical by Jews (i.e., the Tanakh); Protestants (the "Hebrew Bible" and the New Testament); and Roman Catholic, Anglican, and Eastern

Orthodox Communions (i.e., Tobit, Judith, 1 and 2 Maccabees, Wisdom of Solomon, Sirach/Ecclesiasticus, Baruch, including the Letter of Jeremiah, the additions to Esther, and Susanna and Bel and the Dragon in Daniel).

A Symphony of Diverse Voices

Included in the Wisdom Commentary series are voices from scholars of many different religious traditions, of diverse ages, differing sexual identities, and varying cultural, racial, ethnic, and social contexts. Some have been pioneers in feminist biblical interpretation; others are newer contributors from a younger generation. A further distinctive feature of this series is that each volume incorporates voices other than that of the lead author(s). These voices appear alongside the commentary of the lead author(s), in the grayscale inserts. At times, a contributor may offer an alternative interpretation or a critique of the position taken by the lead author(s). At other times, she or he may offer a complementary interpretation from a different cultural context or subject position. Occasionally, portions of previously published material bring in other views. The diverse voices are not intended to be contestants in a debate or a cacophony of discordant notes. The multiple voices reflect that there is no single definitive feminist interpretation of a text. In addition, they show the importance of subject position in the process of interpretation. In this regard, the Wisdom Commentary series takes inspiration from the Talmud and from *The Torah: A Women's Commentary* (ed. Tamara Cohn Eskenazi and Andrea L. Weiss; New York: Women of Reform Judaism, Federation of Temple Sisterhood, 2008), in which many voices, even conflicting ones, are included and not harmonized.

Contributors include biblical scholars, theologians, and readers of Scripture from outside the scholarly and religious guilds. At times, their comments pertain to a particular text. In some instances they address a theme or topic that arises from the text.

Another feature that highlights the collaborative nature of feminist biblical interpretation is that a number of the volumes have two lead authors who have worked in tandem from the inception of the project and whose voices interweave throughout the commentary.

Woman Wisdom

The title, Wisdom Commentary, reflects both the importance to feminists of the figure of Woman Wisdom in the Scriptures and the distinct wisdom that feminist women and men bring to the interpretive process. In the Scriptures, Woman Wisdom appears as "a breath of the power of God, and a pure emanation of the glory of the Almighty" (Wis 7:25), who was present and active in fashioning all that exists (Prov 8:22-31; Wis 8:6). She is a spirit who pervades and penetrates all things (Wis 7:22-23), and she provides guidance and nourishment at her all-inclusive table (Prov 9:1-5). In both postexilic biblical and nonbiblical Jewish sources, Woman Wisdom is often equated with Torah, e.g., Sirach 24:23-34; Baruch 3:9–4:4; 38:2; 46:4-5; 2 Baruch 48:33, 36; 4 Ezra 5:9-10; 13:55; 14:40; 1 Enoch 42.

The New Testament frequently portrays Jesus as Wisdom incarnate. He invites his followers, "take my yoke upon you and learn from me" (Matt 11:29), just as Ben Sira advises, "put your neck under her [Wisdom's] yoke and let your souls receive instruction" (Sir 51:26). Just as Wisdom experiences rejection (Prov 1:23-25; Sir 15:7-8; Wis 10:3; Bar 3:12), so too does Jesus (Mark 8:31; John 1:10-11). Only some accept his invitation to his all-inclusive banquet (Matt 22:1-14; Luke 14:15-24; compare Prov 1:20-21; 9:3-5). Yet, "wisdom is vindicated by her deeds" (Matt 11:19, speaking of Jesus and John the Baptist; in the Lucan parallel at 7:35 they are called "wisdom's children"). There are numerous parallels between what is said of Wisdom and of the *Logos* in the Prologue of the Fourth Gospel (John 1:1-18). These are only a few of many examples. This female embodiment of divine presence and power is an apt image to guide the work of this series.

Feminism

There are many different understandings of the term "feminism." The various meanings, aims, and methods have developed exponentially in recent decades. Feminism is a perspective and a movement that springs from a recognition of inequities toward women, and it advocates for changes in whatever structures prevent full human flourishing. Three waves of feminism in the United States are commonly recognized. The first, arising in the mid-nineteenth century and lasting into the early twentieth, was sparked by women's efforts to be involved in the public sphere and to win the right to vote. In the 1960s and 1970s, the second wave focused on civil rights and equality for women. With the third wave, from the 1980s forward, came global feminism and the emphasis on the contextual nature of interpretation. Now a fourth wave may be emerging, with a stronger emphasis on the intersectionality of women's concerns with those of other marginalized groups and the increased use of the internet as a platform for discussion and activism.[1] As feminism has matured, it has recognized that inequities based on gender are interwoven with power imbalances based on race, class, ethnicity, religion, sexual identity, physical ability, and a host of other social markers.

Feminist Women and Men

Men who choose to identify with and partner with feminist women in the work of deconstructing systems of domination and building structures of equality are rightly regarded as feminists. Some men readily identify with experiences of women who are discriminated against on the basis of sex/gender, having themselves had comparable experiences; others who may not have faced direct discrimination or stereotyping recognize that inequity and problematic characterization still occur, and they seek correction. This series is pleased to include feminist men both as lead authors and as contributing voices.

Feminist Biblical Interpretation

Women interpreting the Bible from the lenses of their own experience is nothing new. Throughout the ages women have recounted the biblical stories, teaching them to their children and others, all the while interpreting them afresh for their time and circumstances.[2] Following is a very brief sketch of select foremothers who laid the groundwork for contemporary feminist biblical interpretation.

One of the earliest known Christian women who challenged patriarchal interpretations of Scripture was a consecrated virgin named Helie, who lived in the second century CE. When she refused to marry, her

---

1. See Martha Rampton, "Four Waves of Feminism" (October 25, 2015), at http://www.pacificu.edu/about-us/news-events/four-waves-feminism; and Ealasaid Munro, "Feminism: A Fourth Wave?," https://www.psa.ac.uk/insight-plus/feminism-fourth-wave.

2. For fuller treatments of this history, see chap. 7, "One Thousand Years of Feminist Bible Criticism," in Gerda Lerner, *Creation of Feminist Consciousness: From the Middle Ages to Eighteen-Seventy* (New York: Oxford University Press, 1993), 138–66; Susanne Scholz, "From the 'Woman's Bible' to the 'Women's Bible,' The History of Feminist Approaches to the Hebrew Bible," in *Introducing the Women's Hebrew Bible*, IFT 13 (New York: T&T Clark, 2007), 12–32; Marion Ann Taylor and Agnes Choi, eds., *Handbook of Women Biblical Interpreters: A Historical and Biographical Guide* (Grand Rapids: Baker Academic, 2012).

parents brought her before a judge, who quoted to her Paul's admonition, "It is better to marry than to be aflame with passion" (1 Cor 7:9). In response, Helie first acknowledges that this is what Scripture says, but then she retorts, "but not for everyone, that is, not for holy virgins."[3] She is one of the first to question the notion that a text has one meaning that is applicable in all situations.

A Jewish woman who also lived in the second century CE, Beruriah, is said to have had "profound knowledge of biblical exegesis and outstanding intelligence."[4] One story preserved in the Talmud (b. Berakot 10a) tells of how she challenged her husband, Rabbi Meir, when he prayed for the destruction of a sinner. Proffering an alternate interpretation, she argued that Psalm 104:35 advocated praying for the destruction of sin, not the sinner.

In medieval times the first written commentaries on Scripture from a critical feminist point of view emerge. While others may have been produced and passed on orally, they are for the most part lost to us now. Among the earliest preserved feminist writings are those of Hildegard of Bingen (1098–1179), German writer, mystic, and abbess of a Benedictine monastery. She reinterpreted the Genesis narratives in a way that presented women and men as complementary and interdependent. She frequently wrote about feminine aspects of the Divine.[5] Along with other women mystics of the time, such as Julian of Norwich (1342–ca. 1416), she spoke authoritatively from her personal experiences of God's revelation in prayer.

In this era, women were also among the scribes who copied biblical manuscripts. Notable among them is Paula Dei Mansi of Verona, from a distinguished family of Jewish scribes. In 1288, she translated from Hebrew into Italian a collection of Bible commentaries written by her father and added her own explanations.[6]

Another pioneer, Christine de Pizan (1365–ca. 1430), was a French court writer and prolific poet. She used allegory and common sense

---

3. Madrid, Escorial MS, a II 9, f. 90 v., as cited in Lerner, *Feminist Consciousness*, 140.

4. See Judith R. Baskin, "Women and Post-Biblical Commentary," in *The Torah: A Women's Commentary*, ed. Tamara Cohn Eskenazi and Andrea L. Weiss (New York: Women of Reform Judaism, Federation of Temple Sisterhood, 2008), xlix–lv, at lii.

5. Hildegard of Bingen, *De Operatione Dei*, 1.4.100; PL 197:885bc, as cited in Lerner, *Feminist Consciousness*, 142–43. See also Barbara Newman, *Sister of Wisdom: St. Hildegard's Theology of the Feminine* (Berkeley: University of California Press, 1987).

6. Emily Taitz, Sondra Henry, Cheryl Tallan, eds., *JPS Guide to Jewish Women 600 B.C.E.–1900 C.E.* (Philadelphia: Jewish Publication Society of America, 2003), 110–11.

to subvert misogynist readings of Scripture and celebrated the accomplishments of female biblical figures to argue for women's active roles in building society.[7]

By the seventeenth century, there were women who asserted that the biblical text needs to be understood and interpreted in its historical context. For example, Rachel Speght (1597–ca. 1630), a Calvinist English poet, elaborates on the historical situation in first-century Corinth that prompted Paul to say, "It is well for a man not to touch a woman" (1 Cor 7:1). Her aim was to show that the biblical texts should not be applied in a literal fashion to all times and circumstances. Similarly, Margaret Fell (1614–1702), one of the founders of the Religious Society of Friends (Quakers) in Britain, addressed the Pauline prohibitions against women speaking in church by insisting that they do not have universal validity. Rather, they need to be understood in their historical context, as addressed to a local church in particular time-bound circumstances.[8]

Along with analyzing the historical context of the biblical writings, women in the eighteenth and nineteenth centuries began to attend to misogynistic interpretations based on faulty translations. One of the first to do so was British feminist Mary Astell (1666–1731).[9] In the United States, the Grimké sisters, Sarah (1792–1873) and Angelina (1805–1879), Quaker women from a slaveholding family in South Carolina, learned biblical Greek and Hebrew so that they could interpret the Bible for themselves. They were prompted to do so after men sought to silence them from speaking out against slavery and for women's rights by claiming that the Bible (e.g., 1 Cor 14:34) prevented women from speaking in public.[10] Another prominent abolitionist, Sojourner Truth (ca. 1797–1883), a former slave, quoted the Bible liberally in her speeches[11] and in so doing challenged cultural assumptions and biblical interpretations that undergird gender inequities.

---

7. See further Taylor and Choi, *Handbook of Women Biblical Interpreters*, 127–32.

8. Her major work, *Women's Speaking Justified, Proved and Allowed by the Scriptures*, published in London in 1667, gave a systematic feminist reading of all biblical texts pertaining to women.

9. Mary Astell, *Some Reflections upon Marriage* (New York: Source Book Press, 1970, reprint of the 1730 edition; earliest edition of this work is 1700), 103–4.

10. See further Sarah Grimké, *Letters on the Equality of the Sexes and the Condition of Woman* (Boston: Isaac Knapp, 1838).

11. See, for example, her most famous speech, "Ain't I a Woman?," delivered in 1851 at the Ohio Women's Rights Convention in Akron, OH; http://www.fordham .edu/halsall/mod/sojtruth-woman.asp.

Another monumental work that emerged in nineteenth-century England was that of Jewish theologian Grace Aguilar (1816–1847), *The Women of Israel*,[12] published in 1845. Aguilar's approach was to make connections between the biblical women and contemporary Jewish women's concerns. She aimed to counter the widespread notion that women were degraded in Jewish law and that only in Christianity were women's dignity and value upheld. Her intent was to help Jewish women find strength and encouragement by seeing the evidence of God's compassionate love in the history of every woman in the Bible. While not a full commentary on the Bible, Aguilar's work stands out for its comprehensive treatment of every female biblical character, including even the most obscure references.[13]

The first person to produce a full-blown feminist commentary on the Bible was Elizabeth Cady Stanton (1815–1902). A leading proponent in the United States for women's right to vote, she found that whenever women tried to make inroads into politics, education, or the work world, the Bible was quoted against them. Along with a team of like-minded women, she produced her own commentary on every text of the Bible that concerned women. Her pioneering two-volume project, *The Woman's Bible*, published in 1895 and 1898, urges women to recognize that texts that degrade women come from the men who wrote the texts, not from God, and to use their common sense to rethink what has been presented to them as sacred.

Nearly a century later, *The Women's Bible Commentary*, edited by Carol Newsom and Sharon Ringe (Louisville: Westminster John Knox, 1992), appeared. This one-volume commentary features North American feminist scholarship on each book of the Protestant canon. Like Cady Stanton's commentary, it does not contain comments on every section of the biblical text but only on those passages deemed relevant to women. It was revised and expanded in 1998 to include the Apocrypha/Deuterocanonical books, and the contributors to this new volume reflect the global face of contemporary feminist scholarship. The revisions made in the third edition, which appeared in 2012, represent the profound advances in feminist biblical scholarship and include newer voices. In both the second and third editions, *The* has been dropped from the title.

12. The full title is *The Women of Israel or Characters and Sketches from the Holy Scriptures and Jewish History Illustrative of the Past History, Present Duty, and Future Destiny of the Hebrew Females, as Based on the Word of God.*
13. See further Eskenazi and Weiss, *The Torah: A Women's Commentary*, xxxviii; Taylor and Choi, *Handbook of Women Biblical Interpreters*, 31–37.

Also appearing at the centennial of Cady Stanton's *The Woman's Bible* were two volumes edited by Elisabeth Schüssler Fiorenza with the assistance of Shelly Matthews. The first, *Searching the Scriptures: A Feminist Introduction* (New York: Crossroad, 1993), charts a comprehensive approach to feminist interpretation from ecumenical, interreligious, and multicultural perspectives. The second volume, published in 1994, provides critical feminist commentary on each book of the New Testament as well as on three books of Jewish Pseudepigrapha and eleven other early Christian writings.

In Europe, similar endeavors have been undertaken, such as the one-volume *Kompendium Feministische Bibelauslegung*, edited by Luise Schottroff and Marie-Theres Wacker (Gütersloh: Gütersloher Verlagshaus, 2007), featuring German feminist biblical interpretation of each book of the Bible, along with apocryphal books, and several extrabiblical writings. This work, now in its third edition, has recently been translated into English.[14] A multivolume project, *The Bible and Women: An Encylopaedia of Exegesis and Cultural History*, edited by Irmtraud Fischer, Adriana Valerio, Mercedes Navarro Puerto, and Christiana de Groot, is currently in production. This project presents a history of the reception of the Bible as embedded in Western cultural history and focuses particularly on gender-relevant biblical themes, biblical female characters, and women recipients of the Bible. The volumes are published in English, Spanish, Italian, and German.[15]

Another groundbreaking work is the collection The Feminist Companion to the Bible Series, edited by Athalya Brenner (Sheffield: Sheffield Academic, 1993–2015), which comprises twenty volumes of commentaries on the Old Testament. The parallel series, Feminist Companion

14. *Feminist Biblical Interpretation: A Compendium of Critical Commentary on the Books of the Bible and Related Literature*, trans. Lisa E. Dahill, Everett R. Kalin, Nancy Lukens, Linda M. Maloney, Barbara Rumscheidt, Martin Rumscheidt, and Tina Steiner (Grand Rapids: Eerdmans, 2012). Another notable collection is the three volumes edited by Susanne Scholz, *Feminist Interpretation of the Hebrew Bible in Retrospect*, Recent Research in Biblical Studies 7, 8, 9 (Sheffield: Sheffield Phoenix, 2013, 2014, 2016).

15. The first volume, on the Torah, appeared in Spanish in 2009, in German and Italian in 2010, and in English in 2011 (Atlanta: SBL Press). Four more volumes are now available: *Feminist Biblical Studies in the Twentieth Century*, ed. Elisabeth Schüssler Fiorenza (2014); *The Writings and Later Wisdom Books*, ed. Christl M. Maier and Nuria Calduch-Benages (2014); *Gospels: Narrative and History*, ed. Mercedes Navarro Puerto and Marinella Perroni (2015); English translation ed. Amy-Jill Levine (2015); and *The High Middle Ages*, ed. Kari Elisabeth Børresen and Adriana Valerio (2015). For further information, see http://www.bibleandwomen.org.

to the New Testament and Early Christian Writings, edited by Amy-Jill Levine with Marianne Blickenstaff and Maria Mayo Robbins (Sheffield: Sheffield Academic, 2001–2009), contains thirteen volumes with one more planned. These two series are not full commentaries on the biblical books but comprise collected essays on discrete biblical texts.

Works by individual feminist biblical scholars in all parts of the world abound, and they are now too numerous to list in this introduction. Feminist biblical interpretation has reached a level of maturity that now makes possible a commentary series on every book of the Bible. In recent decades, women have had greater access to formal theological education, have been able to learn critical analytical tools, have put their own interpretations into writing, and have developed new methods of biblical interpretation. Until recent decades the work of feminist biblical interpreters was largely unknown, both to other women and to their brothers in the synagogue, church, and academy. Feminists now have taken their place in the professional world of biblical scholars, where they build on the work of their foremothers and connect with one another across the globe in ways not previously possible. In a few short decades, feminist biblical criticism has become an integral part of the academy.

Methodologies

Feminist biblical scholars use a variety of methods and often employ a number of them together.[16] In the Wisdom Commentary series, the authors will explain their understanding of feminism and the feminist reading strategies used in their commentary. Each volume treats the biblical text in blocks of material, not an analysis verse by verse. The entire text is considered, not only those passages that feature female characters or that speak specifically about women. When women are not apparent in the narrative, feminist lenses are used to analyze the dynamics in the text between male characters, the models of power, binary ways of thinking, and dynamics of imperialism. Attention is given to how the whole text functions and how it was and is heard, both in its original context and today. Issues of particular concern to women—e.g., poverty, food, health, the environment, water—come to the fore.

---

16. See the seventeen essays in Caroline Vander Stichele and Todd Penner, eds., *Her Master's Tools? Feminist and Postcolonial Engagements of Historical-Critical Discourse* (Atlanta: SBL Press, 2005), which show the complementarity of various approaches.

One of the approaches used by early feminists and still popular today is to lift up the overlooked and forgotten stories of women in the Bible. Studies of women in each of the Testaments have been done, and there are also studies on women in particular biblical books.[17] Feminists recognize that the examples of biblical characters can be both empowering and problematic. The point of the feminist enterprise is not to serve as an apologetic for women; it is rather, in part, to recover women's history and literary roles in all their complexity and to learn from that recovery.

Retrieving the submerged history of biblical women is a crucial step for constructing the story of the past so as to lead to liberative possibilities for the present and future. There are, however, some pitfalls to this approach. Sometimes depictions of biblical women have been naïve and romantic. Some commentators exalt the virtues of both biblical and contemporary women and paint women as superior to men. Such reverse discrimination inhibits movement toward equality for all. In addition, some feminists challenge the idea that one can "pluck positive images out of an admittedly androcentric text, separating literary characterizations from the androcentric interests they were created to serve."[18] Still other feminists find these images to have enormous value.

One other danger with seeking the submerged history of women is the tendency for Christian feminists to paint Jesus and even Paul as liberators of women in a way that demonizes Judaism.[19] Wisdom Commentary aims to enhance understanding of Jesus as well as Paul as Jews of their day and to forge solidarity among Jewish and Christian feminists.

---

17. See, e.g., Alice Bach, ed., *Women in the Hebrew Bible: A Reader* (New York: Routledge, 1998); Tikva Frymer-Kensky, *Reading the Women of the Bible* (New York: Schocken Books, 2002); Carol Meyers, Toni Craven, and Ross S. Kraemer, *Women in Scripture* (Grand Rapids: Eerdmans, 2000); Irene Nowell, *Women in the Old Testament* (Collegeville, MN: Liturgical Press, 1997); Katharine Doob Sakenfeld, *Just Wives? Stories of Power and Survival in the Old Testament and Today* (Louisville: Westminster John Knox, 2003); Mary Ann Getty-Sullivan, *Women in the New Testament* (Collegeville, MN: Liturgical Press, 2001); Bonnie Thurston, *Women in the New Testament: Questions and Commentary*, Companions to the New Testament (New York: Crossroad, 1998).

18. Cheryl Exum, "Second Thoughts about Secondary Characters: Women in Exodus 1.8–2.10," in *A Feminist Companion to Exodus to Deuteronomy*, FCB 6, ed. Athalya Brenner (Sheffield: Sheffield Academic, 1994), 75–97, at 76.

19. See Judith Plaskow, "Anti-Judaism in Feminist Christian Interpretation," in *Searching the Scriptures: A Feminist Introduction*, ed. Elisabeth Schüssler Fiorenza (New York: Crossroad, 1993), 1:117–29; Amy-Jill Levine, "The New Testament and Anti-Judaism," in *The Misunderstood Jew: The Church and the Scandal of the Jewish Jesus* (San Francisco: HarperSanFrancisco, 2006), 87–117.

Feminist scholars who use historical-critical methods analyze the world behind the text; they seek to understand the historical context from which the text emerged and the circumstances of the communities to whom it was addressed. In bringing feminist lenses to this approach, the aim is not to impose modern expectations on ancient cultures but to unmask the ways that ideologically problematic mind-sets that produced the ancient texts are still promulgated through the text. Feminist biblical scholars aim not only to deconstruct but also to reclaim and reconstruct biblical history as women's history, in which women were central and active agents in creating religious heritage.[20] A further step is to construct meaning for contemporary women and men in a liberative movement toward transformation of social, political, economic, and religious structures.[21] In recent years, some feminists have embraced new historicism, which accents the creative role of the interpreter in any construction of history and exposes the power struggles to which the text witnesses.[22]

Literary critics analyze the world of the text: its form, language patterns, and rhetorical function.[23] They do not attempt to separate layers of tradition and redaction but focus on the text holistically, as it is in

---

20. See, for example, Phyllis A. Bird, *Missing Persons and Mistaken Identities: Women and Gender in Ancient Israel* (Minneapolis: Fortress, 1997); Elisabeth Schüssler Fiorenza, *In Memory of Her: A Feminist Theological Reconstruction of Christian Origins* (New York: Crossroad, 1984); Ross Shepard Kraemer and Mary Rose D'Angelo, eds., *Women and Christian Origins* (New York: Oxford University Press, 1999).

21. See, e.g., Sandra M. Schneiders, *The Revelatory Text: Interpreting the New Testament as Sacred Scripture*, rev. ed. (Collegeville, MN: Liturgical Press, 1999), whose aim is to engage in biblical interpretation not only for intellectual enlightenment but, even more important, for personal and communal transformation. Elisabeth Schüssler Fiorenza (*Wisdom Ways: Introducing Feminist Biblical Interpretation* [Maryknoll, NY: Orbis Books, 2001]) envisions the work of feminist biblical interpretation as a dance of Wisdom that consists of seven steps that interweave in spiral movements toward liberation, the final one being transformative action for change.

22. See Gina Hens-Piazza, *The New Historicism*, GBS, Old Testament Series (Minneapolis: Fortress, 2002).

23. Phyllis Trible was among the first to employ this method with texts from Genesis and Ruth in her groundbreaking book *God and the Rhetoric of Sexuality*, OBT (Philadelphia: Fortress, 1978). Another pioneer in feminist literary criticism is Mieke Bal (*Lethal Love: Feminist Literary Readings of Biblical Love Stories* [Bloomington: Indiana University Press, 1987]). For surveys of recent developments in literary methods, see Terry Eagleton, *Literary Theory: An Introduction*, 3rd ed. (Minneapolis: University of Minnesota Press, 2008); Janice Capel Anderson and Stephen D. Moore, eds., *Mark and Method: New Approaches in Biblical Studies*, 2nd ed. (Minneapolis: Fortress, 2008).

its present form. They examine how meaning is created in the interaction between the text and its reader in multiple contexts. Within the arena of literary approaches are reader-oriented approaches, narrative, rhetorical, structuralist, post-structuralist, deconstructive, ideological, autobiographical, and performance criticism.[24] Narrative critics study the interrelation among author, text, and audience through investigation of settings, both spatial and temporal; characters; plot; and narrative techniques (e.g., irony, parody, intertextual allusions). Reader-response critics attend to the impact that the text has on the reader or hearer. They recognize that when a text is detrimental toward women there is the choice either to affirm the text or to read against the grain toward a liberative end. Rhetorical criticism analyzes the style of argumentation and attends to how the author is attempting to shape the thinking or actions of the hearer. Structuralist critics analyze the complex patterns of binary oppositions in the text to derive its meaning.[25] Post-structuralist approaches challenge the notion that there are fixed meanings to any biblical text or that there is one universal truth. They engage in close readings of the text and often engage in intertextual analysis.[26] Within this approach is deconstructionist criticism, which views the text as a site of conflict, with competing narratives. The interpreter aims to expose the fault lines and overturn and reconfigure binaries by elevating the underling of a pair and foregrounding it.[27] Feminists also use other postmodern approaches, such as ideological and autobiographical criticism. The former analyzes the system of ideas that underlies the power and

24. See, e.g., J. Cheryl Exum and David J. A. Clines, eds., *The New Literary Criticism and the Hebrew Bible* (Valley Forge, PA: Trinity Press International, 1993); Edgar V. McKnight and Elizabeth Struthers Malbon, eds., *The New Literary Criticism and the New Testament* (Valley Forge, PA: Trinity Press International, 1994).

25. See, e.g., David Jobling, *The Sense of Biblical Narrative: Three Structural Analyses in the Old Testament*, JSOTSup 7 (Sheffield: University of Sheffield, 1978).

26. See, e.g., Stephen D. Moore, *Poststructuralism and the New Testament: Derrida and Foucault at the Foot of the Cross* (Minneapolis: Fortress, 1994); *The Bible in Theory: Critical and Postcritical Essays* (Atlanta: SBL Press, 2010); Yvonne Sherwood, *A Biblical Text and Its Afterlives: The Survival of Jonah in Western Culture* (Cambridge: Cambridge University Press, 2000).

27. David Penchansky, "Deconstruction," in *The Oxford Encyclopedia of Biblical Interpretation*, ed. Steven McKenzie (New York: Oxford University Press, 2013), 196–205. See, for example, Danna Nolan Fewell and David M. Gunn, *Gender, Power, and Promise: The Subject of the Bible's First Story* (Nashville: Abingdon, 1993); David Rutledge, *Reading Marginally: Feminism, Deconstruction and the Bible*, BibInt 21 (Leiden: Brill, 1996).

values concealed in the text as well as that of the interpreter.[28] The latter involves deliberate self-disclosure while reading the text as a critical exegete.[29] Performance criticism attends to how the text was passed on orally, usually in communal settings, and to the verbal and nonverbal interactions between the performer and the audience.[30]

From the beginning, feminists have understood that interpreting the Bible is an act of power. In recent decades, feminist biblical scholars have developed hermeneutical theories of the ethics and politics of biblical interpretation to challenge the claims to value neutrality of most academic biblical scholarship. Feminist biblical scholars have also turned their attention to how some biblical writings were shaped by the power of empire and how this still shapes readers' self-understandings today. They have developed hermeneutical approaches that reveal, critique, and evaluate the interactions depicted in the text against the context of empire, and they consider implications for contemporary contexts.[31] Feminists also analyze the dynamics of colonization and the mentalities of colonized peoples in the exercise of biblical interpretation. As Kwok Pui-lan explains, "A postcolonial feminist interpretation of the Bible needs to investigate the deployment of gender in the narration of identity, the negotiation of power differentials between the colonizers and the colonized, and the reinforcement of patriarchal control over spheres where these elites could exercise control."[32] Methods and models from sociology and cultural anthropology are used by feminists to investigate

28. See Tina Pippin, ed., *Ideological Criticism of Biblical Texts: Semeia* 59 (1992); Terry Eagleton, *Ideology: An Introduction* (London: Verso, 2007).

29. See, e.g., Ingrid Rose Kitzberger, ed., *Autobiographical Biblical Interpretation: Between Text and Self* (Leiden: Deo, 2002); P. J. W. Schutte, "When *They, We,* and the Passive Become *I*—Introducing Autobiographical Biblical Criticism," *HTS Teologiese Studies / Theological Studies* 61 (2005): 401–16.

30. See, e.g., Holly Hearon and Philip Ruge-Jones, eds., *The Bible in Ancient and Modern Media: Story and Performance* (Eugene, OR: Cascade, 2009).

31. E.g., Gale Yee, ed., *Judges and Method: New Approaches in Biblical Studies* (Minneapolis: Fortress, 1995); Warren Carter, *The Gospel of Matthew in Its Roman Imperial Context* (London: T&T Clark, 2005); *The Roman Empire and the New Testament: An Essential Guide* (Nashville: Abingdon, 2006); Elisabeth Schüssler Fiorenza, *The Power of the Word: Scripture and the Rhetoric of Empire* (Minneapolis: Fortress, 2007); Judith E. McKinlay, *Reframing Her: Biblical Women in Postcolonial Focus* (Sheffield: Sheffield Phoenix, 2004).

32. Kwok Pui-lan, *Postcolonial Imagination and Feminist Theology* (Louisville: Westminster John Knox, 2005), 9. See also, Musa W. Dube, ed., *Postcolonial Feminist Interpretation of the Bible* (St. Louis: Chalice, 2000); Cristl M. Maier and Carolyn J. Sharp,

women's everyday lives, their experiences of marriage, childrearing, labor, money, illness, etc.[33]

As feminists have examined the construction of gender from varying cultural perspectives, they have become ever more cognizant that the way gender roles are defined within differing cultures varies radically. As Mary Ann Tolbert observes, "Attempts to isolate some universal role that cross-culturally defines 'woman' have run into contradictory evidence at every turn."[34] Some women have coined new terms to highlight the particularities of their socio-cultural context. Many African American feminists, for example, call themselves *womanists* to draw attention to the double oppression of racism and sexism they experience.[35] Similarly, many US Hispanic feminists speak of themselves as *mujeristas* (*mujer* is Spanish for "woman").[36] Others prefer to be called "Latina feminists."[37] Both groups emphasize that the context for their theologizing is *mestizaje* and *mulatez* (racial and cultural mixture), done *en conjunto* (in community), with *lo cotidiano* (everyday lived experience) of Hispanic women as starting points for theological reflection and the encounter with the divine. Intercultural analysis has become an indispensable tool for working toward justice for women at the global level.[38]

Prophecy and Power: Jeremiah in Feminist and Postcolonial Perspective (London: Bloomsbury, 2013).

33. See, for example, Carol Meyers, *Discovering Eve: Ancient Israelite Women in Context* (New York: Oxford University Press, 1991); Luise Schottroff, *Lydia's Impatient Sisters: A Feminist Social History of Early Christianity*, trans. Barbara and Martin Rumscheidt (Louisville: Westminster John Knox, 1995); Susan Niditch, *"My Brother Esau Is a Hairy Man": Hair and Identity in Ancient Israel* (Oxford: Oxford University Press, 2008).

34. Mary Ann Tolbert, "Social, Sociological, and Anthropological Methods," in *Searching the Scriptures*, 1:255–71, at 265.

35. Alice Walker coined the term (*In Search of Our Mothers' Gardens: Womanist Prose* [New York: Harcourt Brace Jovanovich, 1967, 1983]). See also Katie G. Cannon, "The Emergence of Black Feminist Consciousness," in *Feminist Interpretation of the Bible*, ed. Letty M. Russell (Philadelphia: Westminster, 1985), 30–40; Renita Weems, *Just a Sister Away: A Womanist Vision of Women's Relationships in the Bible* (San Diego: Lura Media, 1988); Nyasha Junior, *An Introduction to Womanist Biblical Interpretation* (Louisville: Westminster John Knox, 2015).

36. Ada María Isasi-Díaz (*Mujerista Theology: A Theology for the Twenty-First Century* [Maryknoll, NY: Orbis Books, 1996]) is credited with coining the term.

37. E.g., María Pilar Aquino, Daisy L. Machado, and Jeanette Rodríguez, eds., *A Reader in Latina Feminist Theology* (Austin: University of Texas Press, 2002).

38. See, e.g., María Pilar Aquino and María José Rosado-Nunes, eds., *Feminist Intercultural Theology: Latina Explorations for a Just World*, Studies in Latino/a Catholicism (Maryknoll, NY: Orbis Books, 2007).

Some feminists are among those who have developed lesbian, gay, bisexual, and transgender (LGBT) interpretation. This approach focuses on issues of sexual identity and uses various reading strategies. Some point out the ways in which categories that emerged in recent centuries are applied anachronistically to biblical texts to make modern-day judgments. Others show how the Bible is silent on contemporary issues about sexual identity. Still others examine same-sex relationships in the Bible by figures such as Ruth and Naomi or David and Jonathan. In recent years, queer theory has emerged; it emphasizes the blurriness of boundaries not just of sexual identity but also of gender roles. Queer critics often focus on texts in which figures transgress what is traditionally considered proper gender behavior.[39]

Feminists also recognize that the struggle for women's equality and dignity is intimately connected with the struggle for respect for Earth and for the whole of the cosmos. Ecofeminists interpret Scripture in ways that highlight the link between human domination of nature and male subjugation of women. They show how anthropocentric ways of interpreting the Bible have overlooked or dismissed Earth and Earth community. They invite readers to identify not only with human characters in the biblical narrative but also with other Earth creatures and domains of nature, especially those that are the object of injustice. Some use creative imagination to retrieve the interests of Earth implicit in the narrative and enable Earth to speak.[40]

Biblical Authority

By the late nineteenth century, some feminists, such as Elizabeth Cady Stanton, began to question openly whether the Bible could continue to be regarded as authoritative for women. They viewed the Bible itself as

39. See, e.g., Bernadette J. Brooten, *Love between Women: Early Christian Responses to Female Homoeroticism* (Chicago and London: University of Chicago Press, 1996); Mary Rose D'Angelo, "Women Partners in the New Testament," *JFSR* 6 (1990): 65–86; Deirdre J. Good, "Reading Strategies for Biblical Passages on Same-Sex Relations," *Theology and Sexuality* 7 (1997): 70–82; Deryn Guest, *When Deborah Met Jael: Lesbian Feminist Hermeneutics* (London: SCM, 2011); Teresa Hornsby and Ken Stone, eds., *Bible Trouble: Queer Readings at the Boundaries of Biblical Scholarship* (Atlanta: SBL Press, 2011).

40. E.g., Norman C. Habel and Peter Trudinger, *Exploring Ecological Hermeneutics*, SymS 46 (Atlanta: SBL Press, 2008); Mary Judith Ress, *Ecofeminism in Latin America*, Women from the Margins (Maryknoll, NY: Orbis Books, 2006).

the source of women's oppression, and some rejected its sacred origin and saving claims. Some decided that the Bible and the religious traditions that enshrine it are too thoroughly saturated with androcentrism and patriarchy to be redeemable.[41]

In the Wisdom Commentary series, questions such as these may be raised, but the aim of this series is not to lead readers to reject the authority of the biblical text. Rather, the aim is to promote better understanding of the contexts from which the text arose and of the rhetorical effects it has on women and men in contemporary contexts. Such understanding can lead to a deepening of faith, with the Bible serving as an aid to bring flourishing of life.

Language for God

Because of the ways in which the term "God" has been used to symbolize the divine in predominantly male, patriarchal, and monarchical modes, feminists have designed new ways of speaking of the divine. Some have called attention to the inadequacy of the term *God* by trying to visually destabilize our ways of thinking and speaking of the divine. Rosemary Radford Ruether proposed *God/ess*, as an unpronounceable term pointing to the unnameable understanding of the divine that transcends patriarchal limitations.[42] Some have followed traditional Jewish practice, writing *G-d*. Elisabeth Schüssler Fiorenza has adopted *G*d*.[43] Others draw on the biblical tradition to mine female and non-gender-specific metaphors and symbols.[44] In Wisdom Commentary, there is not one standard way of expressing the divine; each author will use her or his preferred ways. The one exception is that when the tetragrammaton, YHWH, the name revealed to Moses in Exodus 3:14, is used, it will be without vowels, respecting the Jewish custom of avoiding pronouncing the divine name out of reverence.

---

41. E.g., Mary Daly, *Beyond God the Father: A Philosophy of Women's Liberation* (Boston: Beacon, 1973).

42. Rosemary Radford Ruether, *Sexism and God-Talk: Toward a Feminist Theology* (Boston: Beacon, 1983).

43. Elisabeth Schüssler Fiorenza, *Jesus: Miriam's Child, Sophia's Prophet; Critical Issues in Feminist Christology* (New York: Continuum, 1994), 191 n. 3.

44. E.g., Sallie McFague, *Models of God: Theology for an Ecological, Nuclear Age* (Philadelphia: Fortress, 1987); Catherine LaCugna, *God for Us: The Trinity and Christian Life* (San Francisco: Harper Collins, 1991); Elizabeth A. Johnson, *She Who Is: The Mystery of God in Feminist Theological Discourse* (New York: Crossroad, 1992). See further Elizabeth A. Johnson, "God," in *Dictionary of Feminist Theologies*, 128–30.

Editor's Introduction to Wisdom Commentary xli

Nomenclature for the Two Testaments

In recent decades, some biblical scholars have begun to call the two Testaments of the Bible by names other than the traditional nomenclature: Old and New Testament. Some regard "Old" as derogatory, implying that it is no longer relevant or that it has been superseded. Consequently, terms like Hebrew Bible, First Testament, and Jewish Scriptures and, correspondingly, Christian Scriptures or Second Testament have come into use. There are a number of difficulties with these designations. The term "Hebrew Bible" does not take into account that parts of the Old Testament are written not in Hebrew but in Aramaic.[45] Moreover, for Roman Catholics and Eastern Orthodox believers, the Old Testament includes books written in Greek—the Deuterocanonical books, considered Apocrypha by Protestants.[46] The term "Jewish Scriptures" is inadequate because these books are also sacred to Christians. Conversely, "Christian Scriptures" is not an accurate designation for the New Testament, since the Old Testament is also part of the Christian Scriptures. Using "First and Second Testament" also has difficulties, in that it can imply a hierarchy and a value judgment.[47] Jews generally use the term Tanakh, an acronym for Torah (Pentateuch), Nevi'im (Prophets), and Ketuvim (Writings).

In Wisdom Commentary, if authors choose to use a designation other than Tanakh, Old Testament, and New Testament, they will explain how they mean the term.

Translation

Modern feminist scholars recognize the complexities connected with biblical translation, as they have delved into questions about philosophy of language, how meanings are produced, and how they are culturally situated. Today it is evident that simply translating into gender-neutral formulations cannot address all the challenges presented by androcentric texts. Efforts at feminist translation must also deal with issues around authority and canonicity.[48]

Because of these complexities, the editors of Wisdom Commentary series have chosen to use an existing translation, the New Revised Standard

---

45. Gen 31:47; Jer 10:11; Ezra 4:7–6:18; 7:12-26; Dan 2:4–7:28.

46. Representing the *via media* between Catholic and reformed, Anglicans generally consider the Apocrypha to be profitable, if not canonical, and utilize select Wisdom texts liturgically.

47. See Levine, *The Misunderstood Jew*, 193–99.

48. Elizabeth Castelli, "*Les Belles Infidèles*/Fidelity or Feminism? The Meanings of Feminist Biblical Translation," in *Searching the Scriptures*, 1:189–204, here 190.

Version (NRSV), which is provided for easy reference at the top of each page of commentary. The NRSV was produced by a team of ecumenical and interreligious scholars, is a fairly literal translation, and uses inclusive language for human beings. Brief discussions about problematic translations appear in the inserts labeled "Translation Matters." When more detailed discussions are available, these will be indicated in footnotes. In the commentary, wherever Hebrew or Greek words are used, English translation is provided. In cases where a wordplay is involved, transliteration is provided to enable understanding.

Art and Poetry

Artistic expression in poetry, music, sculpture, painting, and various other modes is very important to feminist interpretation. Where possible, art and poetry are included in the print volumes of the series. In a number of instances, these are original works created for this project. Regrettably, copyright and production costs prohibit the inclusion of color photographs and other artistic work. It is our hope that the web version will allow a greater collection of such resources.

Glossary

Because there are a number of excellent readily available resources that provide definitions and concise explanations of terms used in feminist theological and biblical studies, this series will not include a glossary. We refer you to works such as *Dictionary of Feminist Theologies*, edited by Letty M. Russell with J. Shannon Clarkson (Louisville: Westminster John Knox, 1996), and volume 1 of *Searching the Scriptures*, edited by Elisabeth Schüssler Fiorenza with the assistance of Shelly Matthews (New York: Crossroad, 1992). Individual authors in the Wisdom Commentary series will define the way they are using terms that may be unfamiliar.

Bibliography

Because bibliographies are quickly outdated and because the space is limited, only a list of Works Cited is included in the print volumes. A comprehensive bibliography for each volume is posted on a dedicated website and is updated regularly. The link for this volume can be found at wisdomcommentary.org.

A Concluding Word

In just a few short decades, feminist biblical studies has grown exponentially, both in the methods that have been developed and in the number of scholars who have embraced it. We realize that this series is limited and will soon need to be revised and updated. It is our hope that Wisdom Commentary, by making the best of current feminist biblical scholarship available in an accessible format to ministers, preachers, teachers, scholars, and students, will aid all readers in their advancement toward God's vision of dignity, equality, and justice for all.

Acknowledgments

There are a great many people who have made this series possible: first, Peter Dwyer, director of Liturgical Press, and Hans Christoffersen, publisher of the academic market at Liturgical Press, who have believed in this project and have shepherded it since it was conceived in 2008. Editorial consultants Athalya Brenner-Idan and Elisabeth Schüssler Fiorenza have not only been an inspiration with their pioneering work but have encouraged us all along the way with their personal involvement. Volume editors Mary Ann Beavis, Carol J. Dempsey, Amy-Jill Levine, Linda M. Maloney, Ahida Pilarski, Sarah Tanzer, Lauress Wilkins Lawrence, and Seung Ai Yang have lent their extraordinary wisdom to the shaping of the series, have used their extensive networks of relationships to secure authors and contributors, and have worked tirelessly to guide their work to completion. Two others who contributed greatly to the shaping of the project at the outset were Linda M. Day and Mignon Jacobs, as well as Barbara E. Bowe of blessed memory (d. 2010). Editorial and research assistant Susan M. Hickman has provided invaluable support with administrative details and arrangements. I am grateful to Brian Eisenschenk and Christine Henderson who have assisted Susan Hickman with the Wiki. There are countless others at Liturgical Press whose daily work makes the production possible. I am especially thankful to Lauren L. Murphy, managing editor, and Justin Howell for their work in copyediting; Colleen Stiller, production manager; Stephanie Nix, production assisstant; and Tara Durheim, associate publisher for academic and monastic markets.

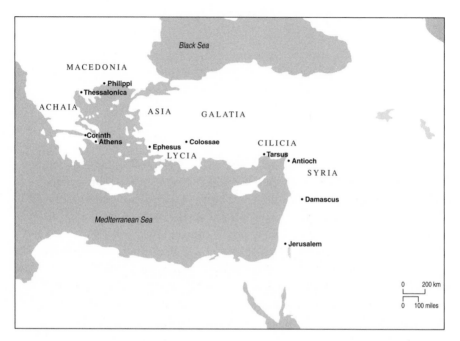

Asia Minor

Author's Introduction

The best-known and most-quoted passage in the letter to the Ephesians is probably the following:

> Wives, be subject to your husbands as you are to the Lord. For the husband is the head of the wife just as Christ is the head of the church, the body of which he is the Savior. Just as the church is subject to Christ, so also wives ought to be, in everything, to their husbands. (Eph 5:22-24)

Sarah Tanzer has therefore correctly stated that "the household code is the inescapable focus of any feminist commentary on Ephesians, because it is the only passage in Ephesians which explicitly addresses women and is about women."[1] Over the centuries, the epistle to the Ephesians has been used, on the one hand, in support of andro/kyriocentric (i.e., male-/ Lord-centered) mind-sets, norms, and texts that continue to inculcate wo/men's[2] second-class status and subordination. On the other hand,

---

1. Sarah J. Tanzer, "Ephesians," in *Searching the Scriptures*, vol. 2: *A Feminist Commentary*, ed. Elisabeth Schüssler Fiorenza (New York: Crossroad, 1994), 325–48, at 325.

2. In order to lift into critical consciousness the linguistic violence of so-called generic male-centered language, I substitute the term "wo/men" with a slash to replace the inclusive "men." To use "wo/men" as an inclusive generic term invites male readers both to think twice and to experience what it means not to be addressed specifically. I also use the term to avoid an essentialist depiction of "woman" and to stress the instability of the term. Wo/man is defined not only by gender but also by race, class, and colonial structures of domination. Thus, "wo/men" can also be equivalent to "subordinated people." Where it is encountered in my writing, the reader is called to reflect on who the term is including, and excluding, in a given instance.

the the*logical[3] vision and cosmic language of Ephesians have fascinated readers and commentators alike. Aware of this double-edged character of Scripture, this commentary series seeks to read Christian Scriptures— the Hebrew Bible and the New* Testament[4]—through a critical feminist lens,[5] searching for the liberating words of Divine Wisdom. Texts like Ephesians 5:22-33 make this task difficult and problematic. Such texts then call for both critical and constructive commentary.

A scriptural text such as Ephesians 5:22-24 continues to justify the religious legitimization of wo/men's second-class citizenship in society and church. Since this text is still proclaimed over and over again at weddings as the "word of G*d" and used in the*logical arguments against wo/men's ordination, a hermeneutics (i.e., a method or theory of interpretation) of suspicion is called for. Such an interpretive approach places on all andro/kyriocentric texts the label, "Caution, could be dangerous to your health and survival," in order to adjudicate "what G*d, for the sake of our [i.e., wo/men's] salvation, wished to see confided to the sacred scriptures [such as Ephesians]."[6]

---

3. Whenever I use the asterisk—most notably, in "the*logy," "G*d," and "New* Testament"—I want to communicate that the word is so marked in order to signal a problem. I write the*logy in this open form in order to avoid the genderization of G*d. The*logy means "speaking about G*d," *theos* being the masculine form of the Greek word for G*d. Carol Christ has suggested that we use the noun *thealogy* (in Greek, *thea* is the feminine form and means "Goddess"). See especially also Carol P. Christ and Judith Plaskow, *Goddess and God in the World: Conversations in Embodied Theology* (Minneapolis: Fortress, 2017). However, this language also reinscribes gender into the Divine. Since Western languages such as Greek, Latin, and even English are gendered and use the masculine as the norm, I seek to interrupt and make conscious this grammatically masculine or feminine determination of the Divine. I have therefore replaced the masculine form of *theos* with the asterisk (*the*s* and the*logy) in order to draw attention to this linguistic problem, which is at one and the same time a theoretical orientation.

4. I write New* Testament, or N*T, also called the "Christian Testament" or "Second Testament," in an effort to call attention to the politics evoked by the designation "new."

5. For the articulation of my own feminist lens, see my recent books *Congress of Wo/men: Religion, Gender and Kyriarchal Power* (Cambridge: FSR Books, 2016); *Transforming Vision: Explorations in Feminist The*logy* (Minneapolis: Fortress, 2011); *Changing Horizons: Explorations of Feminist Interpretation* (Minneapolis: Fortress, 2013); *Empowering Memory and Movement: Thinking and Working across Borders* (Minneapolis: Fortress, 2014).

6. See the Dogmatic Constitution on Divine Revelation (*Dei Verbum*). Different churches have different teachings on how to interpret Scripture. The Dogmatic Con-

Several years ago one of my students worked hard to marshal the scholarly arguments regarding Ephesians 5:22-33 in order to convince the pastor not to read this text in the liturgy at their wedding. After a long conversation the student thought their arguments had convinced the pastor not to use the text. However, on the day of the wedding they learned that the pastor had not respected their wishes. Despite their arguments and requests, the pastor proclaimed and preached on this text, calling for wifely submission. Sharing this experience in class after the wedding, they could barely contain their tears but assured us that they would never visit that church again.

As a text of Sacred Scripture, Ephesians 5:22-33 inscribes and enacts subordination and inequality not only in marriage but also in the church. It continues to shape not only the understanding of Christian marriage and family but also Roman Catholic and Protestant fundamentalist understandings of church and ministry. Official teachings use this text to define "priesthood" (or "ministry") as a male-only function, arguing that, because Christ was male, a priest, as an icon of Christ, must also be male. Christ's maleness is taken as an important sign of their relationship to the *ekklēsia*,[7] which, according to Ephesians 5, is Christ's wife and thereby symbolically typed as feminine. Hence, it is argued, the ordination of wo/men is not merely a matter of church discipline but is divinely revealed in Scripture. Ephesians and other New* Testament

---

stitution on Divine Revelation states: "Since, therefore, all that the inspired authors, or sacred writers, affirm should be regarded as affirmed by the Holy Spirit, we must acknowledge that the books of Scripture, firmly, faithfully and without error, teach that truth which God, for the sake of our salvation, wished to see confided to the sacred scriptures. . . . Seeing that, in sacred scripture, God speaks through human beings in human fashion, it follows that the interpreters of sacred Scriptures, if they are to ascertain what God has wished to communicate to us, should carefully search out the meaning which the sacred writers really had in mind, that meaning which God had thought well to manifest through the medium of their words. In determining the intention of the sacred writers, attention must be paid, among other things, to *literary genres*. The fact is that truth is differently presented and expressed in the various types of historical writing, in prophetical and poetical texts, and in other forms of literary expression." *Vatican Council II: The Basic Sixteen Documents*, ed. Austin Flannery (Collegeville, MN: Liturgical Press, 2013), iii, 11–12.

7. The Greek term ἐκκλησία (*ekklēsia*) is commonly translated as "church." However, the term more accurately refers to the democratic assembly or forum of full citizens who come together to decide issues pertaining to their rights and well-being. Hence, in this commentary, I use the term in its transcribed form, *ekklēsia*, rather than the usual translation, "church."

texts of subordination are used as primary kyriarchal proof-texts for injunctions to subordination and exclusion. These interpretations, too, must be clearly labeled as dangerous to health and survival!

Questions of Interpretation

A critical reading of the letter to the Ephesians as "words of the manifold wisdom/Wisdom of G*d" (Eph 3:10) addressed *both* to freeborn and slave wo/men in the past when the letter was written and to wo/men today when it is read calls for critical evaluation and a feminist hermeneutics of suspicion. What do I mean by the label "feminist"? I work with a bumper-sticker definition of feminism that states: "Feminism is the radical notion that wo/men are people."[8] Wo/men are not beasts of burden, handmaids, or servants; wo/men are full citizens. This definition of feminism alludes to the democratic motto "We, the people!" and asserts that wo/men are full, decision-making citizens with all rights and responsibilities in society and religion.

The slash in "wo/men" also intends to signify that there is no unified essence shared by all wo/men but rather that the category "woman" is always already fractured and inflected by other structures of oppression, including race, class, sexuality, immigrant status, and so many others. Therefore a critical feminist analysis cannot restrict itself to a gender-critical perspective but must go further to an intersectional analysis insofar as wo/men are not just defined by gender but also by race, class, ethnicity, age, and other social-political identity markers.

Since a feminist reading and interpretation seeks to make visible and audible wo/men as social-historical-religious agents, it needs to engage in an analysis not only of gender but more broadly of kyriarchy.[9] Thus, depending on the context, this way of writing "wo/men" can also be understood to include marginalized and subordinated men. The understanding of wo/men as full citizens in society and religious community asserts that all wo/men are empowered to make decisions for their own and their children's well-being.

---

8. This definition of feminism is ascribed to rhetoric scholars Cheris Kramarae and Paula Treichler.

9. I have introduced the analytical terms *kyriarchy/kyriocentrism*, which are derived from the Greek *kyrios* (*emperor, lord, master, father, husband*) in order to specify that in Western societies the system of domination and exploitation is not just patriarchal but kyriarchal—that is, it is defined not just by gender by also by race, class, ethnicity, imperialism, and age. See *Congress of Wo/men: Religion, Gender and Kyriarchal Power* (Cambridge: MA: FSRBooks, 2016), 4 n. 4.

1. Androcentric Language and Translation

A feminist interpretation of Ephesians—or of any other text—must pay special attention to the function of male-centered, androcentric language. To quote *The Inclusive New Testament*, published by Priests for Equality, "Language, seemingly innocuous and inconsequential, is in reality an area which reveals unconscious attitudes, prejudices, stereotypes and patterns of discriminatory thinking. Conversely, care in language is a first and necessary step in raising consciousness."[10]

This translation of the New* Testament recognizes that the androcentric language of the N*T subsumes wo/men under generic terms such as "men" or "slaves." However, N*T texts are not only androcentric, that is, male-centered; they are also kyriocentric, that is, elite male- or master-centered.

Such grammatically and linguistically shaped gendered, raced, and classed language does not simply divide humans into two equal separate groups exclusive of each other: male and female. Rather, it orders them asymmetrically, placing the masculine as the standard, making the feminine the exception in every class and race. In so doing it more highly ranks and valorizes the masculine gender. For instance, in his *Theory of Language*, published in 1788, James Beattie maintains (on the*logical grounds) that biological sex is the primary basis for noun classification because "beings superior to man" are spoken of as masculine in most of the modern tongues of Europe, on account of their dignity. The male being is, according to these theories, the "nobler sex."[11]

In Western language systems, masculine terms function as "generic," connoting both men and women. In such language systems man/male/masculine/he stands for human and male, whereas woman/female/feminine/she lacks this generic sense and connotes only femaleness. In other words, Western languages (including the biblical languages of Hebrew, Greek, and Latin) are androcentric, that is, male-centered. Grammatically, androcentric "generic" Western languages explicitly mention wo/men only as problematic, the exception to the rule, or specifically, as particular individuals. In all cases one has to adjudicate in light of contextual linguistic markers whether wo/men are meant to be included or not.

---

10. Priests for Equality, *The Inclusive New Testament* (Hyattsville, MD: Quixote Center, 1994).

11. James Beattie, *The Theory of Language in Two Parts* (London: A. Strahan, T. Cadell, and W. Creech, 1788).

In addition, Western androcentric languages and discourses do not just marginalize wo/men, or eliminate us from historical cultural-religious records. As andro/kyriocentric languages they also construct the meaning of being a "woman" or being a "man" and do so differently depending on one's social status. What it means to be female/woman/feminine depends not so much on one's sex as on one's location in the social-symbolic kyriarchal status system. The meaning of "woman" is therefore unstable and ever-shifting, depending less on its sex/gender relation than on its socio-systemic contextualization.

For example, the category "woman" is used today interchangeably with female/feminine and thus has become a "naturalized" generic sex-based term, although until very recently it was used as an appellation for lower-class females only, often in distinction to the term "lady" (Greek: κύρια/*kyria*; Latin: *matrona*). In this light, one can perceive the slippage, cultural-constructedness, and historical ambiguity of the term "woman" much more easily, since this discursive appellation readily reveals its race, class, and colonial bias. Not only has "lady" been restricted until very recently to wo/men of higher status or educational refinement; it also has functioned to symbolize femininity and "true womanhood." Thus, a statement such as "slaves were not women" offends our "commonsense" understanding, whereas a statement such as "slaves were not ladies" makes perfect sense.

In the Western androcentric language system the lady/mistress/mother is the "other" of the lord/master/father. All wo/men (both male and female) who are marked as "inferior" by race, class, religion, or culture—as the others of the other—are labeled "feminine." One can illustrate how such supposedly generic language is read, for example, with reference to the famous text of Galatians 3:28, which states that in Christ there is "no longer Jew or Greek, there is no longer slave or free, there is no longer male and female." Generally Galatians 3:28 is understood as referring to three different characterizations: Jew and Greek as religious/ethnic characterizations, slave and free as socio-political class determinations, and male and female as referring to biological sex/gender differences. However, such an understanding of the text tacitly substitutes a gender-specific reading for a generic one when it infers, on the one hand, that Jew and Greek, slave and free are terms naming only man/male and, on the other, that only the third pair, "male and female," refers also to wo/men. However, generic language, terms such as "Jews or Greeks" or "slave or free," connote not only men but also wo/men. Hence the text needs to be read as "neither Jewish nor Greek wo/men, neither slave nor free wo/men, neither male and female." This example indicates the difficulties androcentric language poses for an adequate historical translation and religious-the*logical understanding of biblical texts such as Ephesians.

2. Translation and Interpretation of Androcentric Language

A. TRANSLATION

While the question of how to translate androcentric, male-centered biblical language has received much attention since the 1970s and 1980s in feminist writings, biblical commentaries and scholarly translations have devoted less consideration to this issue. Whereas the NRSV translation renders masculine terms such as "brothers" or "sons" inclusively, to mean "brothers and sisters" or "children," it has retained the masculine pronoun "he" to refer to G*d and has refused to modify the masculine G*d-language of biblical texts. Since the NRSV translation is mandatory for this commentary, a simple reading of the text already inculcates that G*d is male.

Feminists have pointed out since the 1970s that the generic masculine is the epitome of sexism in language[12] and argued that the singular "they" was used by Shakespeare, Charles Dickens, and George Bernard Shaw to indicate inclusion. Jane Austen, for instance, repeatedly uses statements such as "everybody has their failing." However, the Victorian grammarians made it a matter of schoolroom dogma that one could only say "Everybody has *his* failing," with the understanding that "he" stood in for both sexes. As their slogan had it, "The masculine embraces the feminine."[13] Moreover, in 1850 an Act of the British Parliament gave official sanction to the then recently invented concept of "the generic he." This new law declared that "words importing the masculine gender shall be deemed and taken to include females."[14]

---

12. See especially Casey Miller and Kate Swift, *Words and Women: New Language in New Times* (New York: Doubleday, 1977).

13. Geoff Nunberg, "Everyone Uses Singular 'They,' Whether They Realize It or Not," NPR, January 13, 2016, accessed June 7, 2016, http://www.npr.org/2016/01/13/462906419/everyone-uses-singular-they-whether-they-realize-it-or-not. Geoff Nunberg is the linguistic contributor on NPR's *Fresh Air.*

14. Casey Miller and Kate Swift, *The Handbook of Nonsexist Writing for Writers, Editors, and Speakers* (New York: Barnes & Noble Books, 1980), 36–37.

More recently, the American Dialect Society has moved to revive the earlier feminist precedent with respect to the grammatical use of "they" as a gender-neutral singular pronoun, voting it the Word of the Year in its twenty-sixth annual Words of the Year vote in 2015. "They" was recognized by the society for its emerging use as a pronoun to refer to a known person, often as a conscious choice by a person rejecting the traditional gender binary of "he" and "she." Voters in the Word of the Year proceedings singled out its newer usage as an identifier for someone who might identify as "non-binary" in gender terms. Ben Zimmer, chair of the New Words Committee, observed that "[i]n the past year, new expressions of gender identity have generated a great deal of discussion, and singular they has become a particularly significant element of that conversation," noting as well that "while many novel gender-neutral pronouns have been proposed, they has the advantage of already being part of the language."[15]

In short, gender-queer people have launched a new discussion taking "they" into new grammatical territory, using it for alternative genders exactly the way one would use a personal pronoun like "he" or "she." The American Dialect Society focused on this usage when they made "they" their word of the year. It seems that this new gender-queer discussion also reopens the feminist discussion of a biblical translation that could transform our masculine use of G*d language. The feminist historian and reader seeks to recover the generic inclusive "s/he," since in the English language wo/men includes men, she includes he, and female includes male.

In a social-cultural context in which masculine-determined language is no longer understood as generic but as sexist-exclusive, the translator must evaluate whether the androcentric text seeks to enforce "natural" masculine gender in language or whether such a masculine gendering of the generic androcentric text is against the rhetoric of the text and its the*logical meanings. While the appropriate translation of masculine metaphors and androcentric language remains a difficult task, it also has serious ramifications for our understanding of Ephesians as a historical and the*logical re/source.

A feminist translation that is adequate needs to take into account the interpretative implications of androcentric language that functions as inclusive language in a kyriarchal culture. Such androcentric inclusive

15. "Word of the Year Is Singular 'They,'" *American Dialect Society*, January 8, 2015, accessed June 7, 2016, http://www.americandialect.org/2015-word-of-the-year-is -singular-they.

language explicitly mentions wo/men only when wo/men have become a problem, when they are thought to be "exceptional," or when they are mentioned by name (as in greetings). However, such language does not otherwise explicitly acknowledge the presence of wo/men but subsumes them under the generic masculine.

Although androcentric language patterns and linguistic practices have been brought to consciousness in and through feminist work, the implications of this feminist discussion have not yet been fully explored and critically debated with respect to their importance and function in commentary writing. If commentary writing is a language event, then the feminist methodological insight that our sources for early Christian beginnings are written in androcentric language and that archaeological artifacts are explained and interpreted in the same language has far-reaching consequences. Thus commentary writers are confronted with the problem of historically appropriate, philologically correct, and the*logically liberative translation. This problem becomes even more complex when biblical texts are translated into non-androcentric languages such as Japanese or any other status other than gender-stratified language.[16]

B. INTERPRETATION

Scholars understand and interpret such androcentric language in a twofold way, either as generic or as gender-specific. Although in general they no longer refuse to translate the Pauline address, ἀδελφοι, "brothers," as "brothers and sisters," they still often assume that men led the Christian communities to whom Paul writes. Since they generally do not want to claim that early Christianity was a male cult, scholars understand grammatically masculine terms such as ἐκλεκτοί, "elect"; ἅγιοι, "saints"; ἀδελφοί, "brothers"; or υἱοί, "sons," as generic language designating men and wo/men. Such grammatically male designations apply to all members of the Christian community. Grammatically masculine language with respect to community membership is no longer understood in a gender-specific way but rather as inclusive-generic.

However, whenever leadership titles—for example, apostles, prophets, or teachers—occur, readers assume that these terms apply only to men, despite clear instances in which such grammatically masculine titles are

16. See, for instance, Satoko Yamaguchi, "Father Image of G*d and Inclusive Language: A Reflection in Japan," in *Toward a New Heaven and a New Earth: Essays in Honor of Elisabeth Schüssler Fiorenza*, ed. Fernando F. Segovia (Maryknoll, NY: Orbis Books, 2003), 199–224.

also used for wo/men. For instance, Romans 16:1 characterizes Phoebe with the grammatically masculine form of the Greek term *diakonos* (διάκονος) and Titus 2:3 uses the grammatically masculine title for teacher (καλοδιδασκάλος) for wo/men. If, however, we take seriously the issue of androcentric language as generic we can maintain that any interpretation and translation that claims to be historically adequate to the language character of their sources must understand and translate New* Testament androcentric language on the whole as inclusive of wo/men until proven otherwise.

The passages of the New* Testament that directly mention wo/men almost exclusively do so because such wo/men were "exceptional" or their actions had become a problem. These texts must not be taken to be all the available information on wo/men in early Christianity. Thus we can no longer simply assume that only 1 Corinthians 11:2-16 speaks about wo/men prophets, while the rest of chapters 11–14 refer to male charismatics and male prophets. The opposite is the case. In 1 Corinthians 11–14 Paul speaks about the worship of all Christians and singles out wo/men in 1 Corinthians 11:2-16 only because their speaking seems to have constituted a problem. Therefore a historically adequate translation and interpretation must not only take the inclusive function of androcentric language into account but also acknowledge the limitations of such language.

In general, contemporary scholars understand androcentric language as descriptive of historical reality and share in the androcentric-kyriarchal mind-set of Western culture. Hence their literal translation cannot do justice to generic texts that speak about members of the community in grammatically masculine terms, nor is it able to integrate such androcentric language as language about men and women into their reconstructive models. Because it is generally presupposed that men—males—developed religious leadership as apostles, New* Testament texts are still interpreted in terms of an androcentric perspective. For example, many translations assume that Romans 16:7 speaks about two men, Andronicus and Junias, or Junianus, who had already become Christians before Paul and had great authority as apostles. However, there is no reason to understand the Greek word Ἰουνίαν, "Junian," as a form of the male name "Junias," or a shortened form of "Junianus," especially since Junia is a well-known female name.[17] Even patristic exegesis understood the Greek accusative

---

17. Bernadette Brooten, "Junia . . . Outstanding among the Apostles," in *Women Priests: A Catholic Commentary on the Vatican Declaration*, ed. Leonard Swidler and Arlene Swidler (New York: Paulist, 1977); Eldon J. Epp, *Junia: The First Woman Apostle* (Minneapolis: Fortress, 2005).

form Ἰουνίαν, "Junian," as the name of a wo/man. Andronicus and Junia were an influential missionary team who were acknowledged as apostles.

In sum, a critical feminist translation and interpretation of androcentric texts such as Ephesians must pay close attention to the function of androcentric biblical language that derives both its oppressive and its critical power from its cultural-religious contexts. Texts do not have an essential, unchangeable meaning; they always construct meaning in context. Texts are rhetorical. They are always authored by someone and sent to someone as a communication. Texts always construct a symbolic universe that is determined by its historical-symbolic location. The recognition of the rhetorical character of androcentric language has far-reaching consequences for the interpretation of Ephesians. It calls, first, for a critical feminist process of interpretation and, second, for a reading against the grain of the andro/kyriocentric biblical text.

3. Reading Against the Grain

In light of the dominant conventional androcentric language use, a critical feminist reading of Ephesians is called for if we are to appreciate Ephesians as also providing a liberating word of the manifold Wisdom of G*d and not just reject it as an oppressive sacred text. A critical-constructive feminist interpretation calls for a "reading against the grain" of an androcentric, elite male-centered, i.e., kyriocentric text such as Ephesians. Such a reading needs to take into account the "genderedness" of grammar and language. Hence when reading Ephesians it is important to foreground the first-century androcentric language use, which is still operative today. In short, a "reading against the grain" of Ephesians as androcentric text is called for.

A critical feminist historical "reading against the grain" of Ephesians 5:22-33 that situates the text within the context of the whole letter is so significant because it can understand Ephesians 5:22-33 constructively, in a way that is transformative for interpreting the whole letter. It can do so because wo/men are explicitly mentioned here. This passage confirms that the androcentric language in the rest of the letter can be read as gender-inclusive language since wo/men are mentioned here as members of the community to whom Ephesians is written. Since the text does not add σύζυγος, "married," to γυναῖκες, "wo/men," we know that all wo/men are meant here because the wo/men are commanded to subordinate themselves to "their own men." This mentioning of wo/men is like the tip of an iceberg indicating not only that wo/men were present in the Ephesian community but also what historical information we have lost through grammatical andro/kyriocentric language.

Knowing that wo/men of households were members of the community addressed, we can assume that androcentric language functions in Ephesians as generic language. Hence, we can surmise that not only wives but wo/men in general were addressed by the author. Reading the letter's andro/kyriocentric language as inclusive enables and compels us to read the letter to the Ephesians in a different feminist frame. Ephesians, like other New* Testament texts, refers to slaves, Gentiles, and citizens but does not specify whether these social groups are both male and female or only male. The reference to wo/men in Ephesians 5:22-33 enables us to read these androcentric texts not only in an inclusive way but also as "the tip of the iceberg," indicating what is submerged in historical memory.

Ephesians 5:22-33 should not be taken as a descriptive account but as a rhetorical indication of wo/men's presence. Since wo/men are mentioned here, the whole letter can be read against its androcentric grain. We are able to read the whole text as being inclusive of wo/men even though wo/men are not explicitly mentioned throughout the letter. We can engage in such an inclusive reading because we have at least one explicit reference to wo/men, in Ephesians 5:22-33.

A critical feminist analysis of Ephesians needs in the process of reading to deconstruct the androcentric text that erases the presence of both free and slave wo/men. Such a feminist reading seeks to revalorize the emancipatory values and visions that are inscribed in the letter's rhetoric. To read against the kyriarchal grain of the text in this way challenges us not to accept the author(s)'s rhetoric or the androcentric scholarly elaborations of the letter at face value but to stand back and to analyze the letter critically in order not to adopt an interpretive position that automatically and unconsciously takes the side of the author(s).

Reading against the grain compels us to look for and try "to hear into speech" the silenced voices, experiences, and histories of the recipients to whom Ephesians is addressed—voices that are omitted or suppressed by the author. It means searching for the gaps and fissures in the text rather than focusing just on what is forcefully argued by the author and the scholarly interpreters of the text. Reading against the grain involves questioning the kyriarchal norms and values that have informed the arguments inscribed in the letter and its interpretations, which are presented as authoritative because they are said to represent "critical scholarship" or "sacred scripture." To read against the grain is to insist that the biases, attempts at persuasion, and possibly even well-intended manipulations inscribed in the text be acknowledged, so that the values and visions of the author or interpreters are exposed.

Reading against the grain invites us to hear more fully the voices and perspectives of those who are silenced within and by the text. In and through a critical reading of the author's rhetoric one is able to open up the understanding of the letter in terms of a radical democratic equality of the people of G*d, male and female, slave and free, Jew, Greek, Anatolian, and Roman. One must ask why wo/men's subjection is so imperatively necessary. Did married wo/men not act that way? Why are they compared to the *ekklēsia*, the democratic assembly of citizens? Were they, in the author's view, too domineering in the democratic decision-making gatherings of the messianic community?

Although the majority of commentaries translate ἐκκλησία, *ekklēsia*, as "church," this is a mistranslation. The Greek word refers to the democratic decision-making assembly of full citizens, a meaning that has become lost in its translation as "church." As pointed out by Rick Strelan: "It is anachronistic to speak of 'church,' since that term carries too many historical and modern connotations. R. A. Markus rightly suggests that scholars do not always know what they are talking about when speaking of the 'church' in the first and second centuries."[18]

Recovering this democratic lens enables us to shift and nuance the scholarly discussions of the content and function of the letter. "Reading against the grain" of the exhortation, one realizes, moreover, that Ephesians 5:22-33 is not a descriptive but a "should" or prescriptive statement. It does not state that wo/men are willingly subjecting themselves to their men. Rather, it is an imperative statement: Wo/men should submit themselves to their own men in everything. It is important to note as well that the wo/men are admonished to submit to their own men rather than to all men in general.

In short, a feminist reading of Ephesians in general, and of Ephesians 5:22-33 in particular, against its androcentric grain can affirm that wo/men are full members of the *ekklēsia*. This is an important insight for understanding the whole letter, because *ekklēsia* is a key term in Ephesians. Wo/men do not appear in Ephesians as decision-making citizens

---

18. Rick Strelan, *Paul, Artemis, and the Jews in Ephesus*, BZNW 80 (Berlin: de Gruyter, 1996), 14; Robert A. Markus, "The Problem of Self-Definition: From Sect to Church," in *Jewish and Christian Self-Definition*, vol. 1: *The Shaping of Christianity in the Second and Third Centuries*, ed. E. P. Sanders (Philadelphia: Fortress, 1980), 1–15.

(those who make up the *ekklēsia*) but are emphatically told to be subject in everything to their men.

A critical feminist reading against the grain of the reference to wo/men in Ephesians 5:22-33 takes feminist insights regarding androcentric language seriously, transforming our whole understanding of the letter. Such a reading allows us to understand the androcentric language of the whole letter as inclusive language until proven otherwise, enabling us to assume that wo/men were members of the *ekklēsia* and therefore full citizens. We are invited not only to imagine the wo/men of the community hearing or reading the whole letter, as well as responding to it, but also as the*logically questioning claims such as "Ephesians is Holy Scripture that tells us about G*d's relation to his people." The recognition of androcentric language compels us to ask: Why not translate "God's relation to her/his or their people" if one takes seriously that androcentric language is generic language that includes the feminine in the masculine pronoun form? It compels us to read against the grain of the letter's androcentric language rather than to understand it as dramatic script[19] that Christian readers and communities have to perform. Rather than being a script to perform, Ephesians, I suggest, is best understood as rhetoric that seeks to persuade. As rhetoric, the letter calls for reading against the grain of its androcentric language and requires a critical feminist evaluation if we are to discern the words of Divine Wisdom given to us "for the sake of our salvation/well-being."[20] It also requires that we read Ephesians 5:22-33 in its literary and historical context in order to understand its andro/kyriocentric rhetoric and historical situation.

4. A Critical Feminist Hermeneutics

The notion of hermeneutics derives from the Greek word ἑρμενεία (*hermeneia*) and means to interpret, exegete, explain, or translate. Its name is derived from Hermes, the messenger of the G*ds,[21] who has the

---

19. See Timothy G. Gombis, *The Drama of Ephesians: Participating in the Triumph of God* (Downers Grove, IL: InterVarsity Press, 2010).

20. See Vatican II, *Dei Verbum*, Dogmatic Constitution on Divine Revelation (November 18, 1965).

21. During the feminist anti-Judaism debates in the 1980s, the Goddess theologian Carol Christ pointed out that Christian feminists are as much guilty of anti-Paganism as of anti-Judaism. Such a prejudice is expressed in the standard capitalization of the Christian G*d and the writing of other gods and goddesses in lowercase. To become conscious of this prejudice and avoid it, this commentary capitalizes all references to Gods and Goddesses.

task of mediating the announcements, declarations, and messages of the G*ds to mortals. According to Hans Georg Gadamer,[22] hermeneutics is called upon to translate meaning from one "world" to another.[23] Like Hermes, the messenger of the G*ds, hermeneutics not only communicates knowledge but also instructs, directs, and enjoins. As a discipline, hermeneutics is best understood as a theory and practice of interpretation that explores the conditions and possibilities of understanding not just texts but other practices as well.[24] Thus hermeneutics is not so much a disciplined scientific method and technique as it is an epistemological perspective and approach.[25]

Over and against scientific positivism, hermeneutics has maintained that understanding takes place as a process of engagement in the hermeneutical circle or spiral, which is characterized by the part-whole relation. It stresses that understanding is not possible without pre-understandings or prejudices, and therefore that understanding is always contextually dependent.

Hermeneutics insists on the linguisticality of all knowledge, its contextuality and immersion in tradition. It stresses that human understanding can never take place without words and outside of time. From a critical feminist perspective, hermeneutics, which is concerned mainly with the surplus of meaning, does not take sufficiently into account andro/kyriocentric language relations of domination and power. Critical theory, on the other hand, focuses on the lack and distortion of meaning, that is, ideology, through relations of domination.

With the feminist theorist Michèlle Barrett[26] I understand ideology as a process of mystification or misrepresentation. Ideology is distorted communication rather than false consciousness. In this view Ephesians 5:22-33 is distorted communication insofar as the analogy between man and messiah and between woman and *ekklēsia* is based on grammatical gender that

22. See Hans Georg Gadamer, *Truth and Method* and *Philosophical Hermeneutics* (Berkeley: University of California Press, 1976).

23. See Richard Bernstein, "What Is the Difference That Makes a Difference? Gadamer, Habermas, and Rorty," in *Hermeneutics and Modern Philosophy*, ed. Brice R. Wachterhauser (Albany: State University of New York Press, 1986), 343–76.

24. Paul Ricoeur's theory of interpretation has argued that action may be regarded as a text. If an action, like a text, is a meaningful entity, then the "paradigm of reading" can also be applied to socio-religious practices. See Paul Ricoeur, *Hermeneutics and the Human Sciences: Essays on Language, Action, and Interpretation*, trans. John B. Thompson (Cambridge: Cambridge University Press, 1981), 197–221.

25. See Wachterhauser, *Hermeneutics and Modern Philosophy*, 5.

26. Michelle Barrett, *The Politics of Truth: From Marx to Foucault* (Stanford: Stanford University Press, 1991), 177.

is attached to a social group, *ekklēsia*, consisting of wo/men [women and men]. Its grammatical gender assignments are then mistakenly supposed to refer to feminine and masculine dichotomies, that is, the *ekklēsia* is essentialized as female and the messiah as male.

A fundamental assumption of critical feminist theory holds that every form of grammatical and social order contains some elements of domination and that critical emancipatory interests fuel the struggles to change these relations of domination and subordination. Such power relations inscribed in texts and people's lives engender forms of distorted communication that result in self-deception on the parts of agents with respect to their interests, needs, and perceptions of social and religious reality. The*logically speaking, they are structural sin.

A critical feminist emancipatory interpretation seeks not only to understand biblical texts and traditions but also to provide a method of consciousness raising and a space for transforming wo/men's self-understanding, self-perception, and self-alienation in Western male-stream intellectual frameworks, individualistic apolitical practices, and socio-political relations of cultural colonization. By analyzing the Bible's andro/kyriocentric power of persuasion it intends to engender biblical interpretation as a critical feminist praxis against all forms of domination. Liberation the*logies of all colors have not only pointed to the perspectival and contextual nature of biblical interpretation but have also asserted that biblical scholarship and the*logy are—knowingly or not—always engaged for or against the oppressed. Hence a multiplex liberationist feminist framework is needed, one that allows those who traditionally were and still often are non-persons (to use an expression of Gustavo Gutiérrez) to be subjects of interpretation and historical agents of change.

Whenever we read/hear/interpret a biblical or any other text we read/hear/interpret it by engaging one or more of the traditional approaches to interpretation. But whereas the standard modes of interpretation do not call for a critical self-consciousness or demystify grammatical gender systems, a critical feminist emancipatory paradigm makes explicit the interpretive lenses with which it approaches the text. While malestream approaches conceal that they operate with andro/kyriocentric socio-political and religious analytic frameworks, a critical feminist emancipatory approach openly states that it wants to engage in biblical interpretation for the sake of conscientization and change, that is, for the sake of wo/men's salvation or well-being.

Religious biblical identity that is shaped by Scripture must be deconstructed and reconstructed in ever-new readings in terms of a global praxis for the liberation of all wo/men. Equally, cultural identity that is shaped by biblical discourses must be critically interrogated and transformed. Hence it is necessary to reconceptualize the traditional spiritual practice of "discerning the spirits" as a critical ethical-political practice.

In a critical spiraling dance of interpretation, wo/men readers as interpreting subjects learn to reclaim our spiritual authority for assessing both the oppressive and the liberating imagination of particular biblical texts and their interpretations. We are enabled to reject the epistemological blueprints and methodological rules of the linguistic andro/kyriocentered "master template" or "sacred script" that eliminates wo/men from historical texts, often marginalizing and trivializing us as well. In consequence, the feminist label, "Caution, could be dangerous to your health and survival," must be kept in mind, not only when we read sacred texts but especially also when we read scholarly interpretations and commentaries on these texts that fail to take seriously the obfuscating character of andro/kyriocentric language.

Reading Ephesians as a Latina Feminist

Taking into account that by the fourth century of the current era Christianity emerged victoriously as the official religion of the Roman Empire, my reading of Ephesians cannot escape the conviction that this letter, as attributed to the Pauline theological tradition, contributed greatly to making this possible. The letter unfolds a religious rhetoric encouraging everyone to build, in the name of Christ, a "body joined and knit together by every ligament with which it is equipped, as each part is working properly" (4:16). Such a rhetoric of strong social cohesion was highly compatible with the interests and goals of the emperors, who were eager for the unification of imperial powers. Both the emperor Constantine's Edict of Milan (313 CE), declaring religious tolerance, and the emperor Theodosius's Edict of Thessalonica (380 CE), declaring Christianity the official religion of the Roman Empire, functioned politically and theologically as seals validating the long-expected "day of liberation" (4:30) for Christians, whose existence had now shifted from darkness to light (5:8). Ephesians articulates the religious framework that provided legitimization for Christendom as a historical system in which the Holy Roman Empire and Western European Christianity found roots.

As I read this biblical text from a Latina feminist perspective I am often impressed by the sophisticated religious ideology it presents, playing with antinomies in terms of contradicting notions, conflicting meanings, and disconcerting ideas. Here is a powerful kyriocentric religious language that declares docile submission to hierarchical social relationships to be a way of life. More than simply descriptive binaries, one finds throughout the letter the use of antinomies as discursive strategy by which language says one thing but means another, ideologically masking and concealing the political impact and results of discourse. Throughout Ephesians appear antinomies such as earthly masters/ cosmic powers, universal/ domestic, servitude/liberation, alien/citizen, hostility/peace, old self/new self, and so on. This powerful kyriocentric ideology embedded in the text has contributed and still contributes to the forging of entire civilizations. It has also remained so embedded in the mind-set and ordinary thinking of Christians that it appears impervious to change. In my view the message conveyed by Ephesians has been successful in helping to cement hierarchical social systems and relationships, especially by promoting obedience to Christ (but only through and for the church) as well as obedience to earthly masters, and by conveniently transposing the struggles against rulers and authorities as cosmic powers to the ethereal cosmic realm because, according to Ephesians, "our struggle is not against enemies of blood and flesh" (6:12). As a result,

this kyriocentric rhetoric not only conceals conflictive social relationships of power in the name of Christ but also makes of Christianity a religion fully compatible with the interests of every empire or hegemonic social system.

A feminist hermeneutic of critical evaluation has been helpful to my reading of Ephesians. More generally, this hermeneutic is crucial to elucidating the social function and effects of biblical texts and theological traditions. It also allows one to unveil the ideological interests and values conveyed by religious rhetoric. In light of this, a feminist interpretation of Ephesians grounded in contemporary feminist struggles for justice and liberation allows one to expose the incompatibility between Ephesians and feminist the*logy in terms of how they envision a way of life. A radical transformation of kyriarchal social systems and relationships is necessary for a Christian feminist the*logy if one is to maintain that both women and men are members of the one body of Christ and equally belong to the household of God. As created by God, a new humanity freed from exclusion and hostility can flourish only in the setting of a new society freed from kyriarchal powers, so that both humans and world can truly become a praise of God's glory (Eph 1:6, 12, 14).

María Pilar Aquino

Questions of Introduction

Since scholarly discussion on the writings of the New* Testament rarely focuses on questions of andro-kyriocentric language and hermeneutics but centers on questions of historical authorship, recipients, and time and place of publication, I have in a first step tried to establish a feminist framework for exploring such historical issues.

Authorship

The inscribed author of Ephesians is Paul, apostle through the will of G*d (Eph 1:1). However, many scholars today question whether the letter was really written by Paul because of its style, vocabulary, and the*logy, all of which are different from those of the "genuine" Pauline letters such as Romans, Galatians, Corinthians, Philippians, Thessalonians, or Philemon. Hence non-Pauline authorship of the letter is thought to be more likely. Ephesians is then understood to be pseudonymously claiming the authority of the apostle for its communication.

For many Christian readers today the assumption of non-Pauline authorship is troubling. However, the letter's the*logical and spiritual authority is not contingent on its historical Pauline authorship; since the letter is part of the Christian canon, its canonical authority is still valid. The assumption that the historical authorship of Paul is decisive for the the*logical standing of the letter is a very modern assumption because it bases the authority of the letter not on inspiration by the Holy Spirit/Divine Wisdom but on the facticity of whether Paul "actually" wrote the letter. Such an understanding of historical authorship as factual is a very recent notion. Modern concepts of intellectual property and plagiarism were not operative in antiquity in our sense of them. Hence the ancients did not consistently judge borrowing a well-known person's title and writing in that person's name as negative. Rather, they were concerned with the authority and spiritual quality of the content of a writing.

Basing the authority of the letter to the Ephesians on the historical facticity of Paul's authorship hinders critical engagement not only with the the*logical but also with the historical context of the letter. Those scholars who accept the apostle Paul's authorship date the letter in the early 60s CE during Paul's imprisonment in Rome. Scholars who argue that Ephesians is pseudonymous still ascribe the letter to a close disciple of Paul or to a Pauline "school" or circle. Rudolf Schnackenburg pointed out that Catholic exegetes, who in the past defended the authenticity of the letter as Pauline, now think its origins are "post-Pauline" because the language of the letter has greater affinity to post-Pauline literature, marked by differences in style and the*logical divergences.[27]

The authorship debate has consequences that are not so much the*logical but more about our historical understanding of the letter. Considering it post-Pauline makes it difficult for scholars to date the letter and place it in its cultural context. Dating the letter has significant hermeneutical consequences regarding the rhetorical-historical situation of the letter. If Ephesians is best dated in the late 80s or early 90s of the first century rather than in the early 60s, its historical context changes drastically. Not only has the apostolic generation passed but the war against the Roman occupation in the homeland Palestine has also been lost. Thus it is reasonable to conclude that the rhetorical situation in the 80s/90s is quite different from that in the 60s.

Recipients

Whether Ephesians was written by Paul or by a successor of Paul, its Jewish authorship is generally accepted, and the identity of the recipients, who are called "the saints," is assumed to be "Christian." The identity of the recipients is generally not discussed in commentaries because the writer is understood to address "former Gentiles" who, it is presupposed, have become "Christians" rather than "Jews." However, more recently the use of the dualistic nomenclature "Christians"/"Jews," which assumes distinct and oppositional religious and historical identities, has been problematized.

While it is now widely acknowledged that the apostle Paul was Jewish and wrote as a Jew, the time of the "parting of the ways" between Jews and Christians is still a subject for debate. Was it in the late first century, or only in the fourth century when Christianity became the official religion of the Roman Empire? In other words, did the former Gentiles whom the author addresses become "Jewish," or did they become "Christian"? This question presupposes that the categories "Jew" and "Christian" are exclusive of each other, and the question remains whether we can assume that this was already the case at the end of the first century.

The Jewish scholar Daniel Boyarin has argued that we cannot speak about Judaism and Christianity as two distinct, opposing religions until the fourth or fifth centuries CE. Until then there are no sets of features

27. Rudolf Schnackenburg, *Ephesians: A Commentary*, trans. Helen Heron (Edinburgh: T&T Clark, 1991), 24.

that define "Jewish" and "Christian" in such a way that the two categories do not overlap. Boyarin's proposal, which is carefully developed in his book, *Border Lines*, and succinctly argued in *The Jewish Gospels: The Story of the Jewish Christ*, is revolutionary insofar as it opens up the possibility of a non-supersessionist, non-colonizing reading of the New* Testament in general and of Ephesians in particular.

Boyarin convincingly argues that the "parting of the ways," which was supposed in previous scholarship to have taken place after a period of fluidity at the end of the first or the beginning of the second century CE, took place much later. Boyarin points out that the fluidity and diversity of Judaism did not end with the destruction of the temple or the so-called Council of Yavneh (ca. 90 CE)—a Talmudic legend patterned after the famous imperial Council of Nicaea (325 CE) or Constantinople (381 CE). These two ecumenical councils, which were called by the emperor, functioned to establish "a Christianity that was completely separated from Judaism." Boyarin concludes that "[a]t least from a juridical standpoint, then, Judaism and Christianity became completely separate religions only in the fourth century."[28]

To illustrate his point Boyarin translates and quotes a letter sent by Jerome (347–420 CE), a Christian scholar and saint, to his colleague, Augustine of Hippo (354–430 CE):

> In our own days there exists a sect among the Jews throughout all the synagogues of the East, which is called the sect of the Minei, and is even now condemned by the Pharisees. The adherents to this sect are known commonly as Nazarenes; they believe in Christ the Son of God, born of the Virgin Mary; and they say that He who suffered under Pontius Pilate and rose again, is the same as the one in whom we believe. But while they desire to be *both Jews and Christians*, they are neither the one nor the other.[29]

The "parting of the ways" of Judaism and Christianity was completed by Roman imperial power to serve imperial colonial interests. As a result one could no longer be both Jewish and Christian. The canonical consolidation of the Christian Scriptures took place at this same time. Every Christian reading of the Bible that does not question such a colonizing nomenclature is therefore necessarily supersessionist.

---

28. Daniel Boyarin, *The Jewish Gospels: The Story of the Jewish Christ* (New York: New Press, 2012), 12–13. See also Boyarin, *Border Lines: The Partition of Judaeo-Christianity*, Divinations (Philadelphia: University of Pennsylvania Press, 2004).

29. Boyarin, *The Jewish Gospels*, 16; emphasis added.

In order to read New* Testament texts such as Ephesians as fundamentally Jewish texts, Boyarin argues, we must give up the understanding that "religions are fixed sets of convictions with well-defined boundaries," as such a construction does not allow for the possibility that one could be at once both a Jew and a Christian.[30] He suggests, therefore, that we speak of "Christian Jews" and "non-Christian Jews" prior to the fourth or fifth century CE. However, even if one accepts Boyarin's proposal to read Ephesians as a "Christian" Jewish writing one must still defend against supersessionism, since the word "Christian" broadly continues to be understood as "different from" or "over against" the word "Jew." Hence I wonder whether Boyarin's suggested nomenclature "Christian Jews" and "non-Christian Jews," which privileges "Christian or non-Christian" as defining terms for Jews, still allows for the misunderstanding of supersessionism.

Since Boyarin stresses that the coming of a Messiah had been imagined in Jewish Scriptures long before the time of early "Christian Judaism," I suggest a third way of naming is to speak of "Jewish Messianism" instead of "Jewish Christianity" or "Messianic Judaism" in order to overcome the dichotomy Judaism/Christianity and the Christian cooptation of the term "Messianic Judaism."[31]

The Septuagint (LXX), the Greek translation of the Hebrew Bible, renders all thirty-nine instances of the Hebrew word for the "anointed one," משיח, *Mašîaḥ*, as χριστός, *Christos*, an equation the New* Testament writers seem to adopt since we find the Greek transliteration of *Messias* only twice in the New* Testament, in John 1:41 and 4:25. The term Χριστιανός/ Χριστιανοί, *Christianos/Christianoi*, is used in 1 Peter 4:16 and in Acts 11:26; 26:28. Most scholars agree that this designation originated with outsiders.[32] However, it is more difficult to determine whether the term *Christianos* was coined as a popular label, as many suggest,

---

30. Ibid., 8.

31. Messianic Judaism is a syncretistic movement that combines the Christian belief that Jesus is the Jewish Messiah with elements of Jewish tradition and practice. Its current form emerged in the 1960s and 1970s. Salvation is achieved only through acceptance of Jesus as one's savior, and Jewish laws or customs that are followed do not contribute to salvation. Other Christian groups usually accept Messianic Judaism as a form of Christianity. See also David Rudolph and Joel Willetts, eds., *Introduction to Messianic Judaism: Its Ecclesial Context and Biblical Foundations* (Grand Rapids: Zondervan, 2013).

32. David G. Horrell, "The Label Χριστιανός: 1 Peter 4:16 and the Formation of Christian Identity," *JBL* 126 (2007): 361–81.

or whether it was formulated by Roman authorities, as Erik Peterson has argued.[33] If we follow Peterson's lead we can assume that the term was first used in Antioch and may have been coined by members of the Roman administration. According to Peterson the word probably originated in Latin-speaking circles. It appears for the "first" time in Acts 11:26, where it refers "to an official or juridical designation rather than to informal naming."[34] Thus the language seems to convey "a legal or juristic sense, as in legal documents, where it indicates something is now being recorded that will henceforth have force."[35] Finally, in many non-Christian first-century-CE sources the names "Christ" and "Christian" seem to be associated with public disorder.

Since the title *Christos*, i.e., "Messiah"—but not yet the word *Christianoi*—appears in the Ephesian nomenclature we can assume that the recipients still understood themselves as Jewish Messianists. The author speaks of Israel and Gentiles (τὰ ἔθνη). Within the covenant people of Israel we then can identify three distinct groups: the followers of Jesus Messiah, consisting of both Jews and former Gentiles; followers of other Jewish Messianic figures; and those Jews who were not followers of a Messiah (later Rabbinic groups). As we know, at the time there were various Jewish groups claiming different messianic leaders as well as Jews who rejected messianic organizations. Hence we must be careful not to reinscribe the later historical Jew-Christian dichotomy but rather recognize that the dualism being constructed in Ephesians is Jew-Gentile.[36] The recipients of Ephesians are then followers of Messiah Jesus and consist of both Jews and former Gentiles.

Location

Whereas the recipients' Jewish-Messianic identity is for the most part controversially coopted as "Christian" by commentators, their geographical location is much debated, since key manuscripts omit

33. Erik Peterson, "Christianus," in *Frühkirche, Judentum und Gnosis. Studien und Untersuchungen* (Freiburg: Herder, 1959), 64–87.

34. Ibid., 67–69.

35. Ibid., 68.

36. For a somewhat different perspective, see Rikard Roitto, *Behaving as a Christ Believer: A Cognitive Perspective on Identity and Behavior Norms in Ephesians*, ConBNT 46 (Winona Lake, IN: Eisenbrauns, 2011), 198–203. Roitto speaks of Christ-believers rather than Jesus-Messiah followers.

"in Ephesus" as the location of those to whom the letter is sent.[37] That it was sent to the saints (τοῖς ἁγίοις) in Ephesus (ἐν Ἐφέσῳ) was known in the second century, but such a location is not specified in the most trustworthy manuscript witnesses. The omission of the two words "in Ephesus" then makes it difficult to pinpoint the geographical location of the letter's addressees, since we do not have any other information regarding the audience.

Scholars who doubt that the letter was written by Paul argue that it was written to people in Western Asia Minor in general, or to Hierapolis and Laodicea in particular, because of its close literary relationship to Colossians.[38] Whether we consider "in Ephesus" as authentic or assume that the letter was written to the whole province, we can still use the canonical label "Ephesians," since Ephesus was declared the capital of the Roman province of Asia by Augustus. According to the geographer, historian, and philosopher Strabo (born 64 BCE), Ephesus was second only to Rome in importance and size.[39]

We can still fill in information about the community from what we know about it from other Pauline letters as well as from other early Christian and non-Christian historical sources. For instance, Lynn H. Cohick has pointed out that in 1 Corinthians, Paul, who writes this letter from Ephesus, mentions that some people of Chloe have told them of divisions within the Corinthian *ekklēsia*. Hence "we could reasonably surmise that Chloe's people (and perhaps Chloe herself) were members of the Ephesian church."[40]

More important, two apostolic Jewish wo/men[41] are mentioned as having lived either in Ephesus (Prisca) or in Laodicea (Nympha). Paul writes at the end of 1 Corinthians that "the *ekklēsiai* of Asia [Minor] send greetings. Aquila and Prisca, together with the church in their house, greet you warmly in the Lord" (16:19). It is debated whether Prisca and Aquila were a married couple or a missionary pair. We know from Acts 18:2 that they were expelled from Rome by the Roman emperor Claudius's edict

37. On Jewish presence in Ephesus, see Rick Strelan, *Paul*, 192–204, 306–9.

38. Andrew T. Lincoln, *Ephesians*, WBC 42 (Dallas: Word, 1990), 3–4.

39. Strabo, *The Geography of Strabo*, vols. 1–7, trans. Horace Leonard Jones, LCL (Cambridge: Harvard University Press, 1917–1932).

40. Lynn H. Cohick, *Ephesians* (Eugene, OR: Cascade Books, 2010), 34.

41. For the status and role of Jewish wo/men in Asia Minor see also Strelan, *Paul*, 190–91.

against Jews and emigrated to Corinth before Paul arrived there. When Paul wrote 1 Corinthians they had gathered an *ekklēsia* in their house.

According to Acts the history of the church in Ephesus begins with the ministry of Paul on his second missionary journey (Acts 18:18-28). Together with Prisca and Aquila, Paul traveled to Ephesus, preached in the synagogue, and was asked to stay on and teach further. Paul declined, promising to return, but Prisca and Aquila remained in Ephesus. In Ephesus they taught Apollos, a native of Alexandria, who later was a successful preacher in Corinth, "well versed in the Scriptures" (1 Cor 3:4-6; Acts 19:10).[42]

Like Paul, Aquila, Barnabas, Timothy, and Apollos, Prisca was a leading figure in the mission to the Gentiles. The fact that her name is mentioned four times (of six) before that of Aquila indicates that she had a leading position. In Romans 16, Paul calls both of them "coworkers" and emphasizes that not only he but "all Gentile communities are grateful to them." Their house was known as an *ekklēsia* center, not only in Corinth (1 Cor 16:19), but also in Ephesus (Acts 18:18) and Rome (Rom 16:5). That Luke, who focuses on Paul, mentions them in Acts at all indicates that they were so important in the beginning of the messianic Jesus movement that they could not be passed over in silence. As Acts 18:26 indicates, they had great influence, not only on Paul, but also on Apollos, the other great missionary alongside themselves and Paul. Their work shaped the beginnings of the community in Ephesus.

Whether we understand the letter to be penned by Paul or by one of the later followers of the apostle, we still can assert that Prisca was known as a leading wo/man missionary and co-founder of the community in Ephesus. Since Prisca and Aquila were a Jewish couple who founded and nurtured the *ekklēsia* in Ephesus, the so-called household code in Ephesians 5:22–6:8 appears in a new light. This missionary apostolic couple had set an example not only for egalitarian marriage relationships but also for the egalitarian collaboration of wo/men and men in the *ekklēsia*. If Prisca and Aquila were missionary coworkers with Paul it is not likely that Paul would have criticized the example they set by adopting the so-called household code of the letter to the Colossians and reinterpreted it by sharpening the injunction to the wo/men, calling for subordination in everything. This makes it less likely that Paul is the author of Ephesians.

---

42. See Elisabeth Schüssler Fiorenza, *In Memory of Her: A Feminist Theological Reconstruction of Christian Origins* (New York: Crossroad, 1994).

Ephesians's Template: Colossians

If one looks at the relationship between Ephesians and Colossians it also appears more likely that a "student" of Paul used and expanded Colossians than it is that Paul himself did so. Whereas Paul's letters usually speak to a concrete and specific situation within the community addressed, it is difficult to pin down the rhetorical situation of Ephesians. The letter not only takes over segments of Colossians; it also follows the argumentative course taken by Colossians, as indicated in the following chart:[43]

Letter Opening	Eph 1:1-2	Col 1:1-2
Thanksgiving/Intercession	Eph 1:15-17	Col 1:3-8
Coming Alive with Christ	Eph 2:5-6	Col 2:12-13
Exhortation	Eph 4:17-32	Col 3:5-14
Spiritual Worship	Eph 5:19-20	Col 3:16-17
Household	Eph 5:26–6:9	Col 3:18–4:1
Steadfast Prayer	Eph 6:18-20	Col 4:2-4
Sending of Tychicus	Eph 6:21-22	Col 4:7
Concluding Greetings	Eph 6:24	Col 4:18

By following the rhetorical outline of Colossians, the author of Ephesians may have sought to authorize the letter as "Pauline" because Paul was known as the coworker of Prisca and Aquila. If the letter is dated in the late 80s or beginning 90s CE, Prisca was probably still remembered and celebrated in the surrounding areas as a leading missionary and founder of the Ephesian messianic assembly and might have been an inspiration for married wo/men's equal status and leadership in the *ekklēsia*. However, it is interesting that, unlike the letter to the Colossians, which sends greetings to Nympha and the "*ekklēsia* in her house,"[44] no house-*ekklēsia* is mentioned in Ephesians.

Moreover, Ephesians alludes to but omits the pre-Pauline "baptismal reunification formula" (Gal 3:28), which is modified in Colossians 3:11:

---

43. Schnackenburg, *Ephesians*, 30.

44. See Margaret Y. MacDonald, "Can Nympha Rule This House? The Rhetoric of Domesticity in Colossians," in *Rhetoric and Reality in Early Christianity*, ed. Willi Braun (Waterloo, ON: Wilfrid Laurier University Press, 2005), 99–120.

"Here there is no Greek and Jew, circumcision and uncircumcision, barbarian, Scythian, slave, free; but Christ is all and in all." This baptismal formula, which is also mentioned in 1 Corinthians 12:13 (and in noncanonical texts such as Clem. Al. *Strom.* 3.13.92; 2 Clem. 12.2; Gos. Thom. 37.21a, 22b), no longer cites the third pair, "no male and female," but only expands the first two pairs, which are not formulated in Galatians 3:28 in the "and" form but rather in the "neither-nor" form. The text seems to contrast the ethnic, social, and cultural divisions with the new egalitarian cosmic reality in Messiah Jesus, which is also celebrated in the hymn of Colossians 1:15-20.[45]

In addition, by taking over and refocusing large chunks of material from the letter to the Colossians, which was known as a Pauline letter, the author probably also sought to claim Pauline authorization for the message of Ephesians. Of special interest is how the author uses Colossians as a template or source for articulating the so-called domestic code of Ephesians. By appropriating and reshaping the "household code" of Colossians the author may have wanted to suggest that the letter had the approval of the founder Nympha and her house-*ekklēsia* and also wanted to appeal to the memory of the founder of the Ephesian *ekklēsia*, Prisca. A hermeneutics of suspicion and imagination is called for!

A comparison between the so-called household code text of Colossians 3:18–4:1 and that of Ephesians 5:26–6:9 indicates a shift in rhetorical emphasis from admonition to slave wo/men to an address to freeborn wo/men. Whereas in Colossians slaves are the center of attention, the focus in Ephesians is on freeborn wo/men, on the one hand, and the *ekklēsia*, or assembly of free citizens, on the other. Colossians has only a short reciprocal injunction for freeborn[46] wo/men (wives) but a long

---

45. See Margaret Y. MacDonald, *Colossians and Ephesians*, SP 17 (Collegeville, MN: Liturgical Press, 2008), 138–39.

46. Legally, slaves could not marry, although we have evidence that they used kinship terms. Since slave wo/men are mentioned later, it is safe to assume that the text speaks here of freeborn women. I am grateful to Tyler Schwaller for the following references: W. W. Buckland, *The Roman Law of Slavery: The Condition of the Slave in Private Law from Augustus to Justinian* (Cambridge: Cambridge University Press, 1908), 76–79; Dale B. Martin, "Slave Families and Slaves in Families," in *Early Christian Families in Context: An Interdisciplinary Dialogue*, ed. David L. Balch and Carolyn Osiek (Grand Rapids: Eerdmans, 2003), 207–30; Bernadette J. Brooten, "Early Christian Enslaved Families: First to Fourth Century," in *Children and Family in Late Antiquity: Life, Death and Interaction*, ed. Christian Laes, Katariina Mustakallio, and Ville Vuolanto (Leuven: Peeters, 2015), 118–24.

command to slaves (four verses) and concludes with one admonition to masters. Ephesians in turn has a long section on the submission of freeborn wo/men (wives) in everything and the duty of husbands to love their wives. This admonition is intertwined with a comparison between Jesus Messiah and the *ekklēsia*. This shift in emphasis between Colossians and Ephesians indicates the interest of the author in reshaping the Colossian household code instructions as significant not only for the household but also for the *ekklēsia*. Hence it is especially important to pay attention to the divergence of Ephesians from Colossians.

The texts classified as household code, or *Haustafel*, a label derived from Luther's teaching on social status and roles, are concerned with three sets of relationships: husband and wife, fathers/parents and children, and masters/mistresses and slave wo/men. However, it must not be overlooked that it is one and the same person, the *kyrios*-husband-father-slavemaster, who enjoys superordination. The central interest of these texts lies in the enforcement of the submission and obedience of the socially weaker group—freeborn wo/men (wives), slave wo/men, and children—on the one hand, and the authority of the head of the household, the *paterfamilias*, on the other. The so-called household code, with its injunction to submission, also appears in 1 Peter 2:18–3:7; 1 Timothy 2:11-15; 5:3-8; 6:1-2; Titus 2:2-10; 3:1-2; 1 Clement 21.6-8; Ignatius's *To Polycarp* 4.1–6.2; Polycarp's *To the Philippians* 4.2–6.1; Didache 4.9-11; Barnabas 19.5-7. The pattern of subjection need not always include all social-status groups addressed in Colossians and Ephesians. The pattern of the household code can also include obedience and submission to the powers of the empire, as in 1 Peter, or address the governance of the Christian community.

While much of the earlier discussion of the household codes has focused on the context and meaning in ethical instruction, more recent research argues that household codes are part of the political philosophical discussion of *oikonomia* (generally understood as "household management") and *politeia* (understood as civil affairs, i.e., citizenship or politics) in Greco-Roman antiquity. Scholars have long recognized that such household code texts "christianize" kyriarchal social and ecclesial structures and in the past thirty or so years have pointed out the political roots of these texts in Aristotelian philosophy. In contrast to the Sophists, Aristotle stressed that the patri-kyriarchal relationships in the household and city-state, as well as their associated social differences, are based not on social-political convention but on "nature." Aristotle, therefore, insisted that the discussion of political ethics and household management begin with marriage, defined as the union of natural ruler and natural subject (Arist. *Pol.* 1.1252a. 24-28). In the first century CE diverse philosophical schools and directions used this political philosophy to strengthen the kyriarchal household and empire.[47] These discussions assume the interdependence of household (*oikos*) and city-state (*polis*).

Such a political assumption is particularly appropriate for the household code of Ephesians, since the injunctions to wives and husbands are intertwined with the relationship of Jesus Messiah with the *ekklēsia*/ democratic assembly. The household code rhetoric of Ephesians 5 seeks to shape not only the ethos of household relationships but also that of the *ekklēsia*, insofar as it understands the Jesus Messiah–*ekklēsia* relationship in analogy to the husband-wife relation and vice versa. One might have expected the author to pair G*d with the *ekklēsia* in Ephesians 5, given the precedent of the marriage metaphor of G*d and Israel that occurs in the Hebrew Scriptures. But this is not the case. It is not G*d but Jesus Messiah who is "coupled" with the *ekklēsia*. This change in the symbolic "coupling" image could be made because the metaphor of the "marriage" relation between G*d and Israel is still valid and is enhanced by the superordinate/subordinate relationship between Jesus/Messiah and *ekklēsia*/messianic community.

The Symbolic Universe of Ephesians: Political Language and Vision

How, then, does the rhetoric of the household code fit into or shape the overall rhetoric of the letter? Is it only an extraneous addition, or is it intrinsic to the letter's argument? In order to approach this question we have to look at Ephesians's overall rhetoric and vision. A rhetorical analysis[48] pays attention to both the speaker/author and the hearers/ recipients. We have already explored who wrote the letter and who its recipients were in terms of their location and religious affiliation.

---

47. See Elisabeth Schüssler Fiorenza, *Bread Not Stone: The Challenge of Feminist Biblical Interpretation* (Boston: Beacon, 1985), 65–92; Margaret Y. MacDonald, "Beyond Identification of the *Topos* of Household Management: Reading the Household Codes in Light of Recent Methodologies and Theoretical Perspectives in the Study of the New Testament," *NTS* 57 (2011): 65–90. See also Gombis, *Drama of Ephesians*.

48. See Elisabeth Schüssler Fiorenza, *Rhetoric and Ethic: The Politics of Biblical Studies* (Minneapolis: Fortress, 1999).

The rhetorical argument of the letter moves from articulating the*logical "identity"[49] (chaps. 1–2) to narrative telling (chap. 3) to ethical norms (chaps. 4–6). In this arc Ephesians 3 seeks to make the "speaker"— the apostle Paul—present and audible.[50] We touched on the "historical situation" when we looked at the authorship debate and recognized that Prisca, a Jewish wo/man, was the founder of the *ekklēsia* in Ephesus and that the recipients of the letter were Jewish messianic wo/men. This messianic community consisted of Jewish and former Gentile wo/men.

How might we understand the relationship between the historical situation and the overall vision or symbolic universe of the letter? According to Peter L. Berger and Thomas Luckmann, symbolic universes seek to provide legitimation to institutional structures and aim at making the institutionalized structures plausible and acceptable for the individual—who might otherwise not agree with the underlying logic of the institution. As an ideological system the symbolic universe "puts everything in its right place." The symbolic universe also orders history, "locating all collective events in a cohesive unity that includes past, present and future" of humanity and the whole cosmos.[51]

This symbolic political universe of Ephesians is extensively spelled out in the first chapters of the letter. However, it must not be overlooked that its terms are not descriptive but argumentative and constructive. They express the the*logical vision of the author, which must have been at least partially shared by the audience if communication were to take place. The Greek terms οἰκονομία/*oikonomia*, or household management; πολιτεία/*politeia*, or commonwealth; χριστός/*Christos*, or Messiah; and ἐκκλησία/*ekklēsia* are all political terms that define the imagination and symbolic universe of Ephesians. Since I will use them as hermeneutical lenses throughout the commentary, I need to briefly introduce them.

Oikonomia/Housekeeping

Household language is found throughout Ephesians. The Greek word οἰκονομία/*oikonomia*, from which our modern word "economics" is de-

---

49. For the identity discussion, see the introduction by Yair Furstenberg, "The Shared Dimensions of Jewish and Christian Communal Identities," in *Jewish and Christian Communal Identities in the Roman World*, ed. Yair Furstenberg (Boston: Brill, 2016), 1–24.

50. Roitto, *Behaving as a Christ Believer*, 145–218.

51. Peter L. Berger and Thomas Luckmann, *The Social Construction of Reality: A Treatise in the Sociology of Knowledge* (Garden City, NY: Doubleday, 1966), 92–104.

rived, is usually translated as "plan, administration, management, or economy." In several articles Dotan Leshem has elaborated the difference between ancient *oikonomia* and modern economics: whereas ancient economic theory is focused on the elite male and "an action is considered economically rational when taken toward a praiseworthy end, as for instance actively participating in the life of the city-state or being a philosopher," modern understandings of economics stress "the frugal use of means" and independence from "any particular ethical position."[52] The classical οἶκος/*oikos* ("house," "home") was understood as a partnership between the freeborn propertied male head of household and the matron, i.e., the freeborn propertied female head of household. This partnership has as its goal "a happy existence."[53] Leshem points out that

> of all the actors in ancient economics, the matron demonstrates perhaps the greatest resemblance to contemporary *homo economicus*; unlike the slave, she was freeborn, and unlike the master, she spent the bulk of her time in the economic domain as she was excluded from the public sphere of politics and was also barred from engaging in philosophy. . . . [N]o limit was set on her pursuit of happiness through wealth generation, which took place in the economic sphere. . . . The main difference between the ancient matron and the contemporary *homo economicus* was that the matron was expected to govern the interior of the *oikos* by demonstrating the virtue of soundness of mind. . . . In contrast, the wants of contemporary economic man are assumed to know no saturation.[54]

The language of *oikonomia*/housekeeping/household management is found not only within the so-called household code, in the analogy between Christ-*ekklēsia* and husband-wife (Eph 5:21–6:9), but also in Ephesians 1:10; 3:2; and in 3:9 where it articulates G*d's "house-keeping" of the universe. The term shares its root with οἰκοδομή/*oikodomē*, or building (Eph 2:20, 21; 4:12, 16, 29), and with οἰκεῖοι, household/family members (Eph 2:19), and is closely associated with μυστήριον, "mystery" (Eph 1:9; 3:3; 5:22; 6:19) in the argument of Ephesians. The use of "housekeeping" imagery for G*d in Ephesians fashions the Divine in the image of the

---

52. Dotan Leshem, "What Did the Ancient Greeks Mean by Oikonomia?," *Journal of Economic Perspectives* 30 (2016): 225–31.

53. Xenophon, *Ec.* 7.12, in *Xenophon, Oeconomicus: A Social and Historical Commentary*, trans. Sarah B. Pomeroy (Oxford: Clarendon, 1994), 141.

54. Ibid., 233.

ancient *matrona*. She administers, in the fullness of time, the divine plan
or economy of salvation (Eph 1:10).

In short, the lavish grace of G*d/Matrona provides wisdom and insight. Her manifold wisdom and mystery are made known "through the
ekklēsia to the principalities and powers in the heavenly places" (Eph
3:10). The mystery of the "housekeeping" plan of G*d/Matrona/Wisdom
is to gather up all things in Jesus Messiah; the plan was hidden but has
now been revealed and made known to the rulers and authorities in the
heavenly places. This mystery is the fact that Gentile and Jewish followers of Jesus Messiah have been made members of the same the*logical
body politic, Israel, and sharers of the promise in Christ/Messiah Jesus
(Eph 3:4-10).

The *Politeia*/Commonwealth of Israel

The scholarly discussion of the relationship between Jews and Gentiles
in Ephesians has moved from understanding the author and recipients as Gentile Christians and as having separated from Judaism in the
"Christian Church" to seeing the Jewish author challenging the messianic
Ephesians "to remember their past as a Gentile past in relation to Israel
and Israel's God."[55] As pointed out previously, in the past thirty years
or so a drastic change has occurred in Pauline scholarship. Instead of
reading Paul as arguing for abolishing the law and rejecting his Jewish
past, scholars have sought to correct this anti-Jewish reading by show-
ing that Paul was a faithful Jewish rabbi. Paul, then, was not converted
from Judaism to Christianity, which did not exist in the first century CE.
Rather, Paul was called, as a Jew, to become a follower of the Jewish Messiah, Jesus. The Pauline letters do not yet speak about "Christianism" as
a separate religious entity apart from Judaism.

This "new perspective" has also changed the scholarly interpretation
of Ephesians. Scholars have recognized that the characteristic Jewish
language of the letter points to a writer who is steeped in Jewish language
and speech. The author does not write against Judaism in a polemical
fashion. Instead, the author's perspective is "wholly Jewish."[56] Within
this debate, Tet-Lim N. Yee has argued that one cannot construe the

55. Stephen E. Fowl, *Ephesians: Being a Christian at Home and in the Cosmos* (Sheffield:
Sheffield Phoenix, 2014), 45–59.

56. James D. G. Dunn, "Anti-Semitism in the Deutero-Pauline Literature," in *Anti-
Semitism and Early Christianity: Issues of Polemic and Faith*, ed. Craig A. Evans and
Donald A. Hagner (Minneapolis: Fortress, 1993), 151–65.

church as a new and separate entity from Israel. In no way does Ephesians abandon ethnic Judaism in favor of Christian triumphalism. Ephesians, Tet-Lim Yee argues, has a vision of an "inclusive Israel" in which religious and ethnic identity are less bound up in each other.[57] Ephesians represents a particular form of Jewish Messianism that, according to Yee, transcends ethnocentrism. The letter attests to this form of Jewish Messianism by its references to the Messiah by the name "Jesus." The recipients do not follow just any Messiah but the one whose name is "Jesus." In short, this understanding of Ephesians assumes that there were many different messianic movements at the time, one of which was the group of followers of Messiah Jesus. Formerly the recipients were without Messiah Jesus, Gentiles "in the flesh," called the "uncircumcision," and estranged from the commonwealth (*politeia*), the body politic of Israel, but now they are brought near in "Jesus Messiah," who has "broken down the dividing wall," making peace (Eph 2:1-17).

The term *politeia*, which is widely used in the political philosophy of the Greek city-state, has a wide range of meanings. The Jewish writer Philo understands *politeia* as the corporate body of the Jews. Conversion to Judaism required three elements: observance of Jewish Law, devotion to the one G*d of the Jews, and integration into a Jewish civic body, *politeia*.[58] It is the death of Jesus, the blood of the Messiah, that has broken down the dividing wall, marking the end of Gentile separation from Israel and healing the division between Jews and Gentiles in a new messianic space called *ekklēsia*.

Ekklēsia

The term *ekklēsia* is here best translated not as "church" but as "political assembly of citizens." Recent scholarship on *ekklēsia* has confirmed the democratic roots of the term. The groundbreaking work of Anna Miller and Young-Ho Park on 1 Corinthians has demonstrated that *ekklēsia* was still a vibrant political institution and that democratic *ekklēsia* discourse continued to be juxtaposed with imperial discourse in the first-century context of imperial Rome, greatly impacting debates over authority, gender, and speech. Both scholars argue that Paul and the Corinthians shared the understanding of *ekklēsia* as an authoritative

---

57. Tet-Lim N. Yee, *Jews, Gentiles and Ethnic Reconciliation: Paul's Jewish Identity and Ephesians*, SNTSMS 130 (Cambridge: Cambridge University Press, 2005), 228.

58. Philo, *De spec. leg.* 1.314.

democratic assembly in which leadership and "citizenship" were open to all. Whether the *ekklēsia* met *en oikǭ* (in house) or citywide, it engaged in debates and struggles over leadership, community relations, and identity. These citizen assemblies were notably not restricted to male or freeborn members since wo/men are mentioned as leaders of house-*ekklēsiai* in the Pauline letters.

However, the Greek word *ekklēsia* has a different meaning today. For many readers it connotes not the "democratic assembly of full citizens" but the religious Christian community, the church. Interpretation of this Greek word, *ekklēsia*, is today strongly determined by a Christian religious language use and context that distinguishes Christian church from Jewish synagogue, even though the Septuagint (LXX), the Greek translation of the Hebrew Bible, uses *ekklēsia* and *synagogē* interchangeably.[59] *Ekklēsia* is usually translated as "church," although the original root word of church is derived from the Greek word κυριακή/*kyriakē*, "the Lord's."

In the first-century context of Ephesians *ekklēsia* is best understood in political-religious terms as the "democratic assembly or congress" of full, decision-making citizens. Democratic equality, citizenship, and decision-making power are constitutive for the notion of *ekklēsia*. Thus while commonly translated "church," *ekklēsia* should be understood more accurately as the democratic assembly or forum of full citizens who come together to decide issues pertaining to their rights and well-being. Hence, differently from other commentaries, I will use the Greek term *ekklēsia* rather than the usual translation, "church."

The new research on the political aspects of *ekklēsia* also sheds new light on the so-called household code in Ephesians 5:22-33. Whereas most discussions focus on the wife-husband relation, the text itself is interested in a comparison with the *ekklēsia*-Christ/Messiah relation: as the husband is the head of the wife, so Christ/Messiah is the head of the *ekklēsia*; as the *ekklēsia* is subject to Christ/Messiah, so wives should be to their husbands in everything. Just as Christ/Messiah loves the *ekklēsia*, so husbands should love their wives. Jesus Messiah gave himself up on behalf of the *ekklēsia* in order to sanctify *ekklēsia*, cleansing *ekklēsia* by the washing of water by the word, in order that Christ/Messiah might present the *ekklēsia* to themself in splendor, without spot or wrinkle or any such thing, that *ekklēsia* may be holy and without blemish (Eph 5:25-27).

---

59. Young-Ho Park, *Paul's Ekklesia as a Civic Assembly: Understanding the People of God in Their Politico-Social World*, WUNT 2.393 (Tübingen: Mohr Siebeck, 2015), 69–97.

This language thoroughly genderizes and privatizes the political language of *ekklēsia* in order to paint the democratic assembly in a subordinate feminine role. Moreover, the text alludes to baptismal language found in the genuine Pauline letters in order to do so. Why? If we recall that Prisca and Nympha were heads of house-*ekklēsiai* and remember the proclamation of Galatians 3:28 that in Jesus Messiah "there is no Jew or Greek, slave or free, male and female," we can surmise a situation of democratic equality, citizenship, and decision-making power as constitutive for the life of the *ekklēsia*, something the author seeks to modify. The ethos of love is now restricted to Christ/Messiah and the free male members of the *ekklēsia*, whereas the *ekklēsia*, freeborn wo/men, and slave wo/men are called to subordination. Such a trend of restricting the participation of wo/men in the gatherings of the *ekklēsia* is already observable in Paul's first letter to the Corinthians.

Anna Miller has pointed to the limitations of the classic democratic *ekklēsia* concept, in which free speech and decision-making power were masculine gendered and served to maintain the boundaries between citizens and non-citizens.[60] Only the freeborn, propertied, native-born male possessed full citizenship and democratic decision-making powers. The pre-Pauline baptismal proclamation in Galatians 3:28, however, conceives of *ekklēsia* as a citizen-space in which all the baptized—slave and free, Jew and Greek, female and male—could claim free speech, full participation, and decision-making power. It seems that such an understanding of *ekklēsia* was also prevalent among the recipients of the letter to the Ephesians, an *ekklēsia* that was founded by a missionary pair who were engaged in *ekklēsia* work.

Ephesians seeks to correct this egalitarian communal understanding not only by introducing injunctions to subordination but also by distinguishing "head" and "body" when speaking of the "body of Christ," a distinction that is not yet found in the genuine Pauline letters. In 1 Corinthians 12:12, 14-25, Paul uses the metaphor of the body to challenge the hierarchal or, more precisely, kyriarchal understanding of the social-political body. Unlike the author of Ephesians, Paul does not distinguish between head and body but argues for "the reversal of the normal, 'this-worldly' attribution of honor and status," insisting that "greater honor . . . should be given to those normally considered to be

---

60. Anna C. Miller, *Corinthian Democracy: Democratic Discourse in 1 Corinthians* (Eugene, OR: Pickwick Publications, 2015), 115–53.

of low status."[61] Paul is concerned with the ethos of the "body politic" of the *ekklēsia*. He uses the political "body" metaphor for leveling the kyriarchal status and honor system of Greco-Roman society by giving the perceived "lower" parts of the body greater honor, a move that turned the Greco-Roman system upside down. Ephesians seems to do just the opposite by reintroducing the division between head (superiority) and body (subordination). This observation is one of the major reasons why scholars have questioned Pauline authorship. The author of Ephesians does not seek to change the kyriarchal status system of Greco-Roman society but reinscribes it in terms of the status and values of the Roman Empire.

IMPERIAL THE*LOGY AND THE *EKKLĒSIA*

In his very engaging book *Picturing Paul in Empire*, Harry O. Maier has argued that Ephesians mimics the Roman imperial system and ideology through the use of imperial texts and images. However, it is not the Roman emperor but Christ "who delivers imperial triumph, worldwide peace and reconciliation."[62] The rhetoric of Ephesians is thus not anti-imperial but supra-imperial insofar as the letter uses imperial imagery and language to paint an understanding and image of Jesus Messiah that trumps that of the emperor. Whatever claims were made about the emperor and the peace and prosperity the empire has achieved are surpassed by Christ/Messiah. Yet by mimicking the imperial order and using its language and imagery Ephesians reinscribes Roman imperial ideology in the*logical terms.

Ephesians thus mirrors the political situation in Asia Minor, where the democratic city assemblies struggled to preserve their independence and decision-making powers. It is this tension between a democratic and imperial imaginary that shapes the rhetoric and ethos of Ephesians. Its rhetoric promotes the imperial politics of rule by painting Jesus Messiah in imperial colors and subordinating the democratic *ekklēsia* to the imperial order, just as wo/men have to submit to their own men. In line with this imperial politics and following the lead of Colossians, Ephesians—unlike Corinthians—uses the body image for the purpose of kyriarchally differentiating Christ, the head, from the body of believers, the *ekklēsia*.

---

61. Dale B. Martin, *The Corinthian Body* (New Haven: Yale University Press, 1995), 96.
62. Harry O. Maier, *Picturing Paul in Empire: Imperial Image, Text and Persuasion in Colossians, Ephesians and the Pastoral Epistles* (London: Bloomsbury, 2013), 141.

One could argue that the author seeks to undermine this imperial imagery in and through the ethic of love. While that might have been the author's intention, the letter does not preach the mutuality of love between equals. Rather, it calls the lower-status members of the *ekklēsia* to subordination, thereby reinscribing the structural kyriarchal status hierarchy of the Roman Empire. Thus Ephesians ends with a military call to arms. It leaves us with the image not of *ekklēsia* but of imperial war.

In a richly documented work titled *Pax Christi et Pax Caesaris* (*The Peace of Christ and the Peace of Caesar*), Eberhard Faust[63] has argued with reference to Dietmar Kienast[64] that in the time of Emperor Augustus the organic understanding of the Roman city-state was applied to the empire with its provinces, now understood as a body (*corpus*). The emperor is understood as the head of the body-empire. The metaphor of the democratic city-state as a body that expressed the solidarity and mutuality of the citizenry is replaced by the metaphor of the imperial body, now characterized by the mutuality of the members *under the leadership of the imperial head*.

This metaphor of imperial head and body has also determined the Ephesian household code and its understanding of *ekklēsia*. Freeborn wo/men should subordinate themselves to the domination of their husbands, who are their head (κεφαλὴ), just as the *ekklēsia* (citizen assembly) is subordinated to its head, Christ (Eph 5:22-24). The notion of "head" is also used by Paul in 1 Corinthians 11:3, where G*d is understood as head of Christ, Christ as head of man, and man as head of woman. Thus the kyriarchal household is understood as the nucleus of the kyriarchal empire, and Jesus Messiah, who was executed by the Roman Empire, becomes, in Christian imagination, the new emperor who demands subjection. True, the author sought to mitigate this imperial metaphorical-symbolic universe by making the love (*agapē*) of Jesus Messiah the paradigm for the husband to imitate. However, such love is no longer mutual but kyriarchal: top-down love. In short, by masculinizing the Divine and feminizing the *ekklēsia* the author constructs a kyriarchal relationship of domination. Ephesians attempts to mitigate

---

63. Eberhard Faust, *Pax Christi et Pax Caesaris: Religionsgeschichtliche, Traditionsgeschichtliche und Sozialgeschichtliche Studien zum Epheserbrief* (Fribourg: Universitätsverlag, 1993).

64. Dietmar Kienast, "*Corpus Imperii*. Überlegungen zum Reichsgedanken der Römer," in *Romanitas, Christianitas: Untersuchungen zur Geschichte und Literatur der Römischen Kaiserzeit*, ed. Gerhard Wirth, et al. (Berlin: de Gruyter, 1982), 1–17.

this by understanding the masculine Divine in terms of love but does not similarly define the relation of the community, which is construed as feminine and subordinate. The letter thereby undermines the ethical project announced in Ephesians 4:22-24:

> You were taught to put away your former way of life, your old self, corrupt and deluded by its lusts, and to be renewed in the spirit of your minds, and to clothe yourselves with the new self, created according to the likeness of God in true righteousness and holiness.

Insofar as the NRSV translates the Greek words παλαιὸν ἄνθρωπον as "old self" and καινὸν ἄνθρωπον as "new self" it obfuscates the meaning of the Greek text. The Greek text speaks about the "new human being" who, in accordance with G*d's desire, is created in "righteousness and holiness." Although Ephesians 4:24 speaks of the "new human being" in generic, gender-inclusive terms, Ephesians 5:22-33 genderizes the "new human" in masculine kyriocentric terms. Whereas the elite masculine part of humanity is enjoined to love, the majority is called to observe the "order" of kyriarchal subordination. A critical feminist reading "against the grain" is called for! Such a reading must engage in a critical-constructive analysis of the text in such a way that, on the one hand, it can undo the kyriarchal determination of the symbolic world of Ephesians and, on the other hand, it can focus on and strengthen the text's inclusive egalitarian vision.

To sum up this introduction: If one analyzes the structure and argument of Ephesians one can see that it is framed as a letter (Eph 1:1-2; 6:23-24) and that, roughly speaking, it has two major sections (chaps. 1–2 and 4–6), with a connective chapter on the apostle Paul (chapter 3). As previously pointed out, the first section begins with a doxology and sketches the messianic symbolic universe of G*d and Jesus Messiah; the second elaborates the ethos and ethics of the *ekklēsia*. Both parts are connected by chapter 3, which renders Paul as the one who reveals to them "the mystery of Jesus Messiah," so that "the manifold Wisdom of G*d" might be made known to the rulers and authorities in the heavenly places through the *ekklēsia* (Eph 3:10). Ephesians is a "mystery" text that seeks to make known the multifarious Wisdom of G*d. At its heart is the question of power.

Ephesians 1:1–2:22

G*d's Great Love:
Cosmos and *Ekklēsia*

Greetings and *Berakah*/Blessing (1:1-14)

L ike the genuine Pauline letters, Ephesians is framed as a letter by greetings in the beginning and concluding wishes of peace and blessings (postscript). It mentions the apostle Paul explicitly as the sender of the letter. However, this authorship is debated in Ephesian scholarship. The letter's introduction of the apostle Paul points ahead to Ephesians 3:1-12, where Paul's apostolic authority is asserted as integral to the purpose of the letter. As written by a later Pauline follower, this structuring of the letter skillfully claims the voice and authority of the apostle since, as "the reference to Paul as the sole author of the epistle makes clear, the focus is on Paul's unique place in relation to God, Christ/Messiah and community."[1]

Moreover, the preface of the letter is completely patterned on the genuine Pauline letters, since it mentions Paul first, as the sender (Rom 1:1; 1 Cor 1:1; 2 Cor 1:1; Gal 1:1), who has received the title "apostle of

---

1. Margaret Y. MacDonald, *Colossians and Ephesians*, SP 17 (Collegeville, MN: Liturgical Press, 2000), 195.

Ephesians 1:1-14

¹Paul, an apostle of Christ Jesus by the will of God,

To the saints who are in Ephesus and are faithful in Christ Jesus:

²Grace to you and peace from God our Father and the Lord Jesus Christ.

³Blessed be the God and Father of our Lord Jesus Christ, who has blessed us in Christ with every spiritual blessing in the heavenly places, ⁴just as he chose us in Christ before the foundation of the world to be holy and blameless before him in love. ⁵He destined us for adoption as his children through Jesus Christ, according to the good pleasure of his will, ⁶to the praise of his glorious grace that he freely bestowed on us in the Beloved. ⁷In him we have redemption through his blood, the forgiveness of our trespasses, according to the riches of his grace ⁸that he lavished on us. With all wisdom and insight ⁹he has made known to us the mystery of his will, according to his good pleasure that he set forth in Christ, ¹⁰as a plan for the

Jesus Messiah" (1 Cor 1:1; 2 Cor 1:1) according to the will of G*d (2 Cor 1:1; 1 Cor 1:1). It addresses the recipients both as saints (Rom 1:7; 1 Cor 1:2; 2 Cor 1:1; Phil 1:1), who are in certain places (e.g., Corinth, Philippi, Rome, or Ephesus), and as faithful in Messiah Jesus. The name "saints," or "holy ones," is the standard designation for the recipients of the letter (Eph 1:15, 18; 2:19; 3:8, 18; 4:12; 5:3; 6:18).

The preface concludes with a blessing that calls G*d "Father" and Jesus Messiah "*Kyrios.*" *Kyrios* means "Lord," which is an elite male title. Feminist the*logy has problematized both titles: Father and Lord. We therefore need to place here the warning sign: "Caution: could be dangerous to your health and survival!" We must do so, however, not simply to reject these titles but, more important, to draw attention to how their meaning is construed. This is necessary, as we are so used to seeing such domination-, male-centered language in Scripture that we tend to overlook the need to read these titles against their imperial/kyriarchal grain.

As pointed out in the introduction, the location of the saints and faithful "in Ephesus" is controverted, because those words are omitted in a number of the earliest manuscripts. Scholars have proposed different theories to explain this lacuna. The original address might have been to the saints "being in Hierapolis" or "being in Laodicea," locations a later scribe replaced with Ephesus, the metropolis of the Roman province of Asia Minor. Rather than reducing such textual variants to a single "original text," textual critics have argued more recently that we should

fullness of time, to gather up all things in him, things in heaven and things on earth. [11]In Christ we have also obtained an inheritance, having been destined according to the purpose of him who accomplishes all things according to his counsel and will, [12]so that we, who were the first to set our hope on Christ,

might live for the praise of his glory. [13]In him you also, when you had heard the word of truth, the gospel of your salvation, and had believed in him, were marked with the seal of the promised Holy Spirit; [14]this is the pledge of our inheritance toward redemption as God's own people, to the praise of his glory.

appreciate the plurality of textual transmissions.[2] In addition to textual variants, it is important to explore the different possibilities of historical location in order to understand the rhetorical situation of the letter. Rather than placing the male author at the center of interpretation, it is vital to focus on the social location of the recipients when reading against the grain in order to interrogate the text's world of vision. Whether the letter was sent to Laodicea, Hierapolis, or Ephesus, it is important to see that all of these places are located in the Roman province of Asia; hence the rhetorical-historical situation is shaped by the culture and politics of this province.

The Greek text of 1:3-14 consists of one long sentence with a string of subordinate participial and prepositional clauses. Translation into English compels scholars to break up this long sentence into shorter ones. While the NRSV translation clears up the sentence structure, it does not eliminate androcentric/masculine G*d language. Instead, it makes it worse by keeping the masculine for the divine while using inclusive terms for humans.

Conscientized to the problem of generic masculine language, feminist readers will not be able to appreciate this beautiful the*logical blessing because it speaks of G*d and Christ in exclusivist masculine terms. Since such a translation is the*logically incorrect because it ascribes masculine gender to G*d and essentializes Jesus' masculinity rather than Jesus' "Messiahness," it is not able to convey the the*logically rich meaning of this traditional Jewish blessing.

2. See, for example, the work of Eldon J. Epp, e.g., "Textual Criticism," in *The New Testament and Its Modern Interpreters*, ed. idem and G. W. Macrae (Atlanta: Scholars Press, 1989), 75–126.

The Sumerian Pattern of Servitude in Ephesians

[T]hrough an enormous network of mythological narrative, every aspect of culture is cloaked in the relationship of ruler and ruled, creator and created. . . . [Sumerian] *legend endows the Sumerian ruler-gods with creative power; their subjects are recreated as servants. . . .* [This new narrative was] deployed with the purpose of conditioning the mind anew.[3]

This provocative statement is found in a chapter titled "The First Major Sexual Rupture" in a collation of writings, *Liberating Life: Woman's Revolution*, by imprisoned Kurdish leader Abdullah Öcalan. According to Öcalan, who clearly had been reading authors like James Mellaart, Marija Gimbutas, and Heidi Goettner-Abendroth, the values of societies that preceded Sumer in the Near East were entirely different.[4] Earlier societies practiced "primitive socialism, characterized by equality and freedom, [which was] viable because the social order of the matriarchy did not allow ownership." Moreover, in such societies, people regarded nature as "alive and animated, no different from themselves."[5]

Ephesians follows the Sumerian pattern. Expressing a strong doctrine of chosenness and (pre)destination, it reserves all creative power to God. It thus is not surprising that this text enjoins Christians—particularly wives, children, and slaves—"to be subject" to their masters.

It has been argued that biblical monotheism redefines the notion of service when (or insofar as) it insists that only God—not kings or mammon—is worthy of being served. Yet this leaves intact the idea that creativity is restricted to God and that the

3. This argument is more fully developed in Carol P. Christ, "A Servant of All or a Lover of Life," *Feminism and Religion* (June 27, 2016), https://feminismandreligion.com/2016/06/27/shall-i-be-a-servant-to-all-or-shall-i-love-the-world-ever-more-deeply-by-carol-p-christ/.

4. James Mellaart, *The Neolithic of the Near East* (New York: Scribners, 1975); Marija Gimbutas, *The Language of the Goddess: Unearthing the Hidden Symbols of Western Civilization* (San Francisco: Harper & Row, 1989); Heidi Goettner-Abendroth, *Societies of Peace: Matriarchies Past, Present and Future; Selected Papers, First World Congress on Matriarchal Studies, 2003; Second World Congress on Matriarchal Studies, 2005* (Toronto: Inanna Publications, 2009).

5. Öcalan, *Liberating Life: Woman's Revolution*, trans. International Initiative (Cologne: International Initiative Edition; Neuss: Mesopotamian Publishers, 2013), 14–15.

proper human role is to "serve" God. The notion that only God is to be served all too easily reverts to the notion that God's earthly representatives (kings, priests, ministers, rabbis, imams, gurus, holy men, generals, fathers, husbands, the wealthy, landowners, slave owners, and so forth) are to be served in God's name. Certain Christian texts suggest that "the Son of Man came not to be served but to serve" (Mark 10:45; Matt 20:28) yet this also did not prevent Christianity from institutionalizing hierarchical notions of service.

I suggest that all notions that human beings were created to "serve" or "be subject to"

(God or anyone else) should be excised from our religious and political vocabularies.

To understand this insight and to incorporate it into our religious and political vocabularies would require a radical revolution in the way our thoughts and actions continue to be structured by the Sumerian legend.

No more service to God and country.

No more servants of God.

No more servants of all.

Isn't it enough to love the deity with all our hearts and all our neighbors—human and other than human—as ourselves?

Carol P. Christ

TRANSLATION MATTERS

In order to give a sample of an inclusive translation using the gender-neutral singular pronoun "they/them/their," I will add here such an inclusive translation for the beginning of this long sentence. Unfortunately, I cannot change the whole text because publication rules require that the commentary use the NRSV translation.

[3]Blessed be the God and parent (Father) of our leader (Lord) Jesus Messiah (Christ), who has blessed us in Messiah (Christ) with every spiritual blessing in the heavenly places, [4]just as they (he) chose us in Messiah (Christ) before the foundation of the world to be holy and blameless before them (him) in love. [5]They (He) destined us for adoption as their (his) children through Jesus Messiah, according to the good pleasure of their (his) will, [6]to the praise of their (his) glorious grace that they (he) freely bestowed on us in the Beloved. [7]In them (him) we have redemption through their (his) blood, the forgiveness of our trespasses, according to the riches of their (his) grace [8]that they (he) lavished on us.

Whereas the undisputed Pauline letters refer first to the concrete situation of the community addressed, Ephesians begins with a eulogy or *berakah* that, in characteristic Jewish language,[6] spells out the blessings bestowed on the recipients. This introduction is shaped by Jewish liturgical language and blessing formulas, language that is used in the psalms of Scripture and the texts of the Qumran community.[7] In Greco-Roman rhetoric a eulogy is characterized by eloquence and offers a tribute of praise for a benefactor.

This eulogy/blessing/*berakah* is a rich introduction to the whole epistle in the language of liturgy and praise. It is a the*logical introduction in the deepest sense of the word because it starts with G*d, who is not qualified as ruler but as a parent, whereas Jesus, as leader, is called Messiah. Here G*d is seen as the parent of the Messiah as well as a rich benefactor and householder who has bestowed salvation/well-being and spiritual blessings in "the heavenlies" on speaker and audience (us) through the Messiah Jesus (v. 3). Such spiritual blessings are bestowed on the congregation of the holy ones, the saints.

A contrast between "we" and "you" emerges in vv. 13-14, something commentators have struggled to explain. Some scholars argue that the author is contrasting Jewish ("we") and Gentile ("you") Christians. Others have pointed out that there may be an attempt here to distinguish the recipients from other Christians. Pheme Perkins has proposed that, as is the case in other Pauline letters, the speaker distinguishes themself rhetorically from the audience.[8] Andrew Lincoln in turn stresses correctly that "the 'we' and 'us' refers to all believers,"[9] but in so doing they obliterate the distinction. As I have argued in the introduction, I understand the "we" as referring to all members of the Jewish messianic community, including the "you," since the "you" who were formerly Gentiles are now members of this community.

When speaking of the Messiah Jesus the text vacillates between understanding the Messiah as a historical individual called Jesus and as a corporate Messianic realm in which the recipients live, or as an era in

6. Tet-Lim N. Yee, *Jews, Gentiles and Ethnic Reconciliation: Paul's Jewish Identity and Ephesians*, SNTSMS 130 (Cambridge: Cambridge University Press, 2005), 35–45.

7. For the interpretation of Ephesians with reference to the Qumran writings see especially Pheme Perkins, *Ephesians*, ANTC (Nashville: Abingdon, 1997), and Joachim Gnilka, *Der Epheserbrief* (Freiburg: Herder, 1971).

8. Perkins, *Ephesians*, 42–43.

9. Andrew T. Lincoln, *Ephesians*, WBC 42 (Dallas: Word, 1990), 37.

which G*d chose "us" before the foundation of the world to be holy and blameless before G*d in love. G*d destined us, the recipients, for adoption as "children" through the death of Jesus Messiah, in whom we have deliverance from bondage and forgiveness of trespasses, language associated with baptism.[10]

This messianic focus of the eulogy is hard to miss, since "in Messiah Jesus" occurs in nearly every verse and is repeated ten times in one way or another. However, the meaning of "in Messiah Jesus" is difficult to translate since the text vacillates between the understanding of "in the Messiah" as a corporate messianic location and the understanding of Messiah Jesus as a historical individual. Ephesians 1:10 refers to the summing up and bringing together of all things, the whole cosmos, "in Messiah Jesus," who is the Beloved.

G*d chose the recipients in Messiah Jesus before the foundation of the world to be holy and blameless before G*d in love (1:4). The recipients of the letter are in the Messiah Jesus, who is called the Beloved (1:6). Throughout the letter, love (ἀγάπη/*agapē*) is a key *topos*, since the verb and noun are used twenty-one times.[11] The emphasis on the topic of love in Ephesians "seems to furnish the key to the purpose of the book."[12] The place of the believer is being "in love" (ἐν ἀγάπῃ) and being "in Messiah" (ἐν Χριστῷ). This place of the saints "in love" and "in Messiah" is located in the "heavenly places [ἐν τοῖς ἐπουρανίοις, lit.: in the heavenlies]" (1:3, 20; 2:6).

The "heavenlies" are a place that transcends the limits of human experience. They are not only a place where G*d dwells but also a sphere in which hostile powers are active (3:10; 6:12). Whereas the biblical view of the world generally speaks of heaven, earth, and underworld—the place of the dead and the demons—Ephesians does not know a realm that is under the earth, below the human world. Rather, it shares the first-century understanding of the universe in which the earth is at the center of a cosmos, surrounded by the planets that circle from east to west around the earth. The sun, moon, and planets circle the earth. The G*ds were no longer near but far away in the heavens, which were multiple.

10. MacDonald, *Colossians and Ephesians*, 200.

11. Ἀγάπη/*agapē* and its derivatives occur in Ephesians in the following places: 1:4 (2x), 15; 2:4 (2x); 3:17, 19; 4:2, 15, 16; 5:2 (2x), 25 (2x), 28 (3x), 33; 6:21, 23, 24. See John Paul Heil, *Ephesians: Empowerment to Walk in Love for the Unity of All in Christ* (Atlanta: SBL Press, 2007), 2.

12. Harold W. Hoehner, *Ephesians: An Exegetical Commentary* (Grand Rapids: Baker Academic, 2002), 105.

> The region from the earth to the moon was one in which decay and
> death occurred. Earthy, heavy, watery, and dark substances tended
> toward the earth. Fire and air tended toward the heavens. . . . Spiri-
> tual beings, sometimes depicted as demonic, could be associated with
> the planetary spheres and their power to dictate the fate of humans
> and nations.[13]

In its heavenly ascent after death the soul had to travel through the
dangerous world of the demons to the world of G*d.

In the heavenlies, at the right-hand side of G*d's throne, the Messiah
is seated. The realm of the Messiah Jesus is envisioned as above the
realm of the spirits and demons. G*d is seated on top of the realm of
the spirit-powers, which is in the highest of heavens. The "heavenlies"
reach down to earth but do not encompass it. Rather, the expression "all
things" (τὰ πάντα), which is divided into a heavenly and an earthly realm,
is the most comprehensive notion that encompasses heaven and earth, all
beings, angel, demon, and human (1:11, 23; 3:9; 4:10, 15).[14] Messiah Jesus
is enthroned above all the heavens "in order that Messiah Jesus might
fill all things" (4:10). Ephesians envisions Messiah Jesus as completely
filling the cosmos by drawing all things into themself. Messiah Jesus,
the Beloved, is uniting and filling the universe with *agapē*, "love."[15] This
is the mystery, the secret, that has been made known as G*d's will: "the
summing up of the All in Christ."[16]

The language of mystery is used extensively in Ephesians (1:9; 3:3;
4:9; 5:32; 6:19). Scholars now widely agree that this language is derived
from Jewish-apocalyptic the*logy, in which G*d is seen as the revealer
of mysteries.[17] Such a mystery is revealed to the recipients but not to
the public. Whereas in the mystery religions the privileged group who
knows the secret are the initiates, in Judaism they are the people of G*d.
They are now in possession of the mystery that has been hidden and

---

13. Perkins, *Ephesians*, 37–38.

14. Gnilka, *Epheserbrief*, 65.

15. There are different Greek words for the English word "love": ἔρος = erotic
passionate love; φιλία = nonsexual love between friends; ἀγάπη = loving-kindness,
unconditional love. See excursus below (pp. 21–22). The Goddess Isis was called
Agapē Theōn, "Love of Gods." See R. E. Witt, *Isis in the Ancient World* (Baltimore: Johns
Hopkins University Press, 1997).

16. Ernest Best, *Ephesians: A Critical and Exegetical Commentary*, ICC (New York:
T&T Clark, 1998), 137.

17. Raymond E. Brown, *The Semitic Background of the Term "Mystery" in the New
Testament* (Philadelphia: Fortress, 1968), 20–30, 57 n. 168.

unknown until now (see Col 1:26-28; 2 Cor 2:6-10). This mystery "sums up" all things in heaven and on earth in "the Messiah Jesus."

What is the significance of the definite article before the word χριστός, "Christos," Messiah? The author uses the definite article in the phrase "in the Messiah" in 1:10, 12, 20; as well as at 2:5, 13; 3:4, 8, 17, 19; 4:7, 12, 13, 20; 5:2, 5, 14, 23, 24, 25, 29; 6:5—a use of the article before χριστός that is more frequent than in any other writing of the Pauline letter collection. Ernest Best discusses this matter but comes to the conclusion: "The article with Christ has no particular messianic significance at 1.10."[18] However, Best does not discuss the probability that the definite article defines Jesus as the Messiah because he works with the dualism Judaism-Christianity as two different religious communities.

G*d has made known to us in Jesus Messiah a mystery G*d intended "for the administration [οἰκονομίαν] of the fullness of the times." The Greek word οἰκονομία/*oikonomia* is usually translated as "plan" because, it is argued, household management consists in action plans. However, as was pointed out in the introduction, in ancient political discourse *oikonomia*, the management of the household, was the task of the *matrona* (Greek: κύρια), whereas state-management was that of the *dominus* (Greek: κύριος). The All is here envisioned as the household of G*d that is administered in the domain of the Messiah. G*d is envisioned as the *matrona*, the κύρια of the household who takes care of all its members and the whole cosmos. She does so in and through the Messiah, Jesus, who is "the Beloved." This female image of G*d, the "world manager or house-keeper," corrects the male image of G*d as the kyriarchal lord and ruler. The abundance of praise in this introductory eulogy is addressed to G*d imaged as a female householder who takes care of the world.

An Alternative Concept of God

The concept of an all-powerful God who destines certain people for salvation before the creation of the world, distinguishes between children of light and children of darkness, and places all creation under his [*sic*] feet as he rules from the high heavens is profoundly problematic on numerous levels. It attributes all agency to God, negating the possibility of human freedom. It denies the complexity of human beings, all of whom contain some admixture of good and evil. And it turns God into a dominating male other who

18. Best, *Ephesians*, 145.

has been used to justify myriad forms of human domination. But if one rejects this idea of God, what might replace it?

I see God as the creative energy that underlies, animates, and sustains all existence; God is the Ground of Being, the source of all that is, the power of life, death, and regeneration in the universe. God's presence fills all creation, and creation simultaneously dwells in God. God is the reality that unifies creation. Believing in God means affirming that, despite the fractured, scattered, and conflicted nature of experience, there is a unity that embraces and contains diversity and connects all things.

In this view God is neither a locus of consciousness nor a source of unalloyed good. Wholeness or inclusiveness carries more theological weight than goodness. The world as I experience it has little use for human plans and aspirations. The earth, bounteous at one moment, at another can be blighted by drought or washed away by terrible storms. We can be astounded by the care, altruism, and intricate interdependence found everywhere in nature and also by its predation and violence. When we look at ourselves we find the same, often ambiguous, mixture of motives and effects.

To deny God's presence in all this is to leave huge aspects of reality outside of God. Where then do they come from? How are they able to continue in existence?

But while the creative energy flowing through the world may have no moral purpose, the notion of God's unity or oneness provides substantial grounding for moral reflection and action. To say that the divine presence that animates the universe is *one* is to say that we are all bound to each other in the continual unfolding of the adventure of creation. In the human family, for all our differences, we are more alike than unlike. All of us are faces of the God who dwells within each of us; the same standards of justice should apply to everyone. When we harm, diminish, or oppress anyone we harm ourselves. And this is true not simply of human beings but also of the whole of creation. We are linked to each other in a remarkably complex, intricate web of life. God cannot redeem the world for us, but as creatures who, in our better moments, are able to glimpse and appreciate our place in the larger whole, we can act in the interests of that whole and the individuals and human and biotic communities within it.

Judith Plaskow

Prayer for Wisdom and Knowledge (1:15-23)

The thanksgiving usually comes after the opening greetings in the Pauline letters and is unusual after a long eulogy. Like vv. 1-14, this section also consists in the original Greek of one long sentence that must be cut up into segments when translated into English. The text is formulated as a prayer of the letter's sender, who has heard of the recipients' faith in the Lord Jesus and their love for all the saints. Since the authentic Paul had lived in Ephesus for more than two years it is strange that the writer has only "heard" of their faith in Jesus, who is called in v. 15 "Lord Jesus" and in v. 17 "Lord Jesus Messiah." The letter writer gives thanks not only for the recipients' faith but also for their love for the "holy ones" and prays to G*d, who is called the "Father of glory," to give them "a spirit of Wisdom and revelation in full knowledge of the Divine."

How to structure the argument of the text and its division is debated. It seems that a shift in topic-focus is taking place after v. 19, so that the section has a twofold structure: vv. 15-18 and vv. 19-23. The first section explains why the gift of the spirit of Wisdom/wisdom is given by G*d. The reason given is that the recipients may know: the hope to which G*d has called them, the riches of G*d's glorious inheritance among the saints, the greatness of G*d's power for us. The second section, beginning with v. 19, explains how G*d's power worked for the Messiah Jesus whom G*d raised from the dead, who was seated at the right hand of G*d in heavenly places, whose name is above every name, and whose power is greater than any other power. G*d gave the power over the All (τὰ πάντα) to Messiah Jesus, whom G*d appointed as head over the All and at the same time as head of the *ekklēsia*, a word that—as pointed out in the introduction—is wrongly translated as "church." Rather, *ekklēsia* connotes the assembly of free citizens. The *ekklēsia* in turn is defined as the messianic body or corporation (σῶμα); it is the fullness (πλήρωμα) of the All (τὰ πάντα), that is, the filling in all things. The last clause is difficult to understand, but it is generally assumed to mean that the *ekklēsia* is Messiah Jesus' "fullness" (πλήρωμα) and this Messiah is filling the universe in every way.

Ephesians is written in political language and imagery. However, it must not be overlooked that political language, like religious language, also has to work with images and metaphors. Political theory,

Ephesians 1:15-23

[15]I have heard of your faith in the Lord Jesus and your love toward all the saints, and for this reason [16]I do not cease to give thanks for you as I remember you in my prayers. [17]I pray that the God of our Lord Jesus Christ, the Father of glory, may give you a spirit of wisdom and revelation as you come to know him, [18]so that, with the eyes of your heart enlightened, you may know what is the hope to which he has called you, what are the riches of his glorious inheritance among the saints, [19]and what is the immeasurable great- ness of his power for us who believe, according to the working of his great power. [20]God put this power to work in Christ when he raised him from the dead and seated him at his right hand in the heavenly places, [21]far above all rule and authority and power and do- minion, and above every name that is named, not only in this age but also in the age to come. [22]And he has put all things under his feet and has made him the head over all things for the church, [23]which is his body, the fullness of him who fills all in all.

like the*logy, needs literary metaphors.[19] Before the state can be seen it must be personified; before it can be conceptualized it must be imag- ined; before it can be appreciated it must be symbolized. We orient our actions with metaphors of society and community. Hence political terminology and sociological language are not simply descriptive but prescriptive and performative. Such language is significant to what we represent and how we live.[20]

In Ephesians 1:15-23 the metaphor of the "body politic" is prevalent. The Messiah is here imaged as the unifying, universal emperor, the head, whose body is the *ekklēsia*. Roman political theory distinguished between imperial power of ruling and the geographical area of imperial space, the empire. It differentiated between empire as dominion and as *res publica*, loosely translated "public affairs" or "republic." The word "commonwealth" has traditionally also been used as a synonym for it. Cicero could even speak of two social bodies: the social body of the empire, whose head is the emperor, and the democratic social body of all Roman citizens represented by the senate.[21]

19. Michael Walzer, "On the Role of Symbolism in Political Thought," *PSQ* 82 (1967): 191–204.

20. Susannne Lüdemann, *Metaphern der Gesellschaft* (Munich: Fink, 2004), 101–3.

21. See Dietmar Kienast, "*Corpus Imperii*: Überlegungen zum Reichsgedanken der Römer," in *Romanitas, Christianitas: Untersuchungen zur Geschichte und Literatur der Römischen Kaiserzeit*, ed. Gerhard Wirth, et al. (Berlin: de Gruyter, 1982).

This distinction seems also to have shaped the metaphors and discussion of the body politic in Ephesians. Whereas the notion of *ekklēsia* has its roots in democratic imagination, the characterization of Messiah Jesus as ruler over the All, the heavens and the earth, has imperial roots and resonances.[22] Hannah Roose has carefully investigated the reception and kyriarchaliza-tion of the body metaphor in Colossians and Ephesians and traced it back to the uncontested Pauline letters, especially to 1 Corinthians.[23] She argues that Ephesians follows Colossians in understanding Christ as the head of both *ekklēsia* and cosmos but that neither attributes the designation "body" to the cosmos, reserving it for the *ekklēsia*. Since the author introduces this without much explanation we can suppose it is assumed that the recipients are familiar with the metaphor of Colossians and Paul's first letter to the Corinthians, which was sent from Ephesus.

Roose argues that in 4:11-12 the author refers to Paul's democratic understanding of the "body of Christ" in 1 Corinthians 12 but does not take up this democratic understanding. Rather, the reference to the re-lationship between Christ and the *ekklēsia* in 5:29-30 is to the members of the body of Christ; this is intended not to foster democratic equality and collaboration but to define *agapē* as kyriarchal subordination.[24] This indicates that Ephesians does not want to strengthen mutual democratic loving relations between the different members of the body, the *ekklēsia*, as Paul does in 1 Corinthians 12, but rather takes up 1 Corinthians 11:3, where Christ is the head of man, man the head of woman, and G*d the head of Christ.[25] That argument seeks to persuade an audience that has a more democratic-collaborative understanding of *ekklēsia*. Like Paul in 1 Corinthians, Ephesians seeks to change the meaning of *ekklēsia* into a

---

22. For discussion of empire and Scripture, see my book, *The Power of the Word: Scripture and the Rhetoric of Empire* (Minneapolis: Fortress, 2007).

23. Hannah Roose, "Die Hierarchisierung der Leib-Metapher im Kolosser- und Epheserbrief als 'Paulinisierung': Ein Beitrag zur Rezeption Paulinischer Tradition in Pseudo-Paulinischen Briefen," *NovT* 47 (2005): 117–41.

24. Roose uses "hierarchical," but the relation is better characterized as kyriarchal.

25. The author seems here to adopt and theologize the idea of the "great chain of being" developed in the political philosophy of Plato and Aristotle, which "rational-izes and justifies an order in the world in which some beings in the hierarchy dominate others, with a comfortable sense of their innate superiority given them by 'nature' or by God." See Page DuBois, *Centaurs and Amazons: Women and the Pre-History of the Great Chain of Being* (Ann Arbor: University of Michigan Press, 1982), 12; Arthur A. Lovejoy, *The Great Chain of Being: A Study of the History of an Idea* (Cambridge: Harvard University Press, 1936).

kyriarchal one when speaking about wo/men. Thus 1 Corinthians and Ephesians still reveal a struggle over wo/men's full membership in the *ekklēsia*. That struggle occurred in a cultural context in which wo/men were able to exercise such civic leadership.[26]

Kyriarchy and Ekklēsia Language

The difficulty for a critical feminist interpretation is significant when we attempt to read this kyriarchal language and symbolic universe in such a way that the vision of "G*d-as-*agapē*," which is caught up in this kyriarchal imagination, can come to the fore. This difficulty is clearly illustrated in Steve Thomason's YouTube sketch of my book, *Democratizing Biblical Studies*.[27]

Ephesians construes the relation of Messiah Jesus not only to the *ekklēsia* but also to the world, the whole cosmos, in kyriarchal terms. In line with Colossians 1:16; 2:10-15, Ephesians 1:21 enumerates the objects of the Messiah's reign: G*d has seated Messiah Jesus far above every dominion, authority, power, lordship, and domination (κυριότητος), but it explicates this: Messiah Jesus is enthroned at the right of G*d. On the one hand G*d has subjected to this Messiah the whole universe (τὰ πάντα); on the other hand G*d has given this ruler of the universe to the *ekklēsia*. Messiah Jesus is the one who fills all areas of the universe in order to rule and dominate it (4:10).

> A comparison of Ephesians 1:20b-23 with 1 Corinthians 15:24-28 indicates that Ephesians takes up the hierarchical order of domination and even intensifies it. . . . The differences between both texts stem from the different eschatological conceptions of both letters. Whereas 1 Corinthians 15:24 says that Christ hands over dominion to G*d [at the end of time], the author of Ephesians emphasizes that Christ always reigns [or exercises kyriarchy] in the universe.[28]

However, in marked contrast to Greek, Jewish, and other Christian authors, the author of Ephesians is the only one who applies the notion of G*d filling the cosmos to signify a process during which the

---

26. See Katherine Bain, *Women's Socioeconomic Status and Religious Leadership in Asia Minor: In the First Two Centuries CE* (Minneapolis: Fortress, 2014).

27. Steve Thomason, "Sketch of *Democratizing Biblical Studies* by Elizabeth [*sic*] Schüssler Fiorenza," YouTube, 2012, https://www.youtube.com/watch?v=AEwy T21tAG8, accessed September 4, 2016.

28. Roose, "Die Hierarchisierung der Leib-Metapher," 136.

cosmos is increasingly filled with G*d or Christ.[29] The *ekklēsia* is the realm where the fullness of Messiah Jesus is present. All rule, power, lordship, and the whole universe are placed under Messiah Jesus' feet (1:22) in the interest of the *ekklēsia*, which is the body, the fullness, of the Messiah. However, the designation of the *ekklēsia* as the messianic fullness or πλήρωμα in 1:23 indicates a process that is ongoing. Since the *ekklēsia* as body is clearly subordinated to the head we have to critically destabilize these images of the ancient body politic that envision the relationship between the democratic assembly, the *ekklēsia*, and Messiah Jesus in imperial terms. Since we live no longer in an explicitly imperial situation but in a democratic one, we have to carefully identify this political language of Ephesians and ask what it does to us if we submit to its world of vision and imagination.

We also must ask: Does this passage provide another image, one with which we could work toward a more democratic understanding of church and society? I suggest that the *ekklēsia* is the place where such messianic "fullness" (πλήρωμα) is present. G*d's fullness has established itself in Christ in all its density and power, and through our connection with this Messiah Jesus we are drawn into this fullness so that we, too, are filled with G*d's fullness and taken up in it.[30] Here the language of domination and subjection is changed into a horizontal language of connection, satisfaction, richness, and linking. The *ekklēsia* is such a place of interconnection and engagement in which the messianic fullness of G*d is actively realized.

G*d's Great Love (2:1-10)

We have here again a long Greek sentence that the NRSV translation divides into three sentences (2:1-2, 3, and 4-7). Its contents can be seen as two separate sections: vv. 1-3 and vv. 4-7. However, it is important to note that chapter and verse division in the N*T is a later addition to the text.[31] The

29. George H. van Kooten, *Cosmic Christology in Paul and the Pauline School: Colossians and Ephesians in the Context of Graeco-Roman Cosmology, with a New Synopsis of the Greek Texts*, WUNT 2:171 (Tübingen: Mohr Siebeck, 2003), 164.

30. Rudolf Schnackenburg, *Ephesians: A Commentary*, trans. Helen Heron (Edinburgh: T&T Clark, 1991), 8.

31. *The New Schaff-Herzog Encyclopedia of Religious Knowledge*, vol. 2 (New York: Funk & Wagnalls, 1908–1912), 113–14, http://www.bible-researcher.com/chapter-verse.html, accessed June 17, 2016.

²:¹[and] You were dead through the trespasses and sins ²in which you once lived, following the course of this world, following the ruler of the power of the air, the spirit that is now at work among those who are disobedient. ³All of us once lived among them in the passions of our flesh, following the desires of flesh and senses, and we were by nature children of wrath, like everyone else. ⁴But God, who is rich in mercy, out of the great love with which he loved us ⁵even when we were dead through our trespasses, made us alive together with Christ—by grace you have been saved—⁶and raised us up with him

chapter division here obscures that vv. 1-3 are a continuation of the preceding section, 1:15-23, which is indicated by the καὶ ("and") at the beginning of 2:1-3, taking up the "you" and "we" of 1:18-19. Hence the commentaries debate whether this section still belongs to the introduction or already to the body of the letter.[32] I suggest that it is best understood as a "bridge" or "linking section" that connects the introduction to the rest of the letter.

The whole text can also be seen as having a chiastic structure. Chiasm (or chiasmus) is a writing style that uses a unique repetition pattern for clarification and/or emphasis. This chiastic pattern or repetition form appears throughout the Bible, yet it is not well known. One's approach to the Scriptures should be dramatically enhanced by this understanding. Chiasms are structured in a repeating A-B-C . . . C'-B'-A' pattern.[33] The text can then be structured as follows:[34]

A	vv. 1-2
B	v. 3
C	v. 4a
C'	v. 4b
B'	vv. 5-7
A'	vv. 8-10

32. See for instance, Schnackenburg, *Ephesians*, 39, 86–101.
33. Thomas B. Clarke, "What Is a Chiasm (or Chiasmus)? Definition and Explanation of the Chiastic Structure," http://bible-discernments.com/joshua/whatisachiasm.html (accessed June 17, 2016).
34. Heil, *Ephesians*, 93–108.

and seated us with him in the heavenly places in Christ Jesus, [7]so that in the ages to come he might show the immeasurable riches of his grace in kindness toward us in Christ Jesus. [8]For by grace you have been saved through faith, and this is not your own doing; it is the gift of God—[9]not the result of works, so that no one may boast. [10]For we are what he has made us, created in Christ Jesus for good works, which God prepared beforehand to be our way of life.

The coupling of the noun "love" with its cognate verb at the center of the chiasm (2:4) emphatically reinforces the theme of G*d's love that has been developed in the letter. It reminds the audience that the great love with which G*d loved us believers is the love we have received. It is the grace with which G*d graced us in our union with Messiah Jesus as the Beloved (1:6). It is in the Beloved, Jesus Messiah, the one whom G*d preeminently loved, that G*d has graciously loved us with great love, so that we may be holy and blameless before G*d "in love" (1:4b).[35]

The emphatic "you" in 2:1, 2, and 8 is addressing those who were Gentiles as the "others," and it is doing so from a Jewish point of view.[36] What the preceding section says about Christ is now stated about believers: As G*d has raised Messiah Jesus (1:20), so also "you" (2:1); G*d has made you alive (2:5) and co-resurrected (2:6). It is debated who is addressed by the "you" and the "we." John Muddiman, for example, argues that "the variation between the first and second person plural . . . is caused, in part at least, by the fact that the Pauline traditions which are at its core are retained in their 'you' form, while the editor expounds them in the 'we' form."[37] Rudolf Schnackenburg in turn concludes: "It is now easier to see why the author went from 'you' to 'we': it is the common experience of all who have espoused the Christian faith."[38]

In agreement with Tet-Lim N. Yee, I understand the "you" as referring to former Gentiles and the "we" as referring to Jewish Messianists, whom the former Gentiles have joined. The author clearly speaks from a Jewish messianic point of view but does so in order to alleviate the social-religious tension between Jews and Gentiles in the messianic community. The author wants to stress that both are G*d's work, created for good

35. Ibid., 107–8.
36. Yee, *Jews, Gentiles*, 45.
37. John Muddiman, *The Epistle to the Ephesians*, BNTC (London: Continuum, 2001), 101.
38. Schnackenburg, *Ephesians*, 89.

deeds in the sphere of Messiah Jesus. Commentators generally assume that both the "you" and the "we" are now joined "in Christ," that is, in the messianic space consisting of both Gentiles and Jews. The messianic space of G*d's rich love is now extended to embrace both Gentiles and Jews.[39] According to v. 6, this space is "in the heavenlies," where Jews and Gentiles are enthroned together "in Messiah Jesus."

Cosmology

As we already saw in the preceding chapter, Ephesians has a cosmology quite different from our own. The Hebrew Bible envisions the earth as a flat plate, with the underworld, Sheol, underneath it and heaven, like a dome, above it. Sheol connotes the place where those who had died were believed to be congregated. It is a place with gates and seems to have been viewed as divided into compartments, with "farthest corners" one beneath the other. Here the dead meet without distinction of rank or condition—the rich and the poor, the pious and the wicked, the old and the young, the master and the slave. Sheol is a horrible, dreary, dark, disorderly land (Job 10:21-22).[40] It is significant, however, that Ephesians does not speak about Sheol.

The ancient Greeks developed the earliest scientific models of the universe; these were geocentric, placing Earth at the center of the universe. Over the centuries more precise astronomical observations (1473–1543) led to development of the heliocentric model, with the sun at the center of the solar system. As far as we know, the universe includes planets, moons, stars, galaxies, the contents of intergalactic space, and all matter and energy. The observable universe is about twenty-eight billion parsecs (ninety-one billion light-years) in diameter. The size of the entire universe is unknown, but there are many hypotheses about its composition and evolution.[41] In short, our view of the universe is quite different from that of Ephesians.

In contrast with modern views, the ancients believed that spirit beings populated the universe in all its parts. Ephesians 2:2 speaks about cosmic beings such as "the course [αἰών, "age"] of this world," and "the ruler of the power of the air, the spirit that is now at work among those who are

39. Yee, *Jews, Gentiles*, 45–70.

40. Emil G. Hirsch, "SHEOL (שאול)," http://www.jewishencyclopedia.com/articles/13563-sheol, accessed June 17, 2016.

41. Brian Greene, *The Hidden Reality: Parallel Universes and the Deep Laws of the Cosmos* (New York: Knopf, 2011).

disobedient." It is debated whether the αἰών of this world, like the ruler of the power of the air, is also a spiritual being or whether the word is a temporal term referring to the time span of this world. In any case, the ruler of the air-power "clearly refers to a demonic figure responsible for evil in the air."[42] Since we no longer think that a spiritual being is responsible for the evil in the air, how are we to understand this text?

In his three-volume work, *Naming the Powers, Unmasking the Powers,* and *Engaging the Powers,*[43] Walter Wink has argued that we are captive to a materialistic way of thinking, whereas the people of the ancient world could deal with the unknown forces of life only by personifying and treating them as if they were conscious beings, since they did not know the physical laws of the universe uncovered by modern science. He identifies and compares three worldviews: the ancient, the spiritual, and the materialistic.

The ancient worldview is characterized by simultaneity and assumes that everything earthly has its heavenly counterparts, and vice versa. The spiritual worldview in turn divides people into soul and body and believes that the created order is corrupted and

evil, whereas the materialistic worldview maintains the opposite, that there is no heaven, no G*d or spiritual world. Finally, according to Wink, Christian the*logy has invented "the supernatural realm," which cannot be known by the senses and which, unlike the natural realm, is immune to confirmation or refutation.[44]

Wink translates the ancient worldview that thinks in terms of below and above with the modern dualisms, external/peripheral, internal/within, spiritual/institutional, and seeks to interconnect it with the system of power, the domination system, that is, kyriarchy. Rather than working with abstract categories such as "above and below" or "external and internal," I suggest we call this power of the air more concretely by its contemporary name, pollution of the ecosystem. This "spirit" is at work among those who do not appreciate G*d's good creation. There is a connection between the evil powers of 1:21 and the ruler of the power of the air. While we no longer think in terms of personified mythological powers, we are well aware of the power that devastates the ecosystems: modern capitalist consumerism and technological exploitation.

---

42. Perkins, *Ephesians*, 58.

43. Walter Wink, *Engaging the Powers*: *Discernment and Resistance in a World of Domination* (Minneapolis: Fortress, 1992).

44. Ibid., 6.

Ephesians 2:3 sums up the situation: "All of us once lived among them in the passions of our flesh, following the desires of flesh and senses, and we were by nature children of wrath, like everyone else." On the whole, v. 3 probably reflects conventional Jewish notions of the Gentile world, but the "we" asserts that Jewish believers shared the lot of the Gentiles with the rest of the world. Verses 2 and 3 use strikingly strong language regarding the awful situation of believers in the past. This dire picture of believers' past prepares the stage for the proclamation of G*d's saving grace in 2:4-10.

Because of their exalted language and structure, vv. 4-7 are often understood as a traditional hymn celebrating G*d's splendid love and care. The language of being dead and coming alive may have its roots in baptismal proclamation and baptismal liturgy.[45] The whole chapter draws a strong contrast between the "then" of the past of the Messiah Jesus followers and the "now" of life in the messianic realm, the corporate personality of Messiah Jesus, and it does so by emphasizing the great love of G*d. Because of this great love G*d made us, who were dead in sins, alive with the Messiah Jesus, as well as having raised and seated us "in" the realm of Messiah Jesus in the heavenly places (vv. 6-7). Because we are "in" Messiah Jesus, we are enthroned with him in the heavenlies.[46] Obviously Messiah Jesus is here imagined not as an individual but as a messianic collective or corporation that carries the name and shares the destiny of Jesus. Our being, exalted "in" Messiah Jesus to reigning power, is expressed here in royal-imperial terms.

In contrast to this royal characterization of Messiahship, G*d is again pictured in the female figure of the matron, the world-householder who cares for and loves those who are in the messianic domain. G*d is imagined here as the "mistress of the world" whose love takes care not only of the world (cosmos) but also of the followers of Messiah Jesus. G*d's abundance of love and caring, her rich mercy and grace, have raised and enthroned us together "in Messiah/Jesus." Her kindness, grace, and love are overflowing.

As pointed out before, this image of G*d might have invoked, for the audience, the figure of the great Goddess Isis, whose cultic name was ἀγάπη/*agapē* ("love").[47] However, the female G*d-image of "mistress of the world" must also be viewed with a hermeneutics of suspicion, since

45. MacDonald, *Colossians and Ephesians*, 235. She notes that "Eph 2:1-5 are very closely related to Col 2:13 and Eph 2:6 has much in common with Col 3:1-3. . . . It is possible that Colossians and Ephesians are drawing independently from the same liturgical traditions."

46. Hoehner, *Ephesians*, 334–35.

47. Witt, *Isis in the Ancient World*, 266.

it can also invoke the image of self-sacrificing wife and mother. Hence we must be careful not to understand *agapē* in terms of self-sacrificing love that must be imitated.

Love

There are four different Greek words for the English word "love": ἔρος, στοργή, φιλία, and ἀγάπη.[48] Ἔρος (*eros*) means sensual, erotic, passionate love. Στοργή (*storgē*) means familial love, love for one's country, or natural affection, as the love of a parent toward offspring, and vice versa.[49] Φιλία (*philia*) expresses nonsexual love and mutuality between friends, and ἀγάπη (*agapē*) is understood as loving-kindness and unconditional self-sacrificing love, or charity, from the Latin *caritas*.

The Swedish the*logian and bishop Anders Nygren[50] argued in his influential work, *Agape and Eros*, published more than seventy-five years ago, that *eros* is rooted in Greek thought and expresses Greek desire and aspirations, needs, and cravings, whereas *agapē*, by contrast, is the overflowing of divine plenitude, "G*d reaching out to humanity, providing the assurance and inspiration that accounts for any love that we might express."[51] Nygren maintained that the*logians cannot argue that G*d loves G*d's own self, or that the great commandment "to love your neighbor as yourself" is central for Christian love, because self-love is sinful. Moreover, it is not really our love for the other but G*d's love that flows through us; we are its conduits. True Christian *agapē* is purely altruistic and descends from G*d. Although this view is still widespread, it must be critically rejected. All four forms of love—*eros, philia, agapē*, and *storgē*—are Christian religious loves cooperating with G*d's love.[52] Carter Heyward summarizes this feminist understanding of *agapē*:

> God's creative and redemptive love "transforms" culture by working radically through our embodied lives. . . . We know that

48. See Henry George Liddell, Robert Scott, Henry Stuart Jones, and Roderick McKenzie, *A Greek-English Lexicon* (Oxford: Oxford University Press, 1996).

49. Ichykoo, "Four Kinds of Love; Eros, Agape, Phileo & Storge," *Eros to Agape*, October 31, 2015, https://fromerostoagape.wordpress.com/2012/08/09/eros-romantic-love-and-agape-unconditional-love, accessed June 17, 2016.

50. Anders Nygren, *Agape and Eros: The Christian Idea of Love*, trans. Philip S. Watson (Chicago: University of Chicago Press, 1953).

51. Colin Grant, "For the Love of God: Agape," *JRE* 24 (1996): 3–21, at 4.

52. For this summary, see Edward Collins Vacek, "Love, Christian and Diverse: A Response to Colin Grant," *JRE* 24 (1996): 29–34.

this love is sacred because it calls us to life. We realize it is the power of God because it enables us to befriend the world. . . . We know it is agapeic because it goes with us into the depth and suffers with us. We know it is filial because it is the yearning to befriend. We know it is erotic because it is passionate love for the world.[53]

One in Messiah Jesus (2:11-22)

This text can be divided into three sections: (1) vv. 11-13 address the situation of the Gentiles from a Jewish point of view whereas (2) vv. 14-18 focus on Messiah Jesus and their working of peace. Finally, the argument climaxes in (3) vv. 19-22 with the vision of an inclusive Israel as the household of G*d.[54] Whereas the "you" are identified with a Jewish ethno-religious term (Gentiles), the "we" are characterized in political-religious terms as the commonwealth of Israel. The "once-now" pattern in turn announces that the two once-divided groups—Jews and Gentiles—are now one group. Ephesians 2:14-16 echoes Colossians 1:19-22 but introduces the image of the "dividing wall," whose interpretation is crucial for understanding Ephesians. The middle section, vv. 14-18, is the longest, made up of two parts, vv. 14-16 and vv. 17-18, tied together with the watchword "peace."

The interpretation of this passage is difficult, because in a long Christian tradition of interpretation, key terms such as *Christos* or *ekklēsia* are generally understood as "Christian" terms, even though the author clearly writes from a Jewish and not a "Christian" point of view. For that reason it is important to read the whole chapter from such a point of view. This is very difficult for readers to do because the text has been read and interpreted throughout the centuries from a Christian point of view, stressing that the church has replaced Israel as the people of G*d. Hence it is important that we recognize the poison of anti-Judaism in the interpretation of Ephesians and put up the warning sign: Caution, such supersessionist Christian interpretation is dangerous to your health and survival!

---

53. Carter Heyward, "Lamenting the Loss of Love: A Response to Colin Grant," *JRE* 24 (1996): 23–28, at 26.

54. I am following here the outline of Tet-Lim N. Yee, *Jews, Gentiles*.

[11]So then, remember that at one time you Gentiles by birth, called "the uncircumcision" by those who are called "the circumcision"—a physical circumcision made in the flesh by human hands—[12]remember that you were at that time without Christ, being aliens from the commonwealth of Israel, and strangers to the covenants of promise, having no hope and without God in the world. [13]But now in Christ Jesus you who once were far off have been brought near by the blood of Christ. [14]For he is our peace; in his flesh he has made both groups into one and has broken down the dividing wall, that is, the hostility between us. [15]He has abolished the law with its commandments and ordinances, that he might create in himself one new humanity in place of the two, thus making peace, [16]and might reconcile both groups to God in one body through the cross, thus putting to death that hostility through it. [17]So he came and proclaimed peace to you who were far off and peace to those who were near; [18]for through him both of us have access in one Spirit to the Father. [19]So then you are no longer strangers and aliens, but you are citizens with the saints and also members of the household of God, [20]built upon the foundation of the apostles and prophets, with Christ Jesus himself as the cornerstone. [21]In him the whole structure is joined together and grows into a holy temple in the Lord; [22]in whom you also are built together spiritually into a dwelling place for God.

A Resistant Response to Ephesians 2:11-22

My comment offers a resistant response to both the content and the tone of Ephesians 2:11-22. This passage sketches a before-and-after picture for its Gentile readers and hearers. The "before" image consists of a wall dividing two groups: Jews (the circumcised) and Gentiles (the uncircumcised). On the Jews' side of the wall stands a clear path to covenantal relationship with God: the Torah, or, as the translation states, "the law with its commandments and ordinances" (2:15). On their side of the wall the Gentiles are blocked from access, presumably because they are not of the circumcised. The "after" image contains no wall, no separation between Jews and Gentiles, and no law. Instead, "the blood of Christ" or, more prosaically, faith in Jesus as the Christ/Messiah now paves the path to covenantal relationship with God. The tone of the passage is exultant: a long-awaited goal has been reached! The rift has been healed! Gentiles and Jews alike are the holy temple, which, after its destruction at the hands of Roman imperial forces, is now rebuilt on the cornerstone of Christ/Messiah and the foundation of the apostles as the divine dwelling place.

My reading, grounded in my identity as a Jew for whom "the law with its commandments and ordinances" remains a vital and positive element in the divine-human covenant, resists the tone of exultation. It focuses instead on the negation of Jewish identity that seeps through the overtly positive language of the passage. From a historical perspective the covenant to which the Gentiles, according to Ephesians, now have access is not the community of Christians, which in the late first or early second century did not yet exist as a movement that was separate and outside of the variety of Jewish communities. At the same time the passage delegitimizes those Jewish groups (the majority) who did not believe Jesus to be the messiah and for whom Torah, including the laws, ordinances, and ritual practices, was a life-giving source of spiritual sustenance and divine relationship. Whether supersessionism *per se* is present in the passage as such is a matter of debate; nevertheless, a resistant reading reveals that supersessionism is adumbrated by both its tone and its content.

Adele Reinhartz

In vv. 11-13 the author addresses the Gentile recipients of the letter in Jewish religious terms, as former Gentiles, and defines them in relation to the Jewish members of the community. By labeling them as "the un-circumcision" in contrast to the "circumcision," this language not only makes them "the other" but also casts both Jews and Gentiles in generic masculinizing terms. Such language proclaims Jewish preeminence in the covenant G*d made with Israel. In the time past, before Messiah Jesus, the Gentiles ("you") were aliens in relation to the commonwealth of Israel, "god-less" (ἄθεοι) and without hope.

Their situation before the coming of Messiah Jesus is characterized not only in ethnic-religious but in political terms. According to the Jewish writer Philo of Alexandria, conversion to Judaism involved three basic elements: "the practice of Jewish laws; exclusive devotion to the (one) God of the Jews; and integration of proselytes [converts] into the Jewish community."[55] Although they were previously aliens, their conversion through Messiah Jesus made them members of the Jewish community, the commonwealth of Israel (v. 13). Those who were far away are brought

55. Yee, *Jews, Gentiles*, 94.

near through the blood/death of the Messiah Jesus. Their conversion and being brought near makes them not "Christians" but Jewish messianic converts to the commonwealth of Israel.

Recently it has been argued that the function of this "alien rhetoric" is to make sense of Pauline the*logy to an audience that is not (and never has been) wrestling with the issues that produced that the*logy in the first place—that is, the question of Jewish-Gentile reconciliation—saving Paul for the non-Jewish context, if you will.[56] However, the assumption that this the*logical debate around Gentiles and Jews in Paul's time was no longer alive at the end of the first century overlooks the work of scholars who argue that "Jews" and "Christians" were not yet separate groups at the end of the first century. As pointed out in the introduction, Daniel Boyarin, a Jewish scholar, has argued that we cannot speak about Judaism and Christianity as two distinct opposing religions until the fourth or fifth centuries. Until then there are no sets of features that clearly define "Jewish" and "Christian" in such a way that the two categories do not overlap. This proposal, carefully developed in Boyarin's *Border Lines*,[57] and more succinctly argued in *The Jewish Gospels: The Story of the Jewish Christ*,[58] is revolutionary insofar as it opens up the possibility of a non-supersessionist reading of Ephesians and the whole N*T.[59]

However, it must not be overlooked that, even before Boyarin, Markus Barth argued in his book, *The People of God*, which appeared in German in 1959, that Ephesians "speaks of a single people of God, of the citizenship of Israel, into which Gentiles have been accepted."[60] Hence Barth argues that the "church cannot call itself the 'body of the Messiah' or the 'people of God' unless she [*sic*] recognizes that she [*sic*] is participating in the history and community of the Jews."[61] In my opinion Barth has correctly identified the argument of Ephesians,[62] although he assumes

56. Benjamin H. Dunning, "Strangers and Aliens No Longer: Negotiating Identity and Difference in Ephesians 2," *HTR* 99 (2006), 1–16, at 13.

57. Daniel Boyarin, *Border Lines: The Partition of Judaeo-Christianity*, Divinations (Philadelphia: University of Pennsylvania Press, 2004).

58. Daniel Boyarin, *The Jewish Gospels: The Story of the Jewish Christ* (New York: New Press, 2012).

59. See chapter 2 of my commentary on 1 Peter, *1 Peter: Reading against the Grain* (Sheffield: Sheffield Phoenix, 2015), 34–47.

60. Markus Barth, *The People of God* (Sheffield: JSOT Press, 1983), 46.

61. Ibid., 47.

62. Against Andrew T. Lincoln, "The Church and Israel in Ephesians 2," *CBQ* 49 (1987): 605–24.

that the letter is "Pauline." Margaret Y. MacDonald also argues "that Ephesians 2:11-22 is best understood as reflecting significant engagement with the life and fate of the Jewish people."[63]

Moreover, many scholars assume that vv. 14-18 incorporate a hymn (vv. 14-16) similar to the Messiah hymns in Philippians 2:6-11 or Colossians 1:15-20 and debate whether this hymn refers to cosmic reconciliation or to the reconciliation of Jewish and Gentile wo/men.[64] Rather than debating such reconstructions and their meaning productions, it seems more fruitful to attempt to unravel the meaning of the text's difficult constructions in terms of rhetorical argument rather than of a preexisting hymn.

The grammatical argument of this section is convoluted, but its reasoning is straightforward: After the declaration that Gentile wo/men have been brought near through the death (blood) of Messiah Jesus, who is proclaimed as the bringer of reconciliation and the mediator of peace, the statement that Messiah Jesus "made the both one" refers to both Jewish and Gentile wo/men. Messiah Jesus did so by destroying "the dividing wall of partition, the hostility, abolishing the law of the commandments in decrees."

After learning about the destructive activity of Messiah Jesus as our peace, we learn about their constructive activity. Messiah Jesus as our peace made both Jew and Gentile wo/men, that is, two corporate bodies, into one "new" corporate person in themself, so that in Messiah Jesus both are reconciled "in one body to G*d through the cross," "killing the hostility" that existed between both Jewish and Gentile wo/men, on the one hand, and between both groups and G*d on the other. How the argument of the author is transformed in Christian terms can be seen, for example, in the following statement:

> Consequently, now we both—Jews and Gentiles—have the access in "one" (ἑνὶ) Spirit before the Father (2:18). . . . The Christ who is our peace and who brought us peace in himself (ἐν αὐτῷ, 2:15b, 16b) by reconciling both Jews and Gentiles in one body, the church (1:22-23).[65]

John Paul Heil identifies the new "we" with the church, although the argument of vv. 14-18 does not mention the *ekklēsia* but speaks of the

---

63. Margaret Y. MacDonald, "The Politics of Identity in Ephesians," *JSNT* 26 (2004): 419–44, at 419.

64. See, for instance, John Muddiman's proposal comparing his own and Andrew Lincoln's reconstructions of the hymn (Muddiman, *Ephesians*, 123–38).

65. Heil, *Ephesians*, 125.

Jewish πολίτευμα ("commonwealth," "state"). This quotation, which is typical of most Ephesians commentaries, assumes that the "we" that refers to the Jewish people changes here to a new "we" referencing the church. This interpretation contradicts Markus Barth's argument that Ephesians "speaks of a single people of God, the citizenship of Israel, into which Gentiles have been accepted."[66] Indeed, Barth insists, "To be saved means for Gentiles to be grafted into the people of Israel."[67] Moreover, I would point out that the "we" is not identified here as *ekklēsia* (the voting citizen assembly of the *politeia*), the Greek word translated as "church," but as part of the *politeia*, the commonwealth, of Israel. Hence it is important to look more closely at vv. 14-15, which are the focal point of the debate: Messiah Jesus "is our peace; in the flesh and has made both groups into one and broken down the dividing wall, that is, the hostility between us; having abolished in the flesh the enmity, the law with its commandments and ordinances, that Messiah Jesus might create one new humanity in place of the two, thus making peace."

Andrew Lincoln objects to Barth's interpretation of this text, claiming that the whole Law, the Torah, and not just a part of it, has been annulled. He insists that commentators are wrong when they argue that it was only "the ceremonial but not the moral law" or only the casuistic divisive use of the law that has been annulled. Rather, Lincoln maintains that the lengthy phrase "having abolished the law consisting of commandments which are expressed in regulations" clearly states that the whole law, and not just a part of it, is abolished: "The divisiveness was produced by the law as such, by the very fact that Israel possessed the Torah; and so, in order to remove the divisiveness, Christ had to deal with its cause: the law itself."[68]

However, scholarship in line with the "New Perspective" on Paul contests this interpretation. For instance, Tet-Lim N. Yee argues that it is not the Torah as such that is rejected but that the halakhic rulings and teachings are criticized here from a Jewish point of view. The Jewish author is "willing to acknowledge before Gentile readers that the law has played a substantial role in leading to the strains between two ethnic groups. This is not an overt attack on the law itself. What is at stake is not the law *per se*, but 'the law as Jews had used it to consolidate their Jewish

---

66. Barth, *People of God*, 46.
67. Ibid., 20.
68. Lincoln, "The Church and Israel," 612. See also Schnackenburg, *Ephesians*, 114.

identity' and to ethnocentrically cast the Gentiles as 'the other.' "[69] The "body politic of Israel" (*politeia*) and the "law observance" that orders the life of its members are not separable.

In short, the author has spoken critically of the law but this by no means amounts to a personal attack on it. Rather, the author speaks from an insider's perspective on the law, which Jews had regarded as significant but had used as an instrument of division in order to reinforce their distinctive identity (e.g., the circumcision and the uncircumcision) and the "body politic" based on a particular *ethnos*.[70] This ethnic enmity is now abolished through the death of Messiah Jesus, so that in Messiah Jesus the two become one new human, so making peace.

Christian Supersessionism

Already in the late 1970s Judith Plaskow had raised the specter of Feminist Christian anti-Judaism.[71] She pointed not only to Elizabeth Cady Stanton's *The Woman's Bible* but also to the Jesus-was-a-Feminist argument and especially to the constructed dichotomy between a "Jewish" and a "Christian" Paul in Pauline scholarship.[72] This discussion lasted through the 1980s and 1990s but seems no longer center stage in the new millennium. This may be the case partly because of the feminist work on anti-Judaism and the scholarly work on the "New Perspective." Nevertheless, anti-Judaism is still deeply embedded in commentaries and monographs on Ephesians because of Christian supersessionism.

The word "supersessionism" comes from the English verb "to supersede." It signifies one thing being replaced or supplanted by another. According to David Novak a supersessionist reading can understand the N*T either as an addition to the old covenant—the religion of the Torah and Jewish Pharisaic tradition—or as a replacement of the old covenant.[73] When reading the N*T as a Christian, but not

---

69. Yee, *Jews, Gentiles*, 157–58.

70. Ibid., 160.

71. Judith Plaskow, "Christian Feminism and Anti-Judaism," *Cross Currents* 33 (1978): 306–9.

72. Judith Plaskow, "Anti-Judaism in Feminist Christian Interpretation," in *Searching the Scriptures*, vol. 1: *A Feminist Introduction*, ed. Elisabeth Schüssler Fiorenza (New York: Crossroad, 1993), 122–23.

73. David Novak, "The Covenant in Rabbinic Thought," in *Two Faiths, One Covenant? Jewish and Christian Identity in the Presence of the Other*, ed. Eugene B. Korn (Lanham, MD: Rowman & Littlefield, 2004), 65–80.

Jewish, text, such interpretations understand Christianity as the new Israel or the true people of G*d. In such a reading all honorific titles or religious values and visions are transferred from Judaism to Christianity and understood as no longer Jewish.

If we read texts such as Ephesians with the dualistic understanding that Christianity is superior to Judaism we cannot but read the letter in a supersessionist way and in a co-opting colonizing fashion that appropriates and arrogates the positive identity descriptions of Judaism to Christianity, transferring them from the synagogue to the church. It is no longer the Jewish people but the Christian church-communities that are the people of G*d. Such an appropriating reading has become standard because we read the N*T as written by Christians, rather than by Jewish wo/men. Such a reading inculcates the idea of Christian election and superiority over and against Judaism. Recent scholarship, however, has questioned such supersessionist readings of the N*T on historical grounds, arguing that "the parting of the ways" of Judaism and Christianity should be dated to the end of the first century/

beginning of the second century, at the earliest, and the fourth/ fifth century at the latest.

In short, most scholars now agree that Christianity started as a Jewish movement in Palestine. The first Christians were Jewish and the early spread of the Christian movement was aided by the great extent of the Jewish diaspora in the Roman Empire. This revised historical understanding of the beginnings of Christianity as Jewish messianism needs to be activated the*logically when reading the N*T. We must translate such a historical reading and knowledge into a the*logical one that recaptures our Jewish roots so that we no longer formulate Christian identity in the supersessionist way that has engendered centuries of bloody Christian anti-Judaism. A non-supersessionist reading is also critical to an anti-kyriarchal rearticulation of Christian identity. Christians need to learn how to remember our Jewish ancestors who struggled as anti-kyriarchal Jewish Messianists against the dehumanizing powers of empire and for G*d's alternative world of freedom and well-being. Their Jewish writings are collected in the so-called N*T.

The chapter concludes with Ephesians 2:19-22, which refers to the beginning section (vv. 1-3). Those considered Gentile wo/men (you in the flesh, the uncircumcision) are no longer alienated strangers excluded from the citizenship (πολιτεία) of Israel. On the contrary, they are now fellow citizens (συμπολῖται) with the holy ones (τῶν ἁγίων)—that is, with all believers. They are no longer "aliens" (πάροικοι, literally "outside the household") but are now members of the household of G*d (v. 19). Here G*d is seen again in the figure of the caring "housekeeper." This political-the*logical language is grammatically masculine-determined and cultural-religiously kyriocentric. However, we have no indication that it is exclusive of wo/men and therefore it is best understood as generic inclusive language.

In vv. 20-22 the language of the text switches from political to liturgical metaphor. The language of building that had referred to the household now changes to temple language. The addressees are told that they are built on the foundation of the apostles and prophets (v. 20a). Scholars debate whether Messiah Jesus is the cornerstone of the foundation of the building consisting of the apostles and prophets.[74] However, the point is that Messiah/Jesus "has occupied a status of central importance, like the apostles and prophets, in the 'household' to which the Gentiles belong."[75] With Messiah Jesus as cornerstone the building is fitted together and growing into a holy temple (v. 21b) in the Lord (v. 21c), a dwelling place of G*d (v. 22b) in the Spirit.

In sum, as fellow citizens with the "holy ones," as those who are beloved (v. 4) by G*d and love one another, all are growing into a holy temple (v. 21b), a dwelling place of the Spirit (2:22).[76] However, at no point does the author say that this spiritual temple replaces the temple in Jerusalem. According to Yee the high point of the author's argument "underscore[s] the interrelatedness of the Gentiles with other members who constitute the temple."[77]

Careful readers may have noticed that Yee's summary does not directly address the question of whether the recipients are members of the *politeia* of Israel or supersede it. Margaret MacDonald has argued to the contrary: that at the end of the first century, when Gentile Christians in all likelihood outnumbered Jewish Christians, Ephesians probably no longer responds to tensions between Jews and Christians. Rather, she suggests, "the author appropriates the language of Jewish nationhood in vv. 12 and 19 to describe the church. Thus, the writer appeals to the

74. MacDonald, *Colossians and Ephesians*.

75. Yee, *Jews, Gentiles*, 207.

76. For the interpretation of temple language in 1 Peter 2, see Schüssler Fiorenza, *1 Peter*.

77. Yee, *Jews, Gentiles*, 210.

Jewish community on a symbolic level to claim the prestige and honor of Israel for the new community."[78]

In MacDonald's view these verses prevent the assumption that the situation in Ephesians is the same as that in Romans 1, namely, that believers constitute a remnant of Israel to which Gentiles have been added. Instead, Israel "becomes a metaphor for a re-created unified identity (one new person, v. 15) brought about through Christ's agency that has transcended the historical Israel. The Church has become a distinct entity separate from both Judaism and other groups in the Greco-Roman world. Ultimately, 'Israel' like 'body,' 'building' and 'temple' serves as a metaphorical description of this new entity. Unlike Romans 9–11, Eph 2:1-22 is not concerned with the situation of the Jews, who are not part of the church."[79]

In short, against a tendency to supersessionist interpretation I have argued here, in light of Yee's work, that the "New Perspective" needs to be extended to the post-Pauline literature. As alternative to a supersessionist reading we have to recognize that with the language of *politeia* and temple the Jewish author seeks to assure the Gentiles that the community or "body politic" to which they belong transcends the old division of "us" (citizens) and "them" (Gentiles).

This vision, however, can be fully appreciated only if we reject the dualistic descriptive categories of "circumcision" and "uncircumcision," "citizens" and "aliens," "the far off" and "the near," "Gentiles" and "Jews"—in other words, those on the periphery versus those in the center—and refuse to conflate the dominant Christian exclusivist interpretation of Ephesians with the perspective of the author. The beloved "community is marked by undisguised inclusivism and the assumption that Messiah Jesus' work has reconciled Jews and Gentiles."[80] However, we must not overlook that such textual constructions and deconstructions of dualisms in Ephesians go hand in hand with political/ideological/the*logical legitimizations of kyriarchal domination insofar as Messiah Jesus is also characterized in imperial terms of domination.

---

78. MacDonald, *Colossians and Ephesians*, 253.
79. Ibid., 256.
80. Yee, *Jews, Gentiles*, 212.

Ephesians 3:1-21

The Mystery Made Known to Paul

It is debated whether this chapter is still part of the preceding argument and unit or whether it opens up a new section. In my view it is best understood as a "bridge" chapter that connects the first two chapters with chapters 4–6. The formula "for this reason" (τούτου χάριν) noticeably connects the portrayal of Paul as a prisoner "for you Gentiles" (3:1) with the preceding chapter, which placed emphasis on the Gentile wo/men. This opens the way for the author to introduce Paul as the speaker and to describe, in a long digression, the "mystery" given to Paul to reveal (vv. 2-12).

The Mystery Revealed by Paul (3:1-13)

Ephesians 3:2-7 and 3:8-12 consist of two longer statements about the mystery that is central to the Gospel preached by Paul. Whereas the first statement focuses on the mystery of the Gentiles being a part of G*d's[1]

---

1. In order to indicate the brokenness and inadequacy of human language to name the Divine, in my book *Jesus: Miriam's Child, Sophia's Prophet; Critical Issues in Feminist Christology* (New York: Continuum, 1994) I switched from the orthodox Jewish

Ephesians 3:1-13

³:¹This is the reason that I, Paul, am a prisoner for Christ Jesus for the sake of you Gentiles—²for surely you have already heard of the commission of God's grace that was given me for you, ³and how the mystery was made known to me by revelation, as I wrote above in a few words, ⁴a reading of which will enable you to perceive my understanding of the mystery of Christ.

⁵In former generations this mystery was not made known to humankind, as it has now been revealed to his holy apostles and prophets by the Spirit: ⁶that is, the Gentiles have become fellow heirs, members of the same body, and sharers in the promise in Christ Jesus through the gospel.

⁷Of this gospel I have become a servant according to the gift of God's

people, the second connects the mystery with the Divine plan for the cosmos and the *ekklēsia*'s role in it. Ephesians 3:13 takes up the notion of the suffering apostle from v. 1 but uses different language,[2] connecting the section to the one that follows it.[3]

As pointed out in the introduction, most Catholic exegetes are now of the opinion that the apostle Paul is not the author of Ephesians but that the author writes in the name of Paul to promote Paul as an apostle.[4] The portrayal of Paul as the apostle to the Gentiles, to whom special insight into the Mystery of Messiah/Christ was given, vividly underscores Paul's apostolic authority. The special gift bestowed on Paul is his knowledge of the divine mystery of salvation that was revealed to him. Like the prophets and apostles, Paul is a receiver of revelation. Ephesians seeks to persuade the community to remain in continuity with the Pauline tradition. The image of the apostle captive and suffering is intended to strengthen this tradition.

Ephesians 3:1-13 is widely considered a digression. According to rhetorical theory a digression is meant to treat a *topos* that is relevant, but logically unnecessary to the argument, in order to secure the audience's attention and favor. The digression in 3:1-13 is prompted by and based

---

writing of G-d, which I had adopted in *But She Said* and *Discipleship of Equals*, to this spelling, G*d, which seeks to avoid the conservative malestream association that the writing of G-d has for Jewish feminists. Since the*logy means speaking about G*d, or G*d-talk, I write it in the same way.

2. See Andrew T. Lincoln, *Ephesians*, WBC 42 (Dallas: Word, 1990), 168.

3. Joachim Gnilka, *Der Epheserbrief* (Freiburg: Herder, 1971), 179. Gnilka suggests that v. 13 starts the following section rather than concluding the first.

4. See Rudolf Schnackenburg, *Ephesians: A Commentary*, trans. Helen Heron (Edinburgh: T&T Clark, 1991), 24–25.

grace that was given me by the working of his power. [8]Although I am the very least of all the saints, this grace was given to me to bring to the Gentiles the news of the boundless riches of Christ, [9]and to make everyone see what is the plan of the mystery hidden for ages in God who created all things; [10]so that through the church the wisdom of God in its rich variety might now be made known to the rulers and authorities in the heavenly places. [11]This was in accordance with the eternal purpose that he has carried out in Christ Jesus our Lord, [12]in whom we have access to God in boldness and confidence through faith in him. [13]I pray therefore that you may not lose heart over my sufferings for you; they are your glory.

on the text of Colossians 1:23-28, with which it shares the following sequence:

> Introduction of Paul (Col 1:23; Eph 3:1)
> The suffering of the apostle "for you" (Col 1:24; Eph 3:1, 13)
> The "grace" granted to the office of apostle (Col 1:25; Eph 3:2-3a, 7)
> The revelation of the mystery of Christ/Messiah (Col 1:26; Eph 3:5)
> The content of this mystery (Col 1:27; Eph 3:6) and the proclamation to the Gentiles (Col 1:28; Eph 3:8)[5]

In her Wisdom Commentary volume on Colossians, Cynthia Kittredge summarizes the gist of the Colossians statement, which the author of Ephesians has taken as a model:

> The exhortation in the letter to the Colossians to continue right living (walking) has been undergirded by the recollection of baptismal conversion and by the citation of the Christ hymn. It is further supported by an extended passage, spoken in the first-person-singular "I" voice of Paul, that elaborates on his role as "servant [διάκονος] of this gospel" (Col 1:23). Crucial to his authority are Paul's suffering, his divine commission to "make the word of God fully known" (1:25), and his role to "present" (1:28). . . . The length and detail of this passage and Paul's claim to be struggling for "all who have not seen me face to face" (2:1) shows how the claim of authority of the person of Paul is moving beyond personal relationships with particular congregations to general recognition by all/everyone.[6]

---

5. Ibid., 128. See also the chart in Pheme Perkins, *Ephesians*, ANTC (Nashville: Abingdon, 1997), 79–80.

6. Cynthia Briggs Kittredge and Claire Miller Colombo, "Colossians," in *Philippians, Colossians, Philemon*, WCS 51 (Collegeville, MN: Liturgical Press, 2017), 160.

In sum, the lengthy digression on Paul's apostleship in vv. 2-8 serves to establish the character of the speaker Paul and his reliability. Placing emphasis on Paul, the apostle to the Gentiles, serves the same function in Ephesians as it did in Colossians. It determines the whole third chapter of Ephesians but does not explicate his apostolic hardship with reference to the crucified Jesus (cf. 1 Cor 4:1-13 or 2 Cor 6:3-11). Differently from Colossians 1:24, the author does not develop the soteriological nature of apostolic suffering but instead emphasizes Paul's reception of revelation.

This digression, which is patterned after the presentation of Paul in Colossians, is carefully integrated into the overall structure of the letter in that it makes reference to Ephesians 2:11-22 as well as to key terms and concepts in the rest of the letter such as Gentiles, holy apostles and prophets, promise, body of Christ (1:23; 4:12; 5:30), access to G*d (2:18; 3:12), οἰκονομία ("household management," 1:10), grace of G*d (1:6-7; 2:5, 7-8), mystery (1:9), rulers and powers (1:21), and heavenly places (1:3, 20; 2:6). The interconnecting functions of Ephesians 2:2-12 must be kept in mind when analyzing the rhetoric of the digression in 3:2-13.

The rhetoric of this chapter segment (vv. 1-3) confirms the argument of Ephesians 2:11-22. Through the proclamation of the Gospel, the Good News, the Gentile wo/men have become equal heirs in the common-wealth of Israel, members of the same messianic body, and sharers in the promise given in Messiah Jesus. This mystery that was not known to humans in former times has been revealed to the apostles and prophets through the Spirit. It has been made known to Paul, who—as they cer-tainly have heard—is imprisoned for the sake of the Gentile wo/men but is here clearly not counted among the apostles. To him was made known in a revelation "the stewardship or housekeeping plan that is the grace of G*d" for the sake of the Gentiles. Paul is further mentioned as the διάκονος ("servant") of the gospel (v. 7) to whom was given the grace to preach to the nations (τοῖς ἔθνεσιν) the unsearchable riches of the Messiah/Christ (v. 8).[7] The section ends in v. 13 with the statement that Paul prays that they do not "lose heart" because of his sufferings for them, because these are their glory, that is, the glory of their inheri-tance (see also 1:18; 2:7).

The mystery of Messiah Jesus that was revealed to Paul is at the heart of this section. Its revelation is rhetorically placed in the mouth of the

7. The article before Christ defines its meaning to be "Messiah," understood here as a title.

apostle in order to give it persuasive power. The Gentile wo/men are now part of the commonwealth of Israel! Most commentaries miss this point since they assume that the claim is that Gentiles are now part of "the church" consisting of *former* Jewish and Gentile wo/men. In contrast, I have argued in chapter 2, along with Markus Barth and the "New Perspective" in Pauline Studies, that Paul is seen here as the apostolic agent of the incorporation of the Gentile wo/men into the Jewish πολιτεία rather than their incorporation into "the church."

The rhetoric of this section builds up to the goal expressed in vv. 10-12: Although Paul is the very least of all the saints, the apostle received the grace to proclaim to the nations

- the news of the boundless riches of Messiah Jesus (v. 8)

- to bring to light what is the household management (οἰκονομία) of the mystery hidden for ages in G*d, who created all things (v. 9)

- so that through the *ekklēsia* the manifold wisdom of G*d might now be made known to the rulers and authorities in the heavenly places (v. 10)

- in accordance with the eternal purpose carried out in Messiah Jesus, the Lord, in whom we have access to G*d in boldness and confidence by the faithfulness of Messiah Jesus (vv.11-12)[8]

The purpose of the digression is to construct not simply Paul but Paul's ministry. To Paul was given the stewardship or management that results from the grace of G*d (v. 2), which consists in making known to the Gentiles the boundless riches of Messiah Jesus and bringing to light the mystery of the world-management that has been hidden throughout the ages in G*d, the Creator. As pointed out before, according to ancient political discourse, οἰκονομία refers to the management of G*d's world-household. The mystery "involves the Gentiles being joint heirs and joint members of the body and sharers in the promise" in Messiah Jesus "through the Gospel."[9] "In Messiah Jesus" refers to the sphere in which G*d's οἰκονομία is realized.

---

8. For this translation see Markus Barth, *The People of God* (Sheffield: JSOT Press, 1983), 347; C. Leslie Mitton, *The Epistle to the Ephesians: Its Authorship, Origin and Purpose* (Oxford: Clarendon, 1951), 128.

9. Lincoln, *Ephesians*, 181.

The goal of Paul's work is to enable the *ekklēsia* to make known the manifold Divine Wisdom-Sophia to the rulers and authorities in the heavenlies. The bringing together of the whole cosmos in Messiah Jesus is already anticipated, in the present, in the bringing together of Jews and Gentiles in the *ekklēsia*, the democratic assembly of the commonwealth of Israel. It is not Paul but the *ekklēsia*, the assembly of full citizens, that is to proclaim the Wisdom of G*d, which manifests Herself in a great variety of forms and colors. She is described in Wisdom 7:22 as having "a Spirit intelligent, holy, unique of many forms (*polymeres*; cf. *polypoikilos*)."[10] Scholars question whether the text speaks of wisdom as a quality or mode of being sagacious, as in "G*d's wise purpose," or of Wisdom as multidimensional divine personification. Both readings are possible. Although most commentaries choose the first translation, I think it is appropriate to explore the second, which includes the first, since the personification of G*d's Wisdom entails wisdom.[11]

The figure of Divine Wisdom has its roots in Jewish-Hellenistic Wisdom the*logy, which was articulated in interaction with widespread Isis worship. Wisdom was present at creation (Prov 8:27-31; Wis 9:9), as artist and counselor (Wis 8:4, 6), but Wisdom remains hidden (Job 28:12-14). Wisdom is the creator of justice (Prov 8:12-21). Like the Goddess Isis, Divine Wisdom employs the "I am" aretalogical proclamation style in announcing her universal message of salvation (Eccl 24:1, 13-14, 17-21). The aretalogies[12] of Isis were probably known to the author of Wisdom 7:21.[13]

Postexilic wo/men in Israel and Hellenistic Jewish wo/men in Egypt have conceived of Divine Wisdom as prefigured in the language and image of Egyptian Goddesses, like Maat and Isis, or the Greek God-

---

10. Schnackenburg, *Ephesians*, 140.

11. See, for example, Lincoln, MacDonald, Perkins, Heilig, Schnackenburg.

12. Aretalogy is a form of sacred biography (or autobiography, since it is written in the first person); the deity lists their attributes in a poem or other text. Quite frequently each line starts with "I am . . ." and usually, as might be expected, the aretalogy is self-laudatory. Aretalogies are found in the sacred texts of later Egypt and Mesopotamia and in Greco-Roman texts as well. For further discussion, see, e.g., Morton Smith, "Prolegomena to a Discussion of Aretalogies, Divine Men, the Gospels, and Jesus," *JBL* 90 (1971): 174–99; Howard Clark Kee, "Aretalogy and Gospel," *JBL* 92 (1973): 402–22; Jonathan Z. Smith, "Good News Is No News: Aretalogy and Gospel," in *Christianity, Judaism and other Greco-Roman Cults: Studies for Morton Smith at Sixty*, ed. Jacob Neusner, SJLA 12 (Leiden: Brill, 1975), 1–23.

13. See the discussion in Heinrich Schlier, *Der Brief an die Epheser* (Düsseldorf: Patmos, 1957), 158–67.

desses, Athena and Dikē. According to a very well-known prayer, all the different nations and people use divine titles derived from their own local mythologies when they call on the Goddess Isis. They do so in the full knowledge that Isis is one but encompasses all. In the figure of Sophia-Wisdom, also referred to as "Ḥokmah," ancient Jewish Scriptures seek to hold together belief in the "one G*d" of Israel and the language and metaphors of a female Divine being. Hence the texts struggle to subordinate Wisdom to G*d (see Prov 8:23-24, 27, 29-31). In short, Wisdom is a cosmic figure who is expected to return in the messianic period to reveal "the Holy and Righteous One" (i.e., the Messiah), who is filled with the Spirit of Wisdom (1 En. 48:1, 7; cf. 49:3).[14]

Wisdom in Feminist The*logy

In the past several decades feminists have rediscovered and re-created the submerged traditions of Divine Wisdom in all their splendor and possibilities. Feminist the*logians have discovered anew the creativity of wisdom/Wisdom and have searched for Her presence in the spaces "in-between," the blank spaces. We have sought "to hear Wisdom into speech," to use the expression coined by Nelle Morton, one of the first feminist the*logians and teachers of wisdom/Wisdom, who recognized that "Wisdom is feminist and suggests an existence earlier than Word."[15]

In the Bible, "Spirit" (רוח, *ruaḥ*), "Presence" (שכינה, *Shekinah*), and "Wisdom" (חכמה/σοφία, *Ḥokmah/Sophia*) are all grammatically feminine terms. They refer to very similar female figurations in the Hebrew Bible[16] who express G*d's saving presence in the world. They signify the aspect of the Divine that is involved in the affairs of humanity and creation:

> For within Her is a spirit
> intelligent, holy, unique,
> manifold, subtle,

14. Schnackenburg, *Ephesians*, 139.

15. Nelle Morton, *The Journey Is Home* (Boston: Beacon, 1985), 175. See also my books *Wisdom Ways: Introducing Feminist Biblical Interpretation* (Maryknoll, NY: Orbis Books, 2001); *Los Caminos de la Sabiduría. Una Introducción a la interpretación feminista de la Biblia*, trans. José Manuel Lozano Gotor (Santander: Sal Terrae, 2004); and *"En la senda de Sofía": Hermenéutica feminista crítica para la liberación*, trans. Severino Croatto and Cristina Conti (Buenos Aires: Lumen-Isedet, 2003).

16. I use "Hebrew Bible" instead of "Old Testament" and "N*T" instead of "New Testament" because Old and New Testament are Christian designations that announce the superiority of Christianity over Judaism.

active, incisive, unsullied,
  lucid, invulnerable, be-
  nevolent, sharp,
irresistible, beneficent,
  loving humans, stead-
  fast, dependable,
  unperturbed,
almighty, all-surveying,
  penetrating all intel-
  ligence, pure and most
  subtle spirit.
For Wisdom is quicker to
  move than any motion;
She is so pure, she per-
  vades and permeates all
  things.
She is a breath of the power
  of G*d, pure emanation
  of divine glory . . .
In each generation she
  passes into holy souls,
She makes them friends of
  G*d and prophets;
For G*d loves only the one
  who lives with Wisdom
  (Wis 7:22-25, 27-30).[17]

Traditional the*logy has focused on the Spirit, who in Latin is grammatically masculine, whereas feminist the*logy has rediscovered the Divine in female *Gestalt*, or form. Jewish feminists have rediscovered a spirituality of Shekhinah, who plays a significant part in some Jewish traditions; and Christian, especially Catholic, feminists have elaborated the female figure of divine Wisdom (Latin: *Sapientia*). Several books of the Christian Bible speak about Her. Many of these texts, however, are included only as appendices in Protestant versions or are excluded altogether.[18] Divine Wisdom-Sophia-Sapientia plays a significant role in Orthodox the*logy, but less so in the modern West.

In biblical as well as in contemporary religious discourses the word "wisdom" has a double meaning. It can refer either to a quality of life, and in particular to that of a people/person, and/or to a figuration of the Divine. Wisdom in both senses of the word is not exclusive to the biblical traditions but is found in the imagination and writings of all known religions.

---

17. I am quoting from the text of the Revised Standard Version (RSV) of the Bible but have changed masculine language for G*d and humans.

18. The following books are often labeled "apocryphal" or "deuterocanonical" and in Protestant Bible editions they are usually printed in an appendix placed after the N*T. They are included in the Roman Catholic, Greek, and Slavonic canons: Tobit; Judith; Wisdom of Solomon; Ecclesiasticus, also called the Wisdom of Jesus Ben Sirach; Baruch; 1 and 2 Maccabees; 3 Maccabees (only in Greek and Slavonic Bibles); 4 Maccabees (only in an appendix to the Greek Bible); 1 Esdras (in the Greek Bible; 2 Esdras in the Slavonic Bible); Prayer of Manasseh (in Greek and Slavonic Bibles; as appendix in the Vulgate, the Latin translation of the Roman Catholic Bible); Psalm 151 (following Psalm 150 in the Greek Bible); and additions to the books of Daniel and Esther.

It is transcultural, international, and interreligious. Wisdom is practical knowledge gained through experience and daily living as well as through the study of creation and human nature. Both senses, that of capability (wisdom) and that of its female personification (Wisdom), are crucial for articulating a feminist biblical spirituality that seeks to fashion biblical readers as critical interpreting subjects.

Wisdom, however, is most fascinating to feminists as a representation of the Divine in female *Gestalt* (form). She is a Divine female figure who in extra-biblical traditions is represented by a variety of Goddesses and Goddess traditions. The biblical texts about Divine Wisdom-Ḥokmah-Sophia-Sapientia retain the subjugated knowledges and the submerged language of the Goddess within Christian tradition just as the Divine Shekhinah-Presence does within Judaism. Although the feminist scholarly search for the footprints of Wisdom-Ḥokmah-Sophia-Sapientia in biblical writings encounters a host of historical-the*logical problems, it is nevertheless commonly accepted that the biblical image of Wisdom-Ḥokmah-Sophia-

Sapientia has integrated within it Goddess language and traditions.

A similar debate is taking place among Jewish feminists with respect to the Shekinah, a biblical figure akin to Ḥokmah-Sophia-Sapientia-Wisdom. The Bible contains only a few references to "the glory of the Shekinah" and to "the wings of the Shekinah." While the meaning of these verses is not at all obvious, the Rabbinic Sages of the Talmud and Midrash interpreted them as having to do with situations in which the manifestation of G*d and G*d's nearness to humankind or to specific individuals is spoken of.

Feminist objections against the valorization of the biblical Wisdom tradition point out that this tradition is permanently suspect, not only as an elite male tradition, but also as one that, in a dualistic fashion, plays off the "good" woman against the "evil" woman.[19] Such a misogynist tradition, it is argued, cannot be concerned with justice at all. However, other scholars specializing in Wisdom literature have rightly objected to such a negative evaluation of the Wisdom traditions. They have pointed out not only that Wisdom discourses are permeated with

---

19. In fairness to the Wisdom traditions it must be pointed out that the prophetic or apocalyptic traditions are equally suspect because they are also permeated by kyriocentric bias.

the teachings of justice but also that, in the first century, prophetic-apocalyptic and sapiential (Wisdom) traditions were intertwined, integrated, and changed.[20] These traditions espouse a cosmopolitan ethos that can respect local particularities without giving up claims to universality.

In addition the advocates of Wisdom argue that the wisdom traditions had long been democratized and that many of the sapiential traditions of the gospels reflect folk wisdom that could very well have been articulated by and for wo/men. Finally, they point out that feminist exegetical-historical objections against the feminist regeneration of Divine Ḥokmah-Sophia-Wisdom may also be due to different confessional locations and indebtedness to neo-orthodox the*ology.

A closer look at the biblical Wisdom traditions reveals that these traditions do not portray Divine Wisdom in terms of the "lady." Divine Wisdom is a cosmic figure delighting in the dance of creation, a "master" craftswo/man and teacher of justice. She is a leader of her people and accompanies them on their way through history. Very much unlike a lady, she raises her voice in public places and calls to everyone who would hear her. She transgresses boundaries, celebrates life, and nourishes those who will become her friends. Her cosmic house is without walls and her table is set for all.

Hence, biblical discourses on Divine Wisdom are still significant today not only because they are a rich resource of female language for G*d but also, and more important, because they provide a framework for developing a feminist ecological the*logy of creation and a biblical spirituality of nourishment and struggle. Moreover, they embody a religious ethos that is not exclusive of other religious visions but can be understood as a part of them since wisdom/Wisdom is celebrated in all of them. The earliest Sophia traditions that still can be traced in the margins of early Christian works intimate a perspective that combines Jewish prophetic, Wisdom, and *basileia*[21] traditions as central to a political, open-ended, and cosmopolitan religious vision of struggle and well-being for everyone.

---

20. See also Claudia V. Camp, *Wisdom and the Feminine in the Book of Proverbs*, BLS 14 (Sheffield: Almond Press, 1985).

21. *Basileia* refers to the political realm of G*d or G*d's vision of a transformed creation and world.

Paul's mission is to reveal or make known the secret οἰκονομία (world-housekeeping plan) of G*d so that multi-hued Divine Wisdom might now be known to the rulers and authorities in the heavenly places, through the *ekklēsia*, according to the eternal purpose that G*d carried out in the Lord Messiah Jesus. Being a member of the messianic Jesus-corporation, we have the rights and boldness of citizens to speak freely (with παρρησία) and confident access because of the Messiah's own faithfulness (πίστεως αὐτοῦ) (vv.10-12).

As with the first reference to *ekklēsia* in 1:22, so also here in 3:10 *ekklēsia*, the assembly of free citizens, has its location in the heavenly places. The task of the *ekklēsia* is to proclaim the multi-colored Divine Wisdom to the principalities (ἀρχαῖς) and powers (ἐξουσίαις) in the heavenly places (τοῖς ἐπουρανίοις). In 1:3 the recipients of the letter were already told that they are blessed in the Messiah with "every spiritual blessing in the heavenly places," whereas in 2:6 they are characterized as already together, raised up and seated in the heavenly places in Messiah Jesus, who, according to 1:20, was exalted and made to sit at G*d's right hand in the heavenlies. Finally, according to 6:12, "our struggle is not against enemies of blood and flesh, but against the rulers, against the authorities, against the cosmic powers of this present darkness, against the spiritual forces of evil in the heavenly places." To these forces the *ekklēsia* is called to present the multifaceted Wisdom of G*d.

What does "in the heavenlies" mean for people today who think in terms of quite a different universe? As I have pointed out previously, Walter Wink's well-grounded work has examined what the N*T has to say about power in its corporate superhuman manifestations. He attempts to translate the ancient worldview that thinks in terms of below and above by using the modern dualisms—external/peripheral, internal/withinness, spiritual/institutional—and seeks to interconnect it with the system of power, the domination system I have called kyriarchy. Adopting Franz Hinkelammert's distinction "between the material institutions that organize modern society and the Spirit of these institutions," Wink argues that we must focus not only on the physical elements of institutions but also on the spirituality of such institutions: the self-image, corporate personality or institutional spirit, "the unseen power behind the visible elements."[22]

---

22. Walter Wink, *Naming the Powers: The Language of Power in the New Testament* (Philadelphia: Fortress, 1984), 109–10. See also Franz Hinkelammert, *The Ideological Weapons of Death: A Theological Critique of Capitalism* (Maryknoll, NY: Orbis Books, 1986).

Wink develops this thesis in wrestling with Ephesians 3:10 and sums up his interpretation: "If, then, the church must now make known the manifold wisdom of God to the principalities and powers in the heavenlies, it cannot be content with addressing the material aspect of an institution alone. It must speak to the spiritual reality of the institution as well."[23] Wink points to the work of Martin Luther King Jr. as an example of such a "proclamation to the powers":

> With only the powerless at his side, he formulated actions that would provoke and make visible the institutional violence of racism. . . . He resolutely refused to treat racism as a political issue only; he insisted that it be seen also as a moral and spiritual sickness. He did not attack the soul of America, but appealed to its most profound depth. His confrontational tactics were an attempt to address that soul. He called a nation to repent.[24]

In short, for change to take place both institutions and the spirit of these institutions, as well as forms of power, need to be addressed. "In the heavenlies" means for us today that we are able to recognize the spiritual dimensions, the "heavenlies" of our world that promote "love" and not domination.

Ephesians 3:13 is a concluding transitional verse that is in many ways similar to Colossians 1:24, where the afflictions belong to Christ and not to Paul. Ephesians, in contrast to Colossians, stresses that the apostle's afflictions are the recipients' glory. This self-promotion of the apostle sounds like a glorification of suffering. However, according to Margaret MacDonald, in the ancient world "afflictions can act as external manifestations of honor, because in Pauline Christianity they have come to symbolize the promise of salvation. Suffering will be followed by glory (e.g., Rom 8:17-18)."[25] Be that as it may, this text, when understood as Sacred Scripture, is potentially life-threatening when, for example, battered wo/men are told that their sufferings, like Paul's, will also lead to glory. This praise of suffering as leading to glory deserves the label: Caution, could be dangerous to your health and survival.

The Prayer of Paul (3:14-21)

Chapter 3, which links the first part of the letter to the second part, concludes Paul's rhetorical exercise in self-praise with the apostle's prayer.

23. Wink, *Naming the Powers*, 110.

24. Ibid., 129.

25. Margaret Y. MacDonald, *Colossians and Ephesians*, SP 17 (Collegeville, MN: Liturgical Press, 2000), 267.

Ephesians 3:14-21

¹⁴For this reason I bow my knees before the Father, ¹⁵from whom every family in heaven and on earth takes its name. ¹⁶I pray that, according to the riches of his glory, he may grant that you may be strengthened in your inner being with power through his Spirit, ¹⁷and that Christ may dwell in your hearts through faith, as you are being rooted and grounded in love. ¹⁸I pray that you may have the power to comprehend, with all the saints, what is the breadth and length and height and depth, ¹⁹and to know the love of Christ that surpasses knowledge, so that you may be filled with all the fullness of God.

²⁰Now to him who by the power at work within us is able to accomplish abundantly far more than all we can ask or imagine, ²¹to him be glory in the church and in Christ Jesus to all generations, forever and ever. Amen.

The introduction, "for this reason," refers to 3:1, where the same formula is used. The reason given there refers to the unity of Jews and Gentiles, a theme that has been elaborated in chapter 2. Moreover, this prayer is similar to the prayer report in 1:15-23. Paul here adopts the stance of prostration due to a king or emperor and not the usual Jewish position for prayer, which was standing. This stance is appropriate before the Father, from whom every family in heaven and on earth takes its name. Unfortunately, the English translation obscures the wordplay here. In the Greek, G*d is called πατήρ (*patēr*), from whom every πατριά (*patria*) in heaven and on earth takes its name. While the Greek word πατριά derives from the word πατήρ, father, it should not be translated as "family" but as "fatherland."[26] Thus G*d is likened here to the emperor, who was called, in Latin, the *pater patriae*, who ruled the empire. G*d is here imagined as an imperial ruler, whereas in the introductory eulogy (1:9-14) G*d is envisioned as the *matrona*, the caretaker of the household who keeps up the whole cosmos. She does so in and through the Messiah Jesus, who is the "Beloved." This feminine image of G*d as the world's housekeeper balances the masculine image of G*d as the patriarchal lord and ruler. Paul's prayer here may be inspired by Colossians 2:2-10.[27]

As the assembly of free citizens, the *ekklēsia* has access to this G*d of love. However, Paul approaches G*d here as one approaches the emperor, bending one's knee and prostrating oneself. His prayer for the recipients is structured by three consecutive "that" (Greek: ἵνα) clauses:

---

26. See Markus Barth, *Ephesians 1–3*, AB 34 (Garden City, NY: Doubleday, 1974), 380–82.
27. See Schnackenburg, *Ephesians*, 145.

- that you may be strengthened in your inner being with power through G*d's Spirit (v. 16) and Messiah/Christ may dwell in your hearts through faith, as you are being rooted and grounded in love (v. 17)
- that you may have the power to comprehend, with all the saints, what is the breadth and length and height and depth (v. 18) and to know the love of Messiah/Christ that surpasses knowledge
- that you may be filled with all the fullness of God (v. 19)

Unlike the introduction, the love-prayer that follows invokes not the kyriarchal G*d image of the emperor but that of a loving G*d who has been previously invoked with the image of the caring *matrona*. It does so by elaborating the love of Messiah/Christ and the innermost power of the Spirit, so that the members of the community are filled with the fullness of G*d.

The concluding doxology is the only one in the N*T that mentions Messiah Jesus and the *ekklēsia* "as the locus of praise."[28] It declares: "To G*d be glory in the *ekklēsia* and in Messiah Jesus to all generations, forever and ever. Amen" (v. 21). This praise is given to G*d, "who by the power at work within us is able to accomplish abundantly far more than all we can ask or imagine." In the struggles for justice and liberation no "burnout" is possible, because G*d's power "within us" is beyond our imagination. Chapter 3, interlinking chapters 1–2 with chapters 4–6, ends with the affirmation of this divine power "within us." At the same time it names the power that compels and sustains the actions of the *ekklēsia* in its struggles against the kyriarchal powers of racism, sexism, heterosexism, xenophobia, Islamophobia, imperialism, colonialism, and so many more injustices. This divine power of love seeks to work through us.

In reaction to the bombing at Nice, France, on Bastille Day in 2016, Barbara Cullom posted the following on her Facebook page the following day: "Once again, I look to the Children's Sermon preached by Margaret Lacy Dodds at Rockville United Church some 25 years ago, built around the phrase 'God's arms are in our sleeves.' Today, show to others Godde's supportive, compassionate, hopeful, peaceable, peace-making and peaceful arms."

28. Perkins, *Ephesians*, 92.

Ephesians 4:1–5:14

The Way to Walk[1]

In her rhetorical analysis of the letters to the Philippians and Ephesians, Cynthia Briggs Kittredge has made a convincing case that Ephesians 4:1–6:9 should be understood as a rhetorical unit that presents its argument in the form of an exhortation (*exhortatio*), a speech or written passage intended to persuade, inspire, or encourage.[2] In the NRSV this exhortation is laid out under seven section headings: "Unity in the Body

---

1. Whereas in the first part of Ephesians, Colossians is invoked only three times (Col 1:1-2 in Eph 1:1-2; Col 1:38 in Eph 1:15-17; Col 2:12-13 in Eph 2:5-6) and not at all in the transitional connecting chapter (Eph 3), Ephesians 4, 5, and 6 seem to take up and elaborate Colossians 3 and 4, as outlined in the following table (Rudolf Schnackenburg, *Ephesians: A Commentary*, trans. Helen Heron [Edinburgh: T&T Clark, 1991], 30):

Col 3:5-14	Eph 4:17-32
Col 3:16-17	Eph 5:19-20
Col 3:18–4:1	Eph 5:26–6:9
Col 4:2-4	Eph 6:18-20
Col 4:7	Eph 6:21-22
Col 4:18	Eph 6:24

2. Cynthia Briggs Kittredge, *Community and Authority: The Rhetoric of Obedience in the Pauline Tradition*, HTS 45 (Harrisburg, PA: Trinity Press International, 1998), 132–33.

of Christ" (4:1-16), "The Old Life and the New" (4:17-24), "Rules for the New Life" (4:25–5:2), "Renounce Pagan Ways" (5:3-20), "The Christian Household" (5:21-33), "Children and Parents" (6:1-4), and "Slaves and Masters" (6:5-9).

It is difficult to find a clear structure intended by the author for the large segment 4:17–5:20. Margaret MacDonald suggests that it be treated as a single unit. This allows one to see more clearly how two related goals shape the whole section of exhortation, 4:1–6:20: to engender dislike for the way of life of nonbelievers, on the one hand, and, on the other, to encourage unity among the audience.[3] However, it is difficult to follow such a long argument without any textual reading markers. Hence an attempt to set markers differently might reshape the overall interpretation.[4]

It seems that by using transitional grammatical markers the author has given us some pointers for following the argument:[5]

4:17	Now this I affirm and insist, don't walk (περιπατεῖν) . . .
4:25	So then, putting away . . .
5:1	Therefore be imitators . . .
5:15	Be careful then how you walk (περιπατεῖν) . . .

The whole argument is bookended by the Jewish ethical marker of "walking" (4:17; 5:15), as Lincoln has pointed out. Walking (περιπατεῖν) refers to the Hebrew word הלך, which is often translated, "Jewish Law," although

---

3. Margaret Y. MacDonald, *Colossians and Ephesians*, SP 17 (Collegeville, MN: Liturgical Press, 2000), 319–20.

4. Different scholars and interpreters employ different section markers depending on their overall understanding of the work. Andrew Lincoln's widely used scholarly commentary (*Ephesians*, WBC 42 [Dallas: Word, 1990]) uses the verb "to walk" (περιπατεῖν) as a guide, which results in four segments: 4:17-24; 4:25–5:2; 5:3-14; 5:15-20. Rudolf Schnackenburg (*Ephesians*), on the other hand, divides the text into two segments: 4:7–5:14 and 5:15–6:9. Pheme Perkins (*Ephesians*, ANTC [Nashville: Abingdon, 1997]: 4:17-32; 5:1-14; 5:15-21) and John Muddiman (*The Epistle to the Ephesians*, BNTC [London: Continuum, 2001]: 4:17-24; 4:25–5:5; 5:6-14; 5:15-20) also differ, while Ernest Best (*Ephesians: A Critical and Exegetical Commentary*, ICC [New York: T&T Clark, 1998]: 4:17-24; 4:25–5:2; 5:3-14; 5:15-21) agrees for the most part with Lincoln, but like Perkins retains 5:21 for this unit rather than seeing it as the beginning of the household code section.

5. See Rudolf Hoppe, "Ekklesiologie und Paränese im Epheserbrief (Eph 4:17–5:20)," in *Ethik als angewandte Ekklesiologie. Der Brief an die Epheser*, ed. Michael Wolter (Rome: Benedictina, 2005), 139–62.

a more literal translation might be "the way to behave" or "the way to walk." The word הלך derives from the root "to behave" (also "to go" or "to walk"). It commonly occurs in the Greek Bible, the Septuagint (LXX), to refer to ethical behavior and moral living.[6] The word הלכה, derived from this verb, is the collective body of oral and written laws. The written and oral Torah includes the 613 מצות (commandments), subsequent Talmudic and rabbinic law, as well as the customs and traditions known as the "Code of Jewish Law." It guides not only religious practices and beliefs but numerous aspects of day-to-day life.

The segment in 4:17–5:14 is thereby marked as a unit on ethical conduct and moral actions. I divide it into three sections: "Don't Walk Like the Gentiles" (4:17-24), "Grieve Not the Holy Spirit of G*d" (4:25-32), and "Walk in Love" (5:1-14). The overall argument of 4:17–5:14 is determined by opposites and dualistic thinking: old human–new human (4:22-24), lies-truth (4:25), steal-work (4:28), malice-understanding (4:32), darkness-light (5:8-11, 13). The author thinks in exclusive oppositions, using the indicative and imperative, to drive home the argument. Hence I will discuss 4:1–5:14 as a single unit with different segments; it is followed by 5:15–6:20, a concluding unit that contains not only the so-called "household code" or "exhortation to submission" but also an exhortation to continue the struggles with the powers.

Unity in the Body of Christ (4:1-16)

Like Romans 12:1, this section of exhortation begins with "I beseech [or exhort] you," expressions that seek to connect it with the earlier sections. Both of the references in 4:1, to Paul the prisoner and to the recipients' calling, relate this new section to the preceding one in chapter 3 and serve to link the first two and the last three chapters of Ephesians. The author reminds the recipients of their *ekklēsia* calling to make known the multicolored Sophia of G*d to the cosmic principalities and powers (3:10). This section of Ephesians 4 focuses on what unites the *ekklēsia*, the assembly of people, while at the same time acknowledging their differences: each of them has received G*d's grace in a specific way according to the measure of the gift of Messiah/Christ (4:7). This statement of rich diversity in terms of their calling is corroborated in 4:8 with reference to Psalm 67:19 (LXX). It is the culmination of a series of appeals for unity and oneness.

---

6. Lincoln, *Ephesians*, 94.

Ephesians 4:1-16

⁴:¹I therefore, the prisoner in the Lord, beg you to lead a life worthy of the calling to which you have been called, ²with all humility and gentleness, with patience, bearing with one another in love, ³making every effort to maintain the unity of the Spirit in the bond of peace. ⁴There is one body and one Spirit, just as you were called to the one hope of your calling, ⁵one Lord, one faith, one baptism, ⁶one God and Father of all, who is above all and through all and in all.

⁷But each of us was given grace according to the measure of Christ's gift. ⁸Therefore it is said,

"When he ascended on high he made captivity itself a captive; he gave gifts to his people."

⁹(When it says, "He ascended," what does it mean but that he had also descended into the lower parts of the earth? ¹⁰He who descended is the same one who ascended far above all the heavens, so that he might fill all things.) ¹¹The gifts he gave were

The admonition to "lead a life worthy of [their] calling" is an invitation that in Greek literally exhorts the recipients to "walk" in such a worthy manner. This exhortation expresses Jewish understandings that the people of G*d are called to practice humility, gentleness, and patience—virtues that are taken over from Colossians 3:12 by the author, who adds, "in love." Whereas "kindness" is found also in Greco-Roman traditions, "humility" is a typically Jewish ideal, expressed only in Jewish and Christian lists of virtues, because in Greco-Roman culture humility was associated with servility.[7]

The author adds "in love" in order to stress the importance of "being in love" for the life of the community. The members of the *ekklēsia*, who have been called to be holy and blameless before G*d in love (1:4) and are already rooted and grounded in love (3:17), are to bear with one another in love (4:2). Such forbearance requires that differences engendered by religious-ethnic status and practices must be recognized and respected. *Agapē*/love defines the *ekklēsia*, the citizen assembly, and enables it to sustain unity in diversity.

The recipients are admonished to make every effort to maintain the unity of the Spirit in the bond of peace (4:3). *Agapē*/love constitutes the bond of peace that enables the community to maintain the unity of the Spirit. This unity or oneness is explicated in a sevenfold way. There is

---

7. Perkins, *Ephesians*, 95, with reference to Ceslas Spicq, *Theological Lexicon of the New Testament*, trans. and ed. James D. Ernest (Peabody, MA: Hendrickson, 1994).

that some would be apostles, some prophets, some evangelists, some pastors and teachers, [12]to equip the saints for the work of ministry, for building up the body of Christ, [13]until all of us come to the unity of the faith and of the knowledge of the Son of God, to maturity, to the measure of the full stature of Christ. [14]We must no longer be children, tossed to and fro and blown about by every wind of doctrine, by people's trickery, by their craftiness in deceitful scheming. [15]But speaking the truth in love, we must grow up in every way into him who is the head, into Christ, [16]from whom the whole body, joined and knit together by every ligament with which it is equipped, as each part is working properly, promotes the body's growth in building itself up in love.

> one body and
> one Spirit, just as you were called to the
> one hope of your calling,
> one lord,
> one faith,
> one baptism,
> one God and Father of all.

The first three declarations of oneness—one body, one spirit, one hope—explicate the recipients' calling. This calling constitutes the communal body or corporation enlivened by one Spirit or breath. Whereas Colossians emphasizes love and peace (Col 3:14), Ephesians stresses the "unity of Spirit," which is maintained by the "bonds of peace" that are holding together the one body. The Spirit is fundamental for the life of the community. The formulaic character of the reference to the "one body" suggests that it might be based on 1 Corinthians 12:13. Because the recipients belong to the messianic corporation (2:16, 18) they share in a common hope.

Exegetes agree that the formulaic expression "one Lord, one faith, one baptism" seems to be at home in the baptismal discourse, to which Ephesians refers throughout the letter (see 1:11-14; 2:1-6; 4:22-24, 30; 5:25-27).[8] The expression "one *kyrios*/lord" refers the reader/hearer back to 1:21, which celebrates the triumph of Messiah/Christ over all other lords. It also refers the audience back to 2:11-22, a section that announces the unification of Jewish and Gentile wo/men in one Lord. In this context one faith probably refers to the baptismal declaration. The climax of this section is the confession, "one God and father of all who is above all and

8. MacDonald, *Colossians, Ephesians,* 288; Schnackenburg, *Ephesians,* 165–66.

through all and in all." It acknowledges G*d as "father of all things who is permeating all things."

After stressing unity again and again, the author emphasizes diversity in v. 7, stating that G*d has given different gifts to each member. Like Paul in Romans 12:6, the author declares that each member receives gifts from G*d that are different. This statement does not mean that G*d is partial and gives more or less grace or love to some than to others. Rather, this text is best understood as Jerome explains it. Jerome lived around 347–420 CE and is known for his translation of most of the Bible into Latin (the "Vulgate") and for many commentaries. Jerome compares the grace of G*d to the waters of the ocean, which to us seem immeasurable. We are asked to imagine the situation of a person standing in the ocean; many come with jugs and pitchers to be filled with water. While all around them the sea waters are without end, each person can take away only as much water as their vessel would hold. The water is infinite, whereas the vessels are finite. G*d's grace is infinite; our capacity to receive it depends on us.[9]

This emphasis on the diversity of gifts prepares the way for emphasizing the diversity of ministries in vv. 11-16. This declaration of diversity in unity is substantiated by a quotation from Psalm 68:18 (LXX: 67:18): "By ascending to the heights of heaven he made captivity itself a captive and gave gifts to his people." This quotation is then explicated in vv. 9-11. Ephesians has many allusions to Scripture but only two quotations, this one and one in Ephesians 5:31. Although this formulation, which stresses the role of Messiah/Christ as gift-giver, is unique, it shares similar meanings with 1 Corinthians 12:27-28 and Romans 12:5-8. With this citation the author seeks to substantiate the claim of the diversity of gifts received.

Pheme Perkins points out that this early Christian citation of Scripture takes the form of a *pesher*, a Jewish mode of scriptural interpretation in which the citation of a scriptural text is followed by its application. She argues that the opening argument of this *pesher* "is strikingly similar to John 3:13, 'no one has ascended into heaven, except the one who descended from heaven.' . . . Both the form and content of the *pesher* suggest that the regions to which Christ descends refer to the earth."[10]

Messiah Jesus who descended to earth is also the one who ascended above all the heavens, completely filling the cosmos (4:9-10). The descent and ascent are stressed to underscore the cosmic Messianic activity, so that Messiah Jesus may fill the entire cosmos (τὰ πάντα), as was stressed

---

9. Ronald Heine, *The Commentaries of Origen and Jerome on St Paul's Epistle to the Ephesians* (Oxford: Oxford University Press, 2002), 171.

10. Perkins, *Ephesians*, 98–99.

in 1:22-23. The author is interested in the concept of "filling the cosmos," which articulates a process instead of an actual status or completed action. In this process Messiah Jesus becomes more and more the actual head of the cosmos. In Colossians the cosmos, τὰ πάντα, is the body of Messiah Jesus, whereas in Ephesians the *ekklēsia* rather than the cosmos is the messianic body.[11]

Although the cosmos is still in the process of being filled with Messiah Jesus, in the *ekklēsia*, the assembly of the messianic people, Messiah Jesus' fullness has already been implemented. So that the *ekklēsia*, the people's assembly, can fulfill its task to herald G*d's cosmic Sophia, G*d's agent in creation, to the principalities and powers of the cosmos, its members have received messianic gifts. It was this Messiah Jesus who has given gifts to believers for service in the *ekklēsia*.

Ephesians 4:11-16 forms a single sentence in Greek that is broken down in English into several sentences. The gifts given by the exalted Messiah Jesus who fills the universe are not things or offices but persons who exercise different functions. This Messiah calls people who can fulfill specific leadership functions for the saints. Similar lists are found in 1 Corinthians 12:28 and Romans 12:5-8. These leaders—apostles, prophets, evangelists, pastors, and teachers—can all be characterized as teachers. These teachers are not only male, although our historical imagination still tends to see all church leaders as male.

Leading Wo/men in the Pauline Tradition of Ephesians

It is important that we keep in mind what we know about wo/men in the Pauline tradition when reading Ephesians. Only when we understand the history of the early Christian movement according to an egalitarian, non-androcentric interpretive model are we able to adequately integrate the available information on wo/men's leadership that is found in the tradition. Although this information is very fragmentary, it nevertheless permits us to trace wo/men's roles in the churches associated with Paul and the Pauline tradition.

First: When the Pauline letters mention wo/men as Paul's coworkers they give no indication that these wo/men were dependent on Paul or subordinate to him. Only five of

11. George H. van Kooten, *Cosmic Christology in Paul and the Pauline School: Colossians and Ephesians in the Context of Graeco-Roman Cosmology, with a New Synopsis of the Greek Texts*, WUNT 2:171 (Tübingen: Mohr Siebeck, 2003), 189.

Paul's coworkers (Erastus, Mark, Timothy, Titus, and Tychicus) "stand in explicit subordination to Paul, serving him or being subject to his instructions."[12] The genuine Pauline letters apply missionary titles or characterizations like "coworker" (Prisca), "sister" (Apphia), *"diakonos"* (Phoebe), and "apostle" (Junia) to women. In 1 Corinthians 16:16 Paul speaks of those who "have put themselves at the service of the saints" and admonishes the Corinthians to "put yourselves at the service of such people, and of everyone who works and toils with them" and to give recognition to such persons. First Thessalonians 5:12 exhorts the Thessalonians to "respect those who labor among you, and have charge of you in the Lord, and admonish you." It is therefore significant that Paul uses the same Greek verb κοπιάω, "to labor" or "to toil," not only to characterize his own missionary evangelizing and teaching but also that of wo/men. In Romans 16:6, 12 he commends Mary, Tryphaena, Tryphosa, and Persis for having "labored hard" in the Lord.

Paul also affirms that wo/men have worked with him on an equal basis. Philippians 4:2-3 explicitly states that Euodia and Syntyche have "contended" side by side with him. As in an athletic race, these wo/men have competed alongside Paul, Clement, and the rest of Paul's co-missionaries in the cause of the Gospel. Paul considers the authority of both wo/men in the community at Philippi so great that he fears their dissension could do serious damage to the Christian community.[13] These wo/men missionaries commanded the same esteem and respect as Paul's male coworkers in the community at Philippi.

Second: The house-assemblies were a decisive factor in the missionary movement insofar as they provided space, support, and actual leadership for the community.[14] The house-assemblies were where the

12. See E. Earle Ellis, "Paul and his Co-Workers," *NTS* 17 (1971): 437–52, at 439; see also the essay by Mary Ann Getty on *synergos*, "God's Fellow Worker and Apostleship," in *Women Priests: A Catholic Commentary on the Vatican Declaration*, ed. Leonard Swidler and Arlene Swidler (New York: Paulist, 1977), 176–82.

13. See W. Derek Thomas, "The Place of Women in the Church at Philippi," *ExpTim* 83 (1972): 117–20; R. W. Graham, "Women in the Pauline Churches: A Review Article," *LTQ* 11 (1976): 25–33, at 29–30.

14. See Floyd V. Filson, "The Significance of the Early House Churches," *JBL* 58 (1939): 105–12; Edwin A. Judge, *The Social Patterns of Christian Groups in the First Century: Some Prolegomena to the Study of New Testament Ideas of Social Organization* (London: Tyndale Press, 1960), 36: "Not only was the conversion of a household the natural or even necessary way of establishing the cult in unfamiliar surroundings, but the household remained the soundest basis for the meeting of Christians."

early Christians celebrated the Lord's Supper and preached the Good News. The*logically the community is called the "house of God," the "new temple" in which the Spirit dwells.[15] Since wo/men were among the wealthy and prominent converts (see Acts 17:4, 12), they played an important role in the founding, sustaining, and promoting of house-*ekklēsiai*. The following texts that speak of wo/men as leaders of house assemblies demonstrate this: Paul greets Apphia, "our sister," who, together with Philemon and Archippus, was a leader of the house-*ekklēsia* in Colossae, to which the letter to Philemon is written (Phlm 2).[16] Paul also twice mentions the missionary pair Prisca and Aquila and "the *ekklēsia* in their house" (1 Cor 16:19; Rom 16:5). Similarly, the author of the letter to the Colossians refers to Nympha of Laodicea and the "*ekklēsia* in her house" (Col 4:15). According to Acts, the assembly at Philippi began with the conversion of the businesswo/man Lydia from Thyatira, who offered her house to the Christian mission (Acts

16:14). We also know from Acts that a gathering for prayer was held in the house of Mary, the mother of John Mark. We have therefore no reason to assume that wo/men were excluded from the leadership of such house-*ekklēsiai* and from presiding at their worship. The love-patriarchalism of the household-code tradition is, therefore, best understood as a later patri-kyriarchal reaction to the leadership of wo/men within the house-*ekklēsiai*. Love-patriarchalism does not express the original order of the *ekklēsiai*. This is supported by 1 Timothy 2, where the injunctions that wo/men should be submissive are given in the context of regulations for prayer-meetings and teaching as well as in the context of implementing patri-kyriarchal requirements for leadership.

Third: One of the most prominent heads of a house-*ekklēsia* and outstanding coworker of Paul is Prisca or Priscilla who, together with her partner, Aquila, worked with Paul. Like Barnabas or Apollos, she too was independent of Paul and did not stand under his

---

15. See Robert J. McKelvey, *The New Temple: The Church in the New Testament* (Oxford: Oxford University Press, 1969), and my article, "Cultic Language in Qumran and in the New Testament," *CBQ* 38 (1976): 159–79.

16. But see Eduard Lohse, *Colossians and Philemon*, trans. William R. Poehlmann and Robert J. Karris, Hermeneia (Philadelphia: Fortress, 1971), 190: "The lady of the house had to deal daily with the slaves. Therefore she had to give her opinion when the question of taking back a runaway slave was raised." The tendency is clear. Apphia is reduced to a wife and mistress, although like the two men she is given a Christian leadership characterization.

authority.[17] Paul is grateful to both because they have risked their lives for him. Not only he but all the Gentile assemblies, Paul points out, have reasons to give thanks to these outstanding missionaries (Rom 16:4). Their house-assemblies in Corinth, Ephesus, and Rome (if Rom 16 is addressed to that community) were missionary centers. First Corinthians 16:19 has greetings from them. Even though Prisca is mentioned here after Aquila it is remarkable that she is referred to by name at all, since normally the male partner alone is named in such greetings. However, it is significant that whenever Paul sends greetings to them (as in Rom 16:3-4) he addresses Prisca first, thus underscoring that she is the more important of the two (see 2 Tim 4:19).

Acts also mentions Prisca before Aquila, which corresponds to the information provided in the Pauline letters (see Acts 18:2-4, 26).[18] Since the second part of Luke-Acts focuses on the greatness of Paul, this missionary team is referenced only in passing. Even these brief remarks, however, indicate their great influence. We therefore can assume that the author(s) of Luke-Acts had much more information about them than they transmit to us. Like Paul, Priscilla and Aquila were by trade tentmakers and supported their missionary activity through their own work. Like Paul, they were Jews and financially independent from the communities they served. Like Paul, they traveled to spread the Gospel and suffered for their missionary activity. When Claudius banished the Jews from Rome they were expelled from there and moved to Corinth. In Ephesus they converted Apollos, another great apostle and missionary alongside Paul (Acts 18:26), and taught Apollos "the way of God more accurately." The text clearly assumes that Prisca was the teacher of Apollos.[19] While Prisca and Aquila are not explicitly called apostles, another team receives this title in Romans 16:7. Like Aquila and Prisca, Andronicus and Junia were a missionary team who were apostles before Paul.

Fourth: Phoebe appears to have been one of the most

17. Ernst Käsemann, *An die Römer*, HNT 8a (Göttingen: Vandenhoeck & Ruprecht, 1973), 394, asserts that we are justified in counting the couple as outstanding among the early Christian missionaries in the dispersion.

18. The writer of Codex D (second century) mentions the name of Prisca in second place in Acts 18:26. Not only does the writer make Aquila the subject of the sentence in 18:2 by writing "Aquila with his wife Priscilla," but also mentions Aquila three times (18:3, 7, 22), without referring to Priscilla.

19. Therefore Adolf von Harnack, "Probabilia über die Addresse und den Verfasser des Hebräerbriefes," *ZNW* 1 (1900): 16–41, suggests that she authored the letter to the Hebrews. It is significant that scholars always assume male authorship, although in most cases we do not know who wrote the N*T books.

prominent wo/men in the incipient messianic movement. In Romans 16:1-2 she is characterized by three terms: Paul calls her ἀδελφή, "our sister," a διάκονος of the *ekklēsia* at Cenchreae, and a προστάτις "of many and myself as well." Scholars have taken pains to downplay the significance of these titles because they are given to a wo/man. Whenever Paul uses the title διάκονος to refer to himself or another male leader, scholars translate it as "minister," "missionary," or "servant," whereas in the case of Phoebe they usually have rendered it as "deaconess." Yet Phoebe is not a deaconess whose service is limited to wo/men but a minister of the whole *ekklēsia* at Cenchreae. Paul uses the term διάκονος in tandem with συνεργός ("coworker") in 1 Corinthians 3:5, 9, and 2 Corinthians 6:1, 4. According to 1 Corinthians 16:15 the coworkers and laborers are those who "have devoted themselves to the service [διακονία] of the saints." However, in contrast to the coworkers, the διάκονοι appear to be not only traveling missionaries but also leaders of local congregations. The term is used in the N*T and in secular sources to refer to preaching and teaching.[20]

The importance of Phoebe's position as minister of the *ekklēsia* at Cenchreae is underlined by the title προστάτις, which is usually translated as "helper" or "patroness," even though in the literature of the time the term has the connotation of leading officer, president, governor, or superintendent.[21] In 1 Thessalonians 5:12 the related verb προΐστημι characterizes persons with authority in the community, and in 1 Timothy 3:4-5 and 5:17 it designates the functions of the bishop, deacon, or elder. We therefore can assume that Phoebe had a position of great authority within the community of Cenchreae and that her authority was not limited to that congregation but was widely respected, even by Paul himself. Phoebe, in short, receives a recommendation similar to that of Timothy in 1 Corinthians 16:10-11.[22]

In conclusion: When reading the arguments of Ephesians we need to keep such leadership of wo/men before our eyes, and we can do so because the genuine Pauline letters indicate that wo/men were among the most prominent

20. See André Lemaire, "From Services to Ministries: '*Diakoniai*' in the First Two Centuries," *Concilium* 14 (1972): 35–49; Karl Hermann Schelkle, "Ministry and Ministers in the New Testament Church," *Concilium* 11 (1969): 5–11; André Lemaire, "The Ministries in the New Testament: Recent Research," *BTB* 3 (1973): 133–66.

21. Bo Reicke, "*prohistemi*," *TDNT* 6:703: The verb as well as the substantive "have the twofold sense of leadership and care."

22. See Harry Y. Gamble, *The Textual History of the Letter to the Romans: A Study in Textual and Literary Criticism*, SD 42 (Grand Rapids: Eerdmans, 1977), 87.

missionaries and leaders of the early Christian communities. They were coworkers with Paul who did not stand under Paul's authority. They were teachers, preachers, and prophets. As leaders of house-assemblies they had great influence and probably also presided at the worship celebrations. If we compare their leadership with the ministry of the later deaconesses, it is striking that their authority was not restricted to "women's ministry" or to specific "female" functions.

In short, we can assume that wo/men apostles, prophets, evangelists, pastors, and teachers were well known to the Ephesian community. Since the emphasis of Ephesians is on teaching, it is important to notice that we do not find in the letter an injunction against wo/men as teachers such as appears in 1 Timothy 2:11-15:

Let a woman learn in silence with full submission. I permit no woman to teach or to have authority over a man; she is to keep silent. For Adam was formed first, then Eve; and Adam was not deceived, but the woman was deceived and became a transgressor. Yet she will be saved through childbearing, provided they continue in faith and love and holiness, with modesty.

We also know from the works of Anne Jensen, Ute Eisen, and Christina Trevett that such debates were ongoing in the following centuries.[23] Therefore it is significant that Ephesians does not prohibit teaching by wo/men ministers or demand their silence. Ephesians argues the*logically for the subordination of wives, but there is no indication that it seeks to prohibit wo/men from teaching.

The task of ministers is the restoration, training, and discipline of all members of the *ekklēsia*. They are to equip the saints for fulfilling their commission: to make known the divine multicolored Wisdom-Sophia to the powers of the cosmos (3:10). Such ministers are equipped to train the saints for the work of service (διακονία) that builds up the body of Christ. While we today assume that the work of ministry is done by ordained ministers, Ephesians insists that this is the work of the "saints," that is,

23. Anne Jensen, *God's Self-Confident Daughters: Early Christianity and the Liberation of Women*, trans. O. C. Dean (Louisville: Westminster John Knox, 1996); Ute Eisen, *Women Officeholders in Early Christianity: Epigraphical and Literary Studies*, trans. Linda M. Maloney (Collegeville, MN: Liturgical Press, 2000); Christina Trevett, *Christian Women and the Time of the Apostolic Fathers (AD c.80–160): Corinth, Rome and Asia Minor* (Cardiff: University of Wales Press, 2006), who curiously does not acknowledge that *In Memory of Her* is not restricted to the N*T but also discusses her area of inquiry.

of all the members of the body of Christ. The task of the ministers is to enable and to empower the saints to do this work.

In their teaching and leadership the various ministers, who are Messiah Jesus' gifts, are equipped to carry out their service for building up the "body," the saints, to the "measure of the stature of the fullness of Christ," the adult person (v. 13). Although the Greek text uses the masculine form of the word "man/male"(ἄνδρα), most interpreters understand the expression to mean adult person because of the reference to "children" in v. 14. Ephesians 4:13-16 thus creates a vivid contrast between believers (adult vs. baby), between maturity and immaturity.

The recipients are said to be like infants, tossed around by wind and waves, which are metaphorically identified with different teachings and empty words. The next remark refers to "cunning," alluding to 2 Corinthians 11:3, which states that the serpent deceived Eve by its cunning. The positive response to this being tossed around and cunning temptation is "speaking" or "doing" "the truth in love." Speaking truth in love is important for understanding "church teachings" that often have been imposed and enforced with violence rather than enjoined with love. The following quotation speaks of such kyriarchal control: "When as the risen Lord takes control of the world in His body, He is simply actualizing His real power over creation. . . . Hence, the church as His body, when it relates the world to itself, is simply in process of taking over what truly belongs to it."[24]

This kyriarchal interpretation of Ephesians is supported by the understanding that Messiah/Christ is pictured in analogy to the Roman emperor. Andrew Lincoln points out that "the metaphor of Christ as head was originally independent of the metaphor of the Church as body." However, Colossians, followed by Ephesians, telescoped them together.[25] This fusion has opened the door for ascribing the powers of Christ, acclaimed as *kyrios* and imperial lord, to the church. The history of brutal violence against heretics and witches testifies to the failure of the kyriarchal church to "speak the truth in love." The crucial question for the interpretation of Ephesians thus becomes: Does attaining to the status of the full measure of Christ (v. 13) mean that the church is filled with and filling the cosmos with domination or does it do so with *agapē*-love? The text of Ephesians allows for both interpretations. If, in the past, the filling of the cosmos with domination and exploitation was prevalent,

24. Heinrich Schlier, *"Kephalē," TDNT* 3:681.
25. Lincoln, *Ephesians*, 262.

in the face of climate deterioration today our task is to fill it with love. Hence it becomes necessary to spell out carefully what "filling with love" actually entails.

Don't Walk Like the Gentiles (4:17-24)

This section begins with a solemn call to live no longer as the Gentile wo/men do. It refers the reader to 2:11, where the Gentiles who have become part of the Commonwealth of Israel are addressed. The term used here for Gentiles is τὰ ἔθνη, "the nations." It was used by Jews like the author to distinguish themselves in terms of culture, ethnic identity, and religion from those who were not Jewish. As we have seen in chapter 2, those members of the *ekklēsia* who were not native Jewish wo/men were able to become members of the *politeia*, the commonwealth of Israel in Messiah Jesus (2:13). Here they are admonished to live a life different from that of the Gentiles who may have still been members of their families, friends, or neighbors. The language used is emotionally tinged. It is typical of the characterizations of the Gentiles that occur in Paul's letter to the Romans (1:21, 24) and in Colossians (3:5-10), and it reflects a rhetorical repertoire of stereotypes.

The Gentiles/nations are said to be ignorant of G*d. They are locked in immorality and worship of false G*ds. Their understanding is darkened and their thinking is futile and ignorant. They suffer from hardness of heart and lack of sensitivity. The Gentiles have abandoned themselves to licentiousness, eager to practice every kind of impurity. Ernest Best acknowledges that "the first Christians," who were all Jews by birth, continued to think of Gentiles in this stereotyping way. In order to avoid this stereotype he suggests that the word in v. 17 should probably be read as "pagan" or "heathen."[26] However, this switch in terminology does not derail the othering tendencies of the text; it merely shifts them from a Jewish- to a Roman-Christian nomenclature. In either case, Gentiles are the quintessential "other."

Since Simone de Beauvoir the notion of "the Other," expressed also with the verbal forms "othering" or "otherize," articulates a key concept in feminist philosophy and the social sciences.[27] "Otherness" is what is

---

26. Best, *Ephesians*, 417.

27. Simone de Beauvoir, "Woman as Other," in *The Second Sex*, accessed September 2016, https://www.marxists.org/reference/subject/ethics/de-beauvoir/2nd-sex/introduction.htm.

Ephesians 4:17-24

¹⁷Now this I affirm and insist on in the Lord: you must no longer live as the Gentiles live, in the futility of their minds. ¹⁸They are darkened in their understanding, alienated from the life of God because of their ignorance and hardness of heart. ¹⁹They have lost all sensitivity and have abandoned themselves to licentiousness, greedy to practice every kind of impurity. ²⁰That is not the way you learned Christ! ²¹For surely you have heard about him and were taught in him, as truth is in Jesus. ²²You were taught to put away your former way of life, your old self, corrupt and deluded by its lusts, ²³and to be renewed in the spirit of your minds, ²⁴and to clothe yourselves with the new self, created according to the likeness of God in true righteousness and holiness.

alien and divergent from what is supposedly "given": norm, identity, self.[28] The characterization of the Gentiles as unclean, lascivious, and ignorant, or characterized by vanity of mind, is a dangerous case of "othering." Where such "othering" language occurs within Scripture it needs to carry the warning label: "Caution! Could be dangerous to your health and survival!" The negative "othering" process has always as its goal the creation of a positive self by distancing and creating opposition to the "other."

With the transitional emphatic "but you" in 4:20 the author seeks to construct the positive self of the audience: "But you have not so learned the Messiah/Christ!" Indeed, they have heard him and have been taught "in [ἐν] him as/how [καθώς] truth is in Jesus" (v. 21). This truth is that they have put off the "old" corrupted human and put on the "new" human, whom G*d "created in righteousness and true holiness" (v. 24).

The translation and meaning of the statements in 4:20-21 are very much debated. According to Best the unusual phrase is best translated: "But you have learned Christ to that effect, assuming, [as we can] that you heard him and were taught in him, because the truth is in Jesus."[29] Lincoln translates v. 20 as "But this is not the way you learned Christ," and explains that "[j]ust as a Jew learned Torah, so now a Christian can be said to learn Christ." He goes on to suggest that, in v. 21b, Jesus with the article, τῷ Ἰησοῦ, is "likely a stylistic variation and should not immediately be assumed to have major theological significance."[30]

---

28. See J. Mitchell Miller, "Otherness," in *The SAGE Encyclopedia of Qualitative Research Methods*, ed. Lisa Given (Thousand Oaks, CA: SAGE Publications, 2008), 588–91.

29. Best, *Ephesians*, 414, 425–30.

30. Lincoln, *Ephesians*, 270–81.

Markus Barth, on the other hand, correctly translates Χριστόν, "Christ," with "Messiah" ("you have . . . become students of the Messiah. . . . you have . . . listened to him and been taught in his school") but drops the article and understands "in Jesus" as a later interpolation.[31] MacDonald also omits the definite articles before Christ and Jesus, concluding that "[i]n the end, the expression remains somewhat cryptic and the reference 'in Jesus' may simply be a stylistic variation of 'in Christ.' "[32]

One might ask why this long explanation about translation. I wanted to show how context matters. Most scholars interpreting Ephesians are doing so within a Christian framework that has been shaped by centuries of christological teachings. These teachings present Jesus Christ as divine, on the one hand, and as not-Jewish, on the other. The tendency, then, is to assume that Ephesians speaks about a singular divine being, Jesus Christ of Nazareth, who was the Son of G*d. Christian readers do not think of a Jewish Messiah when hearing or reading the word "Christ." Thus the tendency is to explain away the article and to downplay its potential significance.

In this commentary I have therefore used "Messiah Jesus," "Messiah/ Christ," or "Christ/Messiah" to indicate a Jewish understanding of the word Χριστός, "Christ," since the recipients addressed by the Jewish author had become messianic Jews rather than "Christians" in our sense of the word. Therefore I argue here that in translating the text we should retain the definite article before Messiah/Christ or Jesus that occurs in the original Greek, which most translations leave out. We can safely assume that the original audience knew many Messiahs/Christs and also many persons named Jesus. Hence the author had to identify which Messiah/ Christ—and which Jesus—was meant. It was the Jesus Messiah, and not any other Messiah, of whom the text speaks! Such an interpretation understands why the definite article is necessary and explains why the author uses it when talking about the Messiah, identifying him as "the" Jesus, in whom truth is.

The truth of the Messiah Jesus that the recipients have learned requires that they put off the old corrupted human and put on the new human (NRSV: "self") "created according to G*d in righteousness and true holiness." The language of Ephesians 4:22-23 is taken over with modifications from Colossians 3:8-10, except for 4:22b, which has as its

---

31. Markus Barth, *Ephesians 4–6*, AB 34A (Garden City, NY: Doubleday, 1974), 504–5.
32. MacDonald, *Colossians and Ephesians*, 304.

parallel Colossians 3:5. Whereas Colossians speaks of the new human as the image of G*d, Ephesians omits the phrase "according to the image of the one who created them" and says simply that the new human was created according to G*d.[33] The Greek word ἄνθρωπος is used here; it means "human being" rather than "man/male" as it is still often translated. The metaphor of putting on and putting off the old and the new human/ity as a reference to baptism is a central metaphor in Paul's letter to the Galatians (3:27-28). It suggests that one can take off the old human like a garment and be transformed into the new human. The text likens what happens in baptism to changing one's clothing.

Galatians 3:27-28

Form-critical analyses converge in the classification of Galatians 3:26-28 as a baptismal formula that is quoted by Paul:[34]

3:26a	For you are all children of God.
3:27a	For as many as were baptized into Christ
3:27b	have put on Christ
3:28a	There is [valid] neither Jew nor Greek
3:28b	There is neither slave nor free
3:28c	There is no male and female
3:28d	for you are all one

Though scholars differ on the delineation of the individual lines, they agree that the core of the traditional formula is Galatians 3:28abc. The three parallel statements of v. 28 express the self-understanding of the newly baptized. Because of the opposition reference "Jew/Greek," exegetes assume that this text was formulated in a Jewish-Hellenistic community. Therefore it seems reasonable to attribute this baptismal formula to the pre-Pauline missionary movement that probably

---

33. See Perkins, *Ephesians*, 105.

34. [26]Πάντες γὰρ υἱοὶ θεοῦ ἐστε διὰ τῆς πίστεως ἐν Χριστῷ Ἰησοῦ. [27]ὅσοι γὰρ εἰς Χριστὸν ἐβαπτίσθητε, Χριστὸν ἐνεδύσασθε· [28]οὐκ ἔνι Ἰουδαῖος οὐδὲ Ἕλλην, οὐκ ἔνι δοῦλος οὐδὲ ἐλεύθερος, οὐκ ἔνι ἄρσεν καὶ θῆλυ· πάντες γὰρ ὑμεῖς εἷς ἐστε ἐν Χριστῷ Ἰησοῦ (Gal 3:26-28, N/A[26]).

centered around Antioch and to understand it as an integral part of that movement's the*logy of the Spirit rather than as a the*logical "peak formulation" of Paul.

Hans Dieter Betz has acknowledged that commentaries on Galatians "have consistently denied that Paul's statements have political implications."[35] Such commentaries are prepared, in Betz's view, to state the opposite of what Paul actually says in order to preserve a "purely religious" interpretation. In doing so they tend to emphasize the reality of equality before G*d and at the same time to "deny that any conclusions can be drawn from this in regard to the ecclesiastical offices (!) and the political order."[36]

Others argue that Galatians 3:28 does not yet reflect the same notion of anthropological unification and androcentric perspective that have determined the understanding of equality found in later Gnostic and patristic writings. According to those texts, for a wo/man to become a disciple means her becoming "male," and "like man," because the male principle stands for the heavenly, angelic, divine realm whereas the female principle represents either human weakness or evil. While patristic and so-called Gnostic writers could

express the equality of Christian wo/men with men only as "manliness" or as vilification of wo/men's sexuality, Galatians 3:28 does not extol ontological maleness but instead exalts the social oneness of the messianic community in which social, cultural, religious, national, and biological gender divisions and status differences are no longer valid. On this reading, the pre-Pauline formula of Galatians 3:28 rejects all structures of kyriarchal domination.

Hence, the androcentric language of Galatians 3:28 must be translated, I argue, as generic language to mean "neither Jewish nor Greek wo/men, neither slave nor freeborn wo/men, neither husband and wife." Such a translation does not suppress the notion that the first two pairs of the baptismal proclamation, Jews or Greeks, slaves or free, are gendered. It also underscores that patriarchal heterosexual marriage is at the root of the kyriarchal socio-political status system that reproduces kyriarchy and is produced by it. In short, gender is overdetermined by kyriarchal structures and differently constructed for freeborn wo/men or slave wo/men, for Jewish or Gentile wo/men, for Roman or Asia Minor wo/men.

In a careful analysis of the extant materials on circumcision,

---

35. Hans Dieter Betz, *Galatians*, Hermeneia (Philadelphia: Fortress, 1979), 189.
36. Ibid.

Judith Lieu has pointed out that, as far as we can tell from written and inscriptional evidence,[37] no clear ritualization and the*logical understanding of wo/men's conversion to Judaism existed in the first century.[38] However, at the turn from the first to the second century a clarification of the status of proselytes and an explication of the understanding and rite of conversion seems to have occurred. Shaye Cohen has argued, for instance, that one of the factors in developing a structured ritual may have been the need of wo/men converts.[39] Hence one may assume that this discussion was already active in the first century when Ephesians was written. Accordingly, Lieu reads the challenge of Justin, the Christian, to Trypho, the Jew, as part of this ongoing debate: "I might also cite Sarah, the wife of Abraham, Rebecca, the wife of Isaac, Rachel, the wife of Jacob and Leah, and all the other such women up to the Mother of Moses, the faithful servant, who observed none of these—do you think they will be saved?"[40] Interestingly, this argument lists the foremothers in terms of their family status as wives and mothers. If, as in Greco-Roman religion, a tradition existed in Judaism that defined the membership of wo/men in terms of their affiliation as wives and mothers, then the declaration in Galatians 3:28c could be understood as standing over and against such a tradition.[41]

37. See Bernadette Brooten, *Women Leaders in the Ancient Synagogue: Inscriptional Evidence and Background Issues*, BJS 36 (Chico, CA: Scholars Press, 1982).

38. Judith Lieu, "Circumcision, Women, and Salvation," *NTS* 40 (1994): 358–70.

39. Shaye J. D. Cohen, "The Rabbinic Conversion Ceremony," *JJS* 41 (1990): 177–203; idem, "Crossing the Boundaries and Becoming a Jew," *HTR* 82 (1989): 13–33; idem, "The Origins of the Matrilineal Principle in Rabbinic Law," *AJSR* 10 (1985): 19–53.

40. Justin, *Dial.* 46.3.

41. See my discussion of the household code trajectory in *In Memory of Her: A Feminist Theological Reconstruction of Christian Origins* (New York: Crossroad, 1983) and *Bread Not Stone: The Challenge of Biblical Interpretation* (Boston: Beacon, 1984). See also Clarice Martin, "The *Haustafeln* (Household Codes) in African American Biblical Interpretation: 'Free Slaves' and 'Subordinate Women,'" in *Stony the Road We Trod: African American Biblical Interpretation*, ed. Cain Hope Felder (Minneapolis: Fortress, 1991), 206–31. Lieu, "Circumcision," 369, cites my statement "If it was no longer circumcision but baptism which was the primary rite of initiation, then women became full members of the people of God with the same rights and duties" (*In Memory of Her*, 210). Granted that this statement is ambiguous, I still would want to insist that the baptismal formula asserted the full membership of wo/men—independently of male family affiliation—with the full rights and duties of "citizenship" in the *ekklēsia*. With this assertion I did not and do not want to suggest that wo/men were not full members in Judaism. However, in light of my analysis above I would no longer follow the lead of Paul and connect this assertion with the debate on circumcision.

Earlier in the debate Justin had sought to refute Trypho's argument that circumcision was already enjoined upon Abraham by making reference to the biblical wo/men. Justin argues that women are part of the people of G*d; they predate the giving of the commandment of circumcision to Abraham and their sons but are excluded from circumcision by virtue of their not having a penis. "Furthermore, that the female sex is unable to receive fleshly circumcision demonstrates that this circumcision was given as a sign and not as a work of righteousness. For G*d made wo/men equally able to observe all that is right and virtuous. We see that in physical form male and female have been made differently, but we are confident that neither is righteous or unrighteous on this basis but only on the basis of piety and righteousness."[42]

This argument fits with the tenor of the pre-Pauline baptismal formula. It also underscores that Paul's argument in 1 Corinthians 11 and 14 is contrary to it. One must ask whether Paul masculinizes the generic language of the baptismal formula or whether he still understands it in generic terms so as to include wo/men, since the baptismal formula in Galatians 3:28 is framed in vv. 26 and 29 by the kyriocentric Pauline statements that the baptized are sons of G*d, Abraham's offspring, and heirs according to the promise. Galatians 4:1-7 explicates the meaning of "sons of G*d" in Galatians 3:26-29. Paul applies a legal metaphor (vv. 1-2) to the present situation of the Galatians (v. 3) and explicates it in vv. 4-6 with traditional christological formulae and legal concepts. Verse 7 draws the conclusion in terms of the pronouncements in 3:26 and 29: "Therefore you are no longer a slave but a son, and if a son then also an heir through G*d."

The observation of andro- and kyriocentric language also makes it clear why Paul did not add the phrase "neither male and female" in 1 Corinthians 12:13, since Paul addresses problems in 1 Corinthians 7 that relate to sexuality and marriage.[43] The same applies to the enumeration in Colossians 3:11, which is followed in 3:18 by the so-called *Haustafel* (household code), the rules for the household, which begin with the exhortation to wives to subordinate themselves to their husbands.[44]

---

42. Justin, *Dial.* 23.5.

43. καὶ γὰρ ἐν ἑνὶ πνεύματι ἡμεῖς πάντες εἰς ἓν σῶμα ἐβαπτίσθημεν, εἴτε Ἰουδαῖοι εἴτε Ἕλληνες, εἴτε δοῦλοι εἴτε ἐλεύθεροι, καὶ πάντες ἓν πνεῦμα ἐποτίσθημεν (1 Cor 12:13, N/A²⁶).

44. ὅπου οὐκ ἔνι Ἕλλην καὶ Ἰουδαῖος, περιτομὴ καὶ ἀκροβυστία, βάρβαρος, Σκύθης, δοῦλος, ἐλεύθερος, ἀλλὰ [τὰ] πάντα καὶ ἐν πᾶσιν Χριστός (Col 3:11, N/A²⁶).

The metaphor of putting off the old human/ity and putting on the new, which Ephesians takes over from Colossians, is inspired by the baptismal tradition of Galatians 3:27-29. The NRSV translates the Greek word ἄνθρωπος with "self" rather than with "human/ity." However, the text is not talking about the internal self of the individual but about a new and different space "in Christ."[45] In light of a critical feminist interpretation for liberation, the "old human/ity" is characterized by intersecting kyriarchal structures of gender, race, religious-ethnic exclusion, exploitation, or imperial domination, which are dubbed in Ephesians "deceitful desires" (ἐπιθυμίας) that "corrupt our minds." To be able to get rid of ideologies we need first of all to be "renewed in the spirit of our minds." Such a renewal of our spirit and mind means transformation (Rom 12:2). The new human/ity we are to put on is created "according to G*d." Ephesians omits the expression "image of G*d" (Col 3:10) but stresses that we are patterned after G*d's self and not just God's image. To be created according to G*d means to be shaped by justice and the holiness of truth. To put on the new human/ity, not according to Paul or Caesar, but according to G*d, means to envision and practice human relationships of equality, respect, and love.

Such a metaphor must be seen in the context of the socio-political world in which it was formulated and in which it is proclaimed today. The baptismal clothing imagery signifies a change of identities shaped by slavery, Roman imperialism, ethnic strife, racism, heterosexism, poverty, imperialism, ageism, and other -isms. It articulates a change in what it means to live as new human/ity "according to/patterned after G*d." The *ekklēsia* is the assembly of the citizenry constituted by this new human/ity. The identity of the "new human/ity according to G*d," which is put on in baptism, reshaped the old identity of those who were joining the *ekklēsia*.

It is significant that the metaphor of clothing is chosen here. As Kelly Olson has pointed out: "In the ancient world as still today, clothing is an important part of the sign system of every society, a central aspect of its visual language. Clothing has the power to express rank, communicate status, wealth, and power, express the relation between the sexes, reflect values, exemplify anxieties. . . . Clothing therefore embodies social structure and is important

---

45. See also Timothy G. Gombis, *The Drama of Ephesians: Participating in the Triumph of God* (Downers Grove, IL: InterVarsity Press, 2010), 165–66.

to a society's sense of itself."[46] If dress and clothing signify social structure, then the metaphor of being clothed in "the new human according to G*d" announces the radical equality of all the baptized. The author of Ephesians spells out the equality of Jewish and Gentile wo/men in the *ekklēsia* but argues against the equality of slave and free as well as married wo/men and men. However, such an argument presupposes that slave wo/men or freeborn wives may have understood their being clothed with the new human in a different way.

As pointed out earlier, G*d is understood in Ephesians as *Matrona*. Dress was an important signifier of the status difference between matron and slave wo/man. For instance, M. Antistius Labeo points to the consequences of clothing.

> If someone accosts virgins in slaves' garb, his offence is regarded as venial, even more so if women are in prostitutes' dress and not that of matrons. There-fore, if a woman is not in the dress of a matron and someone accosts her or ab-ducts her attendant, he will not be liable to the action for insult.[47]

When freeborn wives or slave wo/men, whose humanity was in question, heard this baptismal proclamation about them being clothed in a new human/ity, they must have understood this baptismal statement as proclaiming their equality "according to G*d."[48] The author in turn sought only to proclaim the equality between Jews and Gentiles but followed Colossians in rejecting the equality between slave and free and correcting the third pair "neither male and female" of the baptismal formula (Gal 3:28), which, in referring to "male and female," did not speak of the abolition of gender but of marriage. The so-called "household code" can then be understood as an attempt to correct the baptismal proclamation of equality. The following exhortations seek to establish what it means not to "walk in the way of the Gentiles" but to imitate G*d, in whose likeness they have been formed in baptism.

---

46. Kelly Olson, "Matrona and Whore: The Clothing of Women in Roman Antiq-uity," *Fashion Theory: The Journal of Dress, Body and Culture* 6 (2002): 387–420.

47. Justinian, *Digest* 47.10.15.15; see Olson, "Matrona and Whore," 397.

48. See Elisabeth Schüssler Fiorenza, "Slave Wo/men and Freedom: Some Meth-odological Reflections," in *Empowering Memory and Movement: Thinking and Working across Borders* (Minneapolis: Fortress, 2014), 447–70.

²⁵So then, putting away falsehood, let all of us speak the truth to our neighbors, for we are members of one another. ²⁶Be angry but do not sin; do not let the sun go down on your anger, ²⁷and do not make room for the devil. ²⁸Thieves must give up stealing; rather let them labor and work honestly with their own hands, so as to have something to share with the needy. ²⁹Let no evil talk come out of your mouths, but only what is useful for building up, as there is need, so that your words may give grace to those who hear. ³⁰And do not grieve the Holy Spirit of God, with which you were marked with a seal for the day of redemption. ³¹Put away from you all bitterness and wrath and anger and wrangling and slander, together with all malice, ³²and be kind to one another, tenderhearted, forgiving one another, as God in Christ has forgiven you.

Grieve Not the Holy Spirit of G*d (4:25-32)

The "so then" (διὸ) in v. 25 marks the transition from the baptismal statement to the exhortation, which in a series of imperatives spells out what the "putting off" and "putting on" of the new human concretely entails. These exhortations seek to validate and correct the self-understanding of the audience as created equal "according to G*d." The audience is admonished now to "walk" no longer in the way of the Gentiles but in the likeness of G*d.

This is expressed in a list of virtues and vices that exhorts the audience to avoid foul language and speech that hurt community life. Such lists of vices and virtues were at home in Greco-Roman ethical discourse and mediated through Hellenistic Judaism to early "Christian" writings such as Romans 1:29-32 or Galatians 5:19-21. While Hellenistic moral exhortation argued for rational behavior that is not swept away by irrational passions, Hellenistic Jewish thinkers argued that moral activity and insight would not be possible without the knowledge of the Law of the true G*d.⁴⁹

This unit is based on Colossians 3:8-9, 12-13 and seeks to make clear in seven concrete injunctions how the new way of being should be lived in community. Each of these imperatives spells out what is to be done and makes suggestions and gives a reason why it should be done. To that end Ephesians contrasts foul speech with edifying and gracious speech (4:29) and words of forgiveness (4:32). Such exhortations and warnings against deceptive language are intermingled with references to the*logical incentives, such as the *ekklēsia* as body (4:25), the devil (4:27), the Spirit (4:30), and Messiah/Christ (4:32).

---

49. "Philosophy, Jewish," *Encyclopaedia Judaica*, accessed September 2016, https://www.jewishvirtuallibrary.org/jsource/judaica/ejud_0002_0016_0_15718.html.

All but one of these imperatives are negative, but they have a positive goal that is articulated in the seventh one:

> Put aside lying: speak truth with your neighbor. (4:25)
> Be angry, but do not sin: end your anger before sundown. (4:26)
> A thief no longer should steal, but work with their hands, so that they may have something to share with those in need. (4:28)
> Let no corrupt communication come from your mouth, but only good words for upbuilding. (4:29)
> Do not grieve the Holy Spirit of G*d: [respect] the seal of redemption. (4:30)
> Let all bitterness, shouting, slander, malice depart from you. (4:31)
> Be kind/forgiving to one another, just as G*d in the Messiah forgave you. (4:32)

Gender Subordination and Anger in East Asian Christian Communities

I would like to situate Ephesians 4:26a in a context of East Asian Christianity, briefly examining how such kyriarchal Christian teachings have been incorporated into Asian cultural norms. First of all, it is undeniable that modern Western Christianity as brought to East Asia retained imperial aspects. Second, an example introduced by Korean feminist the*logian Chung Hyun Kyung[50] shows how such Christian teachings have fortified existing Asian patriarchy, especially within Asian conservative[51] congregations.

Chung writes that she witnessed a Korean woman who shared her testimony in front of the congregation. She "confessed" her sinful disobedience to her "unreasonable and unfair" husband, who, one day during a fight, threw a kitchen knife[52]— which missed her. The speaker described this incident as an experience of divine judgment, death on the cross, resurrection,

50. This story is also commented on by Elisabeth Schüssler Fiorenza. See her *But She Said: Feminist Practices of Biblical Interpretation* (Boston: Beacon, 1992), 37.

51. Lisa Isherwood reports, "Bible-believing Christians are highly represented amongst batterers since they believe their wives should be submissive (1 Pet 3:5-6)," and women also "accept the blame for the violence far more readily than non-Christian women." Lisa Isherwood, "The Violence of Gender: Christian Marriage as a Test Case," in *Weep Not for Your Children: Essays on Religion and Violence*, ed. Lisa Isherwood and Rosemary Radford Ruether (London: Equinox, 2008), 54–64, at 60.

52. Chung Hyun Kyung, *Struggle to Be the Sun Again: Introducing Asian Women's Theology* (Maryknoll, NY: Orbis Books, 1990), Kindle Edition, location 2886-2894.

and surrender to God: through this incident God expressed love and taught her the obedience to her husband. When she concluded that she became a new person who maintained "peace" in her family, the congregation responded with a loud "Hallelujah!"[53]

In this story the kyriarchal and subordinating aspects of Ephesians are pressure-cooked. Initially the woman was angry at or frustrated with her abusive spouse but, accepting domestic violence, she interpreted obedience to patriarchy as God's will. Performing such "testimony" in a congregation that reaffirms kyriarchal teaching, the woman would also create future victims who would bury their anger and be silent under the will of God.

Here it should be noted that such suppression of "churched" women's anger could also be grounded in sociocultural gender subordination. Although we cannot easily assess to what degree suppression of anger

is rooted in traditional ethics, the seventeenth- to eighteenth-century Japanese discourse on personal health care (*yojo*) furnishes an example of insistence that women's bodies are fundamentally inferior to those of men; thus women are incapable of controlling emotions such as jealousy and anger.[54] Therefore the expression of anger incurred shame. Moreover, a Confucian teaching of "three obediences" (三従), which entails women's submission to "fathers before marriage, husbands in marriage, and sons in widowhood,"[55] can strengthen gendered teachings of anger as a part of women's obedience to patriarchy.

Susan Brooks Thistlethwaite writes that women with strong religious backgrounds are often unable to admit the wrongness of violence inflicted on them: "They believe what they have been taught, that resistance to this injustice is unbiblical and unchristian."[56] Kyriarchal religious teachings reinforce

53. Ibid.

54. Miyoko Katafuchi, "Children's Bodies and Women's Bodies: Viewing Their Lives from the Discourse of Personal Health Care in the Edo Era" [in Japanese], *Journal of Wakayama University* 63 (2013): 49–56, at 49, 54.

55. Chung Hyun Kyung, *Struggle to Be the Sun Again*, location 1359.

56. Susan Brooks Thistlethwaite, "Every Two Minutes: Battered Women and Feminist Interpretation," in *Weaving the Visions: New Patterns in Feminist Spirituality*, ed. Judith Plaskow and Carol P. Christ (San Francisco: Harper & Row, 1989), 300. As a basis for her feminist methodology Thistlethwaite cites Elisabeth Schüssler Fiorenza's *In Memory of Her* and says that one's method of investigation should be shaped in living in the texts themselves, simultaneously in the midst of women's experiences and movements. She writes from her experiences as a theologian and a pastor, and especially about battered and abused women.

subordination of wo/men with a theological legitimation of "dominance and submission in the household in God."[57] How can women recover their voices and the sense of holistic being? How and in what ways should they recognize, embrace, and express their accumulated and silenced anger in constructive ways, without creating another victim?

Haruka Umetsu Cho

It is noteworthy that one injunction in this series of exhortations has nothing to do with issues of speech. Although theft is frequently mentioned in moral discourse and is also found in Paul's genuine letters (Rom 2:21; 13:9; 1 Cor 6:10), the exhortation to thieves "to work with their own hands so that they have something to share with the community" is, strictly speaking, not about speech but about sharing and giving. A thief does not give to the community but takes things away from its members.

This injunction against thieves stealing from the community has become a cultural stereotype that is heavily gendered and racialized. To illustrate this point I refer to the stereotype of the "welfare queen," popularized in Ronald Reagan's 1976 campaign for the Republican nomination for president. In the popular imagination the notion of "welfare fraud" suggests that poor wo/men take advantage of the welfare system. In the process of Reagan's campaign, however, the term became thoroughly racialized. The media's image of poverty shifted from the 1960s focus on the plight of farmers and factory workers to a more racially divisive image of poor blacks in urban areas, and the term "welfare queen" came to signify an indolent black woman who is stealing and living off the largesse of taxpayers rather than contributing her share to the common good. The term thus functions as a dog whistle, a way to play on gendered racial anxieties without summoning them directly.

Rather than seeing this injunction as "no more than a flag-waving platitude,"[58] some exegetes have suggested that "slaves"[59] or "day-laborers and shop-keepers"[60] might have been taking food and clothing from their owners in order to help other poor people in the community

---

57. Ibid., 310.

58. Muddiman, *Ephesians*, 226.

59. See Joachim Gnilka, *Der Epheserbrief* (Freiburg: Herder, 1971), 271; G. B. Caird, *Paul's Letters from Prison: Ephesians, Philippians, Colossians, Philemon* (Oxford: Oxford University Press, 1976), 82.

60. Best, *Ephesians*, 453.

but may not have seen this as "stealing." These are the circumstances under which they are told not to become thieves but to do hard work in support of the community.

This text caused me great ethical problems when I was a child refugee in Germany. Our neighbors had a big apple tree and in the fall they would not always collect all the apples that had fallen from the tree. Since we could not afford to buy much food and fruit I would sometimes climb over the fence and collect these juicy apples, which our neighbor had not collected. Yet such "stealing" troubled my conscience. When I confessed it to my pastor, he asked whether I took the apples only for myself. When I assured him that I had shared them with my brother and friends without asking for pay, he told me: "You are not a thief, but have done a good work of sharing!" If those scholars who suggest that the author had slave-, day-laborer-, and shopkeeper-wo/men in mind are right, we too reject the author's injunction. We have to value these wo/men's practices rather than the*logically legitimating (because the author is said to be divinely inspired!) the stereotype that sees the poor as thieves who neither work nor contribute.

Pheme Perkins sums up the content and gist of this segment's series of exhortations as advocating "communal harmony."[61] The community is encouraged to abstain from "all bitterness, rage, wrath, shouting, and slander," attitudes that would jeopardize such communal harmony. Those who were sealed with the Holy Spirit of G*d should be kind to each other, compassionate, and forgiving (4:30-32).[62] Just as G*d forgave them in Jesus Messiah, so they should imitate G*d as G*d's beloved children and forgive each other. Thus the whole section concludes with an affirmative appeal that facilitates the transition to the next section.

Walk in Love (5:1-14)

It is debated whether the first two verses of chapter 5 are the climax and conclusion of the previous section—as leading scholars such as Best, Schnackenburg, and Lincoln maintain—or whether 5:1 starts a new section. Pheme Perkins has convincingly argued that vv. 1-2 are best understood as an introduction to the verses that follow, since lists of vices "do not typically open sections of parenesis."[63] She points out

61. Perkins, *Ephesians*, 110.
62. The Spirit has a key role in Ephesians; see 1:17; 3:16; 4:3; 5:18; 6:18.
63. Perkins, *Ephesians*, 112.

Ephesians 5:1-14

⁵:¹Therefore be imitators of God, as beloved children, ²and live in love, as Christ loved us and gave himself up for us, a fragrant offering and sacrifice to God.

³But fornication and impurity of any kind, or greed, must not even be mentioned among you, as is proper among saints. ⁴Entirely out of place is obscene, silly, and vulgar talk; but instead, let there be thanksgiving. ⁵Be sure of this, that no fornicator or impure person, or one who is greedy (that is, an idolater), has any inheritance in the kingdom of Christ and of God.

⁶Let no one deceive you with empty words, for because of these things the wrath of God comes on those who are

that vv. 3-8 draw on the list of vices in Colossians 3:5-8 and refer to the previous section on "impurity and greed (4:19), immorality as a consequence of idolatry (4:18), unguarded, degenerate speech (4:29), and divine judgment (4:30)."[64] Encouragement to imitate a model was a key element of ancient discourses of exhortation. This model of imitation has an antithetical form: what one should aim for and what one needed to dodge.[65] This model of imitation also structures 5:1-14.

This segment of 4:1–5:21 begins with a call to imitate G*d as G*d's beloved children and to live in love, as Jesus Messiah loved us. Its stress on "walking" harks back to 4:17 (see also 2:2-10) and points forward to 5:8-15, 17. This ethical-the*logical metaphor of walking marks the recipients' difference with respect to the Gentiles. The section ends by citing a fragment of an early Christian hymnic prayer (5:21).[66]

The appeal to imitate G*d in 5:1 recalls 4:32, where the recipients are admonished to forgive each other as G*d has done for Christ/Messiah's sake. This call to imitate G*d is not only found here in the N*T but also used in the work of the Hellenistic Jewish philosopher Philo when he exhorts those who rule to imitate G*d's beneficence.[67] To imitate G*d in Ephesians means to "walk in love." Those who live in the dynamic realm of "being in love" (5:2a; see also 1:4; 3:17; 4:2, 15, 16; 5:2) should imitate G*d, which means walking in love. Christ/Messiah, who in 1:6 is

64. Ibid.

65. Abraham Malherbe, "Hellenistic Moralists in the New Testament," in *ANRW* 2.26.1, ed. Hildegard Temporini and Wolfgang Haase (Berlin: de Gruyter, 1992), 267–333.

66. See Schnackenburg, *Ephesians*, 228–29.

67. *Spec. Leg.* 4, 34.186–87.

disobedient. [7]Therefore do not be associated with them. [8]For once you were darkness, but now in the Lord you are light. Live as children of light—[9]for the fruit of the light is found in all that is good and right and true. [10]Try to find out what is pleasing to the Lord. [11]Take no part in the unfruitful works of darkness, but instead expose them. [12]For it is shameful even to mention what such people do secretly; [13]but everything exposed by the light becomes visible, [14]for everything that becomes visible is light. Therefore it says,

> "Sleeper, awake!
>   Rise from the dead,
> and Christ will shine on you."

called "beloved," is the paradigmatic example of what it means "to walk in love" because "Christ selflessly handed himself over as a gift of love on our behalf in a sacrificial death offered to G*d."[68] Christ/Messiah's sacrificial death serves as paradigm for self-sacrificial love.

The emphasis on love in Ephesians recalls the hymn to love in 1 Corinthians 13:1-13, a central Christian text that contrasts love with other spiritual gifts. It asserts:

> Love is patient; love is kind; love is not envious or boastful or arrogant or rude. It does not insist on its own way; it is not irritable or resentful; it does not rejoice in wrongdoing, but rejoices in the truth. It bears all things, believes all things, hopes all things, endures all things. Love never ends.

Much later, and in a different historical-ecclesial context, the author of 1 John writes:

> Beloved, let us love one another, because love is from God; everyone who loves is born of God and knows God. Whoever does not love does not know God, for God is love. God's love was revealed among us in this way: God sent his only Son into the world so that we might live through him. In this is love, not that we loved God but that he loved us and sent his Son to be the atoning sacrifice for our sins. Beloved, since God loved us so much, we also ought to love one another. No one has ever seen God; if we love one another, God lives in us, and his love is perfected in us. (1 John 4:7-12)

---

68. John Paul Heil, *Ephesians: Empowerment to Walk in Love for the Unity of All in Christ* (Atlanta: SBL Press, 2007), 209.

Love and Violence
Against Wo/men

As beautiful as these statements on "love" may be, such scriptural texts must be read with a contextual hermeneutics of suspicion that seeks to explore their impact, since they are proclaimed or read as "word of G*d" in socio-political, cultural-religious situations of violence against wo/men. Violence against wo/men is not limited to one specific class, geographical area, or type of person. Rather, it cuts across all social and religious differences and status lines.

In modernity, the word "love" has been not only privatized and individualized but also deeply genderized. A whole relationships industry with know-how sessions, techniques for making love, courses in romance, mountains of self-help books and TV serials promotes heterosexual love relationships. "Love," according to these cultural standards, is woman's (and not man's) natural calling and G*d-given vocation. Fully actualized femininity is said to express itself in romantic love and self-sacrificing motherhood, whereas masculinity actualizes itself in the exercise of freedom, autonomy, and equality.[69] Traditional Christian preaching on love tends to reinforce this cultural ethos of romantic love, feminine calling, and sacrificial service. Domestic violence against wo/men and their children is the logical outcome.[70]

In a poem published more than forty years ago the African American writer Ntozake Shange summed up this life-threatening violence in which we wo/men of all classes, races, religions, and cultures find ourselves caught up daily:

> Every 3 minutes a woman
>   is beaten
> every five minutes a
> woman is raped/every ten
>   minutes
> a lil girl is molested . . .
> every day
> women's bodies are found
> in alleys & bedrooms/at the
>   top of the stairs . . .[71]

In the intervening years, feminist work has documented

---

69. For Japan, see, e.g., Haruko Okono, "Weiblichkeitssymbolik und Sexismus in alten und neuen Religionen Japans," in *Japan: Ein Land der Frauen?*, ed. Elisabeth Gössmann (Munich: Iudicium, 1991), 117–29; see also Usui Atsuko, "Women's 'Experience' in New Religious Movements: The Case of Shinnyoen," *JJRS* 30 (2003): 217–42.

70. Ann Jones, *Next Time She Will Be Dead* (Boston: Beacon, 1993), problematizes the expression "domestic violence" as insinuating "domesticated violence." However, I would argue that the concept of domestic violence underscores that the patrikyriarchal household—the paradigm of society, religion, and state—produces, sustains, and legitimates violence against wo/men.

71. "With No Immediate Cause," in Ntozake Shange, *Nappy Edges* (New York: St. Martin's Press, 1972), 114.

and analyzed the multifarious forms of violent attacks against wo/men that occur just because we are wo/men.[72] Such violence can take many forms.[73] Moreover, such violence is not always forced on wo/men but also can be self-inflicted in the interest of feminine identity, love, and marriage. Femicide, the murder of wo/men, is the deadly outcome of domestic violence. Finally, the election of Donald Trump has documented that such sexual abuse is still publicly accepted rather than rejected as making someone unfit to be president.

Feminist the*logical work on violence against wo/men and child abuse has pointed to four key traditional the*logical discourses of "love" that are major roadblocks in the way of abused wo/men and children who seek to change their violent situations.[74] These four roadblocks consist of the following: first, "love" enacting a pattern of domination/ subordination; second, the association of wo/men with evil and sin; third, the christological valorization of suffering; fourth, the preaching of forgiveness without redress.

At the heart of Christian faith is the maxim: trust in G*d, the Father, and belief in redemption through the suffering of our Lord Jesus Christ.[75] By ritualizing the

---

72. See Jalna Hanmer and Mary Maynard, eds., *Women, Violence, and Social Control* (London: Macmillan, 1987); Kate Young, Carol Wolkowitz, and Roslyn McGullagh, *Of Marriage and the Market: Women's Subordination in International Perspective* (London: CSE Books, 1981); Roxana Carillo, *Battered Dreams: Violence against Women as an Obstacle to Development* (New York: United Nations Development Fund for Women, 1992); Margaret Schuler, ed., *Freedom from Violence: Women's Strategies from Around the World* (New York: United Nations Development Fund for Women, 1992); Jessie Tellis Nayak, "Institutional Violence Against Women in Different Cultures," *In God's Image* 8 (1989): 4–14.

73. Jill Radford and Diana E. H. Russell, *Femicide: The Politics of Woman Killing* (New York: Twayne Publishers, 1992); Louis B. Schlesinger, *Sexual Murder: Catathymic and Compulsive Homicides* (Boca Raton, FL: CRC Press, 2004).

74. For a review of the discussion see, for instance, Regula Strobel, "Der Beihilfe beschuldigt. Christliche Theologie auf der Anklagebank," *Fama. Feministisch Theologische Zeitschrift* 9 (1993): 3–6. See also eadem, "New Ways of Speaking about the Cross: A New Basis for Christian Identity," in *Toward a New Heaven and a New Earth: Essays in Honor of Elisabeth Schüssler Fiorenza*, ed. Fernando F. Segovia (Maryknoll, NY: Orbis Books, 2003), 351–68.

75. Rita Nakashima Brock, "And a Little Child Will Lead Us: Christology and Child Abuse," in *Christianity, Patriarchy, and Abuse: A Feminist Critique*, ed. Joanne Carlson Brown and Carole R. Bohn (New York: Pilgrim Press, 1989), 42–61. See also her books *Journeys by Heart: A Christology of Erotic Power* (New York: Crossroad, 1988) and (with Rebecca Ann Parker) *Proverbs of Ashes: Violence, Redemptive Suffering, and the Search for What Saves Us* (Boston: Beacon, 2001).

suffering and death of Jesus and by calling the powerless in society and church to imitate his perfect obedience and self-sacrificing love, Christian ministry and the*logy do not interrupt but rather continue to foster the cycle of violence. Central Christian values such as love and forgiveness help to sustain relations of domination and the acceptance of domestic and sexual violence. Hence scriptural texts and Christian ethics often continue the cycle of violence by preventing resistance to it. If victims are taught that it is essential for Christians to suffer as Jesus suffered for love's sake, to trust and to love unconditionally, to remain sexually inexperienced, to be obedient to and to forgive beloved authority figures, it becomes virtually impossible for us, particularly for little girls, either to recover their damaged self-image and self-worth or to speak about sexual abuse by a beloved father, priest, relative, or teacher.[76]

As long as Christian the*logy and pastoral practice do not publicly repent their preaching of unconditional love, the victims of such violence are forced to choose between remaining victims or rejecting their Christian birthright. Such an alternative deprives religious wo/men who refuse to be victimized any longer not just of their communal support but also of the belief systems that give meaning to their lives. Contrary to Ephesians's insistence that love must be self-sacrificial and Paul's hymn to love in 1 Corinthians, love does not endure everything. It does not accept and endure inequality, injustice, violence, abuse, and dehumanization. Love is dangerous if it is not an expression of self-esteem, respect, dignity, independence, and self-determination. Love is nothing without justice.[77] Love is nothing without engaging G*d's power to bring about the *ekklēsia* of wo/men as the harbinger of a more just world.

76. This the*logical construct overlooks that Jesus was executed and suffered a violent death because he was thought to be a political insurrectionist against the Roman Empire. See also Sheila Redmond, "Christian 'Virtues' and Recovery from Child Sexual Abuse," in Carlson Brown and Bohn, eds., *Christianity, Patriarchy, and Abuse*, 70–88.

77. It is important not to reinscribe the traditional Christian the*logical prejudice that claims that Christianity is a religion of love whereas Judaism is one of justice, because this repeats a Christian anti-Jewish stereotype. The G*d of Judaism and of justice is one and the same G*d as the G*d of Christianity and love.

The invitation to imitate G*d is followed in 5:3-7 by a list of vices, associated with the exposition in 4:8-14 on the dualism of darkness and light. The list of vices, arranged in groups of three, is taken over from Colossians 3:5-8 and modified by Ephesians. This list underscores sexual immorality (πορνεία), foolish talk, and greed (which is seen as equal to idolatry). This list of vices stresses the need for the community to cleanse itself from sexual immorality and impurity (also stressed in other lists of vices) and gives as reason "as is fitting among saints."[78] The people who are "holy" should not be involved in such immorality.

Greed is defined by Merriam-Webster as "a selfish and excessive desire for more of something (such as money) than is needed." Such greed could be understood as sexual, but it also could refer to an accumulation of wealth. In both cases it is a source of pollution and should not be mentioned among them. Instead of silly, vulgar, or obscene talk (v. 4), which is not appropriate for the holy ones, there should be the sound of thanksgiving.

Rudolf Schnackenburg points to Jesus, who contrasted serving Mammon to serving G*d (Matt 6:24; Luke 16:13) as well as to Philo, who "accuses the avaricious of guarding their riches like an idol in secret chambers and of honoring their riches like Gods."[79] No fornicator, or impure or greedy person (identified in v. 5 as idolater), can have "any inheritance in the *basileia* of Messiah Jesus and of G*d." Galatians 5:21, which has a related list of vices, similarly states that those who are involved in fornication and uncleanness "will not inherit the *basileia*, the kingdom, of G*d," but omits "of Messiah."

Verses 6 and 7 underscore that the recipients should be wary of those who seek to beguile and deceive them with empty words. This is the third reference in Ephesians to inappropriate speech. Those referred to as "sons of disobedience" are not to be associated with, because the wrath of G*d comes upon those who are disobedient. It is not clear whether "with empty words" refers to false teachers or to those who practice immorality. At any rate, those with whom they should not associate seem to be persons who practice the vices elaborated in the preceding verses.

After detailing the evildoing the recipients should avoid, the author turns to positive, challenging exhortations in vv. 8-14, employing the metaphor of darkness and light. However, the text does not say that the

78. Compare the lists of vices in Galatians 5:19; 1 Thessalonians 4:3, 7; 2 Corinthians 12:21.

79. Schnackenburg, *Ephesians*, 220, with reference to Philo, *Spec. Leg.* 1.23-25.

recipients were in the realm of darkness and are now in that of light, but rather that they *were* darkness and *are* now light. Their being or essence is defined by the contrast between darkness and light. Such language can evoke subliminal racist understandings of people with dark skin as bad and those with light skin as good. Hence, it requires the label: "Dangerous to your health and survival!

Since their previous existence was darkness but now they are light "in the *kyrios*/lord," they should walk as "children of light," an expression that harks back to 5:1, where they are called G*d's beloved children. As is the case with the "then-now" language in 2:1-22, so also here the "darkness-light" language draws a sharp contrast between their past and their new life. Similar dualistic language is found in the Qumran writings,[80] the Testaments of the Twelve Patriarchs, the Jewish-Hellenistic writing "Joseph and Aseneth,"[81] and the pre-Pauline fragment preserved in 2 Corinthians 6:14–7:1.[82] In a contemporary racist context this darkness-light language is unwittingly reinscribing such dualism as racial.

The Pre-Pauline Fragment (2 Cor 6:14–7:1)

Do not get misyoked (or mismatched) with unbelievers! For what partnership have righteousness and lawlessness Or what community has light with darkness? Or what common lot a believer with an unbeliever? What agreement is there between G*d's temple and idols? For we are the temple of the living G*d; as G*d has said: "I will dwell in them and walk among them; And I will be their G*d And they shall be my people. Therefore come out of their midst and separate, says the *Kyrios*. And touch nothing unclean. Then I will receive you, And I will be a father to you,

80. For Qumran scholarship on wo/men, see Cecilia Wassen, *Women in the Damascus Document*, AcBib21 (Atlanta: SBL Press, 2005), 2–11.

81. Ross S. Kraemer, "The Book of Aseneth," in *Searching the Scriptures*, vol. 2: *A Feminist Commentary*, ed. Elisabeth Schüssler Fiorenza (New York: Crossroad, 1994), 859–88.

82. See Schnackenburg, *Ephesians*, 223.

> And you shall be my
>   sons and daughters,"
> Says the *Kyrios* who
>   holds all power.
> Since we have these prom-
>   ises, beloved,
> Let us cleanse ourselves
>   from every defilement
>   of the flesh and spirit,
> Making holiness perfect in
>   the fear of G*d.

The affinities between this text and Ephesians are striking. If one does not translate the first imperative of the pre-Pauline text transmitted in 2 Corinthians as "mismatch" or "cross-bred" but as "mis-yoke" or "unevenly yoked together," the anticolonial political overtones of such an oppositional the*logical consciousness come to the fore. Since the metaphor of the yoke usually refers to burdens imposed by political oppressors (Isa 9:4; 10:27; 14:25; Jer 27:8, 11, 12; Gen 27:40; 1 Kgs 12:4), the community addressed by the fragment might have understood itself in opposition to Roman imperial rule. The most striking adaptation of scriptural texts, however, is the alteration of the promise given to King David in 2 Samuel 7:14: "I will be a father to him and he shall be a son to me." In the fragment of 2 Corinthians, G*d's promise of "sonship" in 2 Samuel 7:14 is modified to include both "sons" and

"daughters" as members of G*d's elect people and royal priesthood.

Scholars have argued that the oppositional consciousness expressed here in the language of Scripture cannot be of Jewish provenance. However, nothing speaks against a Jewish-Christian origin for this pre-Pauline tradition that seems also to inform the the*logical universe of the recipients of 1 Peter. Rather, it seems to fit well into the the*logy of the (Hellenistic) Jewish (Christian) missionary movement. The members of this movement conceived of themselves as a new creation through Messiah Jesus' resurrection and as the eschatological people gifted with the presence of Divine Wisdom. Both daughters and sons, both young and old, both male and female slaves are graced with the gifts of the Spirit and have received prophetic endowment (see also Acts 2:17-18 and Joel 2:28). They are children of G*d, the holy people, the temple-community among whom the Spirit dwells.

As children of light, Ephesians stresses, they should bring forth the "fruits of light," that is, the fruits of the Spirit, which are goodness, righteousness, and truth, proving what is acceptable to G*d.[83] Whereas vv. 8-10 speak of the children of light,

---

83. Note that the Greek text has no verb.

vv. 11-12 warn the recipients not to take part in the works of darkness but instead to expose them. What they do in secret is so shameful that one cannot even speak of it. In 5:2 they were told that fornication and impurity of any kind should not even be mentioned among them because such speaking is improper for the holy ones. It is therefore likely that sexual acts are here alluded to also. Exposing the works of darkness to the light makes them visible. "As the children of light expose the deeds of darkness by their living, so what is exposed itself becomes illuminated by the sphere of light."[84] Ernest Best summarizes the argument as follows:

> Believers are light; some in the community have sinned; believers reprove them and so bring light to bear on their faults; when their faults are reproved, they are revealed and every sin that is revealed is no longer sin and the one who has committed it, is light, i.e., restored to his [*sic*] proper nature as light.[85]

Following this rather unclear and difficult Greek sentence, an early Christian hymn of unknown origin is cited: "Awake, O sleeper, and rise from the dead and Messiah Jesus will shine on you." The Messiah is here identified as the light that continues to shine on them. The act of baptism is expressed here metaphorically as "rising from the dead" (see Eph 2:1, 5). Their life as Gentile wo/men is likened to sleep and death and contrasted with being awakened and coming alive at the moment of their baptism. The Messianic sun of justice warms them and continues to shine on and enliven them.

84. Lincoln, *Ephesians*, 331.
85. Best, *Ephesians*, 496.

Ephesians 5:15–6:24

The Ekklēsia *of the Wise*

With this section of Ephesians we approach what is historically the most influential and most controverted chapter of Ephesians. Malestream commentaries and interpretations clash with feminist interpretations and evaluations of the text. This text is read at millions of Christian marriage celebrations and at the same time has served to prevent wo/men from representing Christ in the ministry of the church. Much less attention has been paid to the political meaning of *ekklēsia*, which does not denote "church," as commentators almost universally translate it, but signifies the democratic assembly of the people.

It is debated whether Ephesians 5:21, "Be subject to one another out of reverence for Christ," is the conclusion of the segment 5:15-20 or the introduction to the next segment, the so-called "household code." This problem disappears, however, if the whole segment is understood as starting with 5:15 and ending with 6:20. Rudolf Schnackenburg agrees that 5:15 begins a new segment, but he argues that this segment ends with 6:9, since 6:10-20 "depicts something new" and "the horizon widens on a universal, cosmic level."[1] He argues that the preceding section speaks both of the life of the congregation and that of the family, and he titles the overall section (5:15–6:9) "the life of the Christian congregation."[2]

---

1. Rudolf Schnackenburg, *Ephesians: A Commentary*, trans. Helen Heron (Edinburgh: T&T Clark, 1991), 266.
2. Ibid., 231.

What is still unclear, however, is the function of v. 21. "Be subject to one another out of reverence for Christ" seems best understood as a bridge sentence connecting 5:15-20 with the imperatives in 5:22-33. Ephesians 5:22-33 exhorts wo/men to "be subject to their own man/husband." Scholars understand this imperative of wifely subjection/submission either as concluding an introductory segment or as an introduction to the so-called household code segment that follows in 5:22-33.

It seems that the text serves both functions; hence it is best to consider 5:15–6:20 as a single section, which I have headlined "the *ekklēsia* of the wise." If the section is understood in this way, then 6:10-20 belongs to it as the climactic concluding argument of this section and of Ephesians as a whole. The previous references to the *ekklēsia* in 1:22 and 3:10-21 speak of it in cosmic terms and state that the *ekklēsia*'s task is to make known to the powers "the manifold Wisdom of G*d," whereas in this section, 5:15–6:20, the *ekklēsia* is imagined both in the figure of the beloved free-born wife/*matrona* and as a military cohort.

As was pointed out in the introduction, Ephesians can be divided roughly into three parts: chapters 1–2, which serve an introductory function; chapters 4–6, which conclude the letter; and chapter 3, which serves as a bridge between the two. The concluding part consists of two sections: 4:1–5:14 and 5:15–6:20. Ephesians 5:15–6:20, in turn, is made up of four segments, 5:15-20; 5:21-33; 6:1-9; and 6:10-20. The recipients are told at the beginning (5:15-20) that they should live as wise wo/men so that they can accomplish their task to proclaim G*d's manifold Wisdom, and at the close (6:10-20) they are called with a military image to continue the struggles against the evil powers and to do so by "praying in the Spirit at all times in every prayer and supplication" (6:18). Finally, Ephesians 6:21-24 consists of the letter's concluding greetings.

Live as Wise and not as Fools (5:15-20)

This short first segment, which has an introductory function, can be divided into two main exhortative statements: "Live, not as unwise people but as wise" (vv. 15-16) and "Be filled with the Spirit . . ." (vv. 17-20).

Live as Wise Wo/men (5:15-17)

Ephesians changes the imperative of Colossians 4:5, "walk in wisdom toward outsiders," to "walk as wise people." Unlike foolish people, wise people understand what the will of the *kyrios* is and make the most of the time they have, because the "days are evil" (v. 15). The days in which the

Ephesians 5:15-20

¹⁵Be careful then how you live, not as unwise people but as wise, ¹⁶making the most of the time, because the days are evil. ¹⁷So do not be foolish, but understand what the will of the Lord is. ¹⁸Do not get drunk with wine, for that is debauchery; but be filled with the Spirit, ¹⁹as you sing psalms and hymns and spiritual songs among yourselves, singing and making melody to the Lord in your hearts, ²⁰giving thanks to God the Father at all times and for everything in the name of our Lord Jesus Christ.

recipients live are characterized by the influence of evil spiritual powers (2:1-3) and not necessarily as the end-of-all-time. This exhortation points to the concluding segment of this section, 6:9-20, where the recipients are exhorted to struggle against the evil spiritual powers.

This imperative to live as wise and not foolish people contrasts wise people and fools. This contrast is widespread in Jewish Wisdom literature: Proverbs, Ecclesiastes, Job, the deuterocanonical books of Ben Sira/Sirach (also known as Ecclesiasticus), and the Wisdom of Solomon. These writings, especially Proverbs and the Wisdom of Solomon, picture Wisdom-Sophia, whom we encountered in chapter 3, as a divine wo/man, Wo/man Wisdom. Since in Hebrew, as well as in Greek, the word "wisdom" is grammatically feminine, Wo/man Wisdom is understood either as a metaphor for the Divine or as its female personification.[3] The female imagery for Wo/man Wisdom is closely connected to that of her negative counterpart in Proverbs, referred to as the "loose" or "strange," Wo/man Stranger.[4]

Since it is generally assumed that the writers of the wisdom texts were male sages, and because Ephesians uses the grammatically masculine form for "wise" (σοφοί), scholars generally conclude that the text speaks about men only. However, we have some indications that, historically, σοφοί can be read in inclusive generic terms as addressing both men and women in the wisdom-community. Fortunately we have a text that explicitly refers to wo/men as members of the community of the wise.

In *On the Contemplative Life* (*De vita contemplativa*), the Jewish philosopher Philo of Alexandria (25 BCE–50 CE) describes just such a Jewish group, whose members are called "Therapeutae" and "Therapeutrides,"

3. See Michael S. Moore, " 'Wise Women' or Wisdom Woman? A Biblical Study of Women's Roles," *RQ* 35 (1993): 147–58.
4. Claudia V. Camp, "Woman Wisdom: Bible," *The Jewish Women's Archive*, accessed September 2016, http://jwa.org/encyclopedia/article/woman-wisdom-bible.

meaning "those who serve [θεραπεύω] G*d." Most important, Philo refers to them not only with the generic masculine but explicitly uses both the masculine and feminine grammatical forms. In antiquity women as well as men could be servants of the G*ds but were especially known as devotees of the Goddess Isis. Philo points out that those who participate in the contemplative life are found in many areas of the world, but Philo focuses on those close to home who live in the suburbs of Alexandria.[5]

In her highly acclaimed work, *Jewish Women Philosophers of First-Century Alexandria: Philo's "Therapeutae" Reconsidered*, Joan E. Taylor has argued that the "communities of the wise" or "sages" included well-to-do Jewish wo/men in the first century.[6] The Therapeutrides were highly educated philosophers. These philosophers, who have dedicated themselves to the service of G*d and have left their possessions to their families to dwell outside urban centers, do so because "they are seized by a heavenly passion" and have "the same zeal and purpose."[7] They have joined the community

> because of a zeal and yearning for Wisdom, with which they are eager to live. They take no heed of the pleasures of the body and desire not a mortal offspring, but an immortal one, to which only a soul that is loved by God is able to give birth by itself, because the Father has sown in it lights of intelligence that enable her to see the doctrines of Wisdom.[8]

The relations between the genders are constructed as positive, since they make music together and "compose psalms and hymns to God in all kinds of meters and melodies which they have to write down in dignified rhythms."[9] Such choral singing was also connected to dancing.[10] In short, the community seems to have consisted of well-to-do people who followed the call of devotion to the Divine. It is also important to note that the community did not have slaves in its midst, but "all are free."[11] Like that of 1 Peter, this community seems to have been structured according to a senior/junior model. The junior people who serve

5. For this section on the Therapeutae, see Joan E. Taylor and Philip R. Davies, "The So-Called Therapeutae of *De Vita Contemplativa*: Identity and Character," *HTR* 91 (1998): 3–24.

6. Joan E. Taylor, *Jewish Women Philosophers of First-Century Alexandria: Philo's "Therapeutae" Reconsidered* (Oxford: Oxford University Press, 2003).

7. Philo, *De vita contemplativa* 12, 32.

8. Ibid., 68.

9. Ibid., 29.

10. Ibid., 80.

11. Ibid., 71–72.

are called διάκονοι, "servers," a title given to Paul and also to Phoebe of Cenchreae (Rom 16:1). However, this senior-junior organizational model is not explicitly found in Ephesians.

The community of the wise are exhorted to make wise use of their time, because the days are evil. To make good use of one's time (καιρός) is a standard virtue in the moral discourse of the Hebrew Bible and in Greco-Roman moral traditions. They should not be foolish, lacking insight and good judgment. Rather, they should seek to understand the wishes and will of the Lord.[12] Like the congregation of the Therapeutae, the *ekklēsia* in Ephesians is characterized by music as a sign that they are filled with the Spirit.

Be Filled with the Spirit . . . (5:17-20)

The imperative "be filled with the Spirit" is accompanied by "and be not drunk with wine, in which is debauchery, sin, and corruption." Since the subsequent text exhorts the recipients to "speak in psalms, hymns, and spiritual songs, making melody in their hearts" as spirit-filled persons, one wonders why the author contrasts "being drunk with wine" and "filled with the Spirit." The effects of the Spirit are here likened to those of wine. Is this expression just used to underscore the contrast to debauchery, depravity, and corruption, or is another contrast intended here?

To explain this contrast, scholars point to another religious community of the day: those initiated into the mysteries of Dionysos, the G*d of wine. Mysteries were widespread in the ancient world and the mystery cult of Dionysos was not the only one. The mystery cult of Isis and those at Eleusis were also very famous, and they too attracted many devotees who wanted to be initiated. The initiation rituals of these mystery communities resemble and fuse with each other.

> In the name of whatever deity they are performed, [they] exhibit the same basic pattern: the fate of the initiand is radically altered by a ritual in which he [*sic*] is purified, instructed, sees and hears sacred things, together with . . . the eating of a special meal and the assumption of a special dress. . . . For example, initiation into the Dionysiac secret society (or *thiasos*) may be incorporated into an actual living community, which is nevertheless a community of the next world.[13]

12. See Daniel D. Darko, *No Longer Living as the Gentiles: Differentiation and Shared Ethical Values in Ephesians 4.17–6.9* (London: T&T Clark, 2008), 258–59.
13. R. A. S. Seaford, "The Mysteries of Dionysos at Pompeii," accessed August 2016, http://www.stoa.org/diotima/essays/seaford.shtml.

Initiation always also meant entry into a followership and community, called the *thiasos*. The Dionysiac communities attracted many followers, especially among wo/men, including the poor. "Those who had no part in the society of the day found a sense of belonging in the *thiasos*."[14] Many wo/men were associated with the cult. They are called Maenads or Bacchantes in Latin.

Being filled up (πληροῦσθε) with the Spirit is contrasted here with "being drunk with wine." Since the rituals of the *ekklēsia* involved wine as well as dancing and singing, the community could easily be mistaken by outsiders (and maybe also some of its members) for a *thiasos* like that of the Divine Dionysos, because wo/men played a leading role in its worship. Since the purpose of the intoxication was to fill the participants with ecstasy and the Spirit of G*d, the author could have had a contrast with the Dionysian rituals and community in mind.

If the filling with the Spirit has to do with a supernatural infilling with the Spirit of the living G*d it would only be logical to suppose that "drunk with wine" could have a supernatural implication. The significance would then be a contrast between the filling with the "spirit" of Bacchus through wine and the filling of the true and living G*d by the Spirit. The wisdom and power, the intellectual and artistic ability, the freedom from the drudgery of daily life, as well as the prophetic message of G*d, are not to be found in the Dionysian drunkenness but in the control of the Spirit of the true G*d.[15]

In short, this segment calls into view two distinct ancient communities, the Jewish community of the Therapeutae/Therapeutrides and the international community of the mysteries of Dionysos (also called Bacchus), the G*d of wine. Both communities are known by their ecstatic worship and by wo/men in their midst. Since we do not know who the Ephesians were (if they were Ephesians), whom the author seeks to address and persuade, we have to resort to historical imagination. In light of the interpretation of 5:15-20 we can assume that wo/men were among "the wise," as inspired wo/men leaders of the mysteries and communal celebrations.

While the study of the Therapeutae suggests that these wo/men were well-to-do, research on the Dionysian mysteries cautions us not to overlook the fact that wo/men members would have come from all walks of life. Hence the community would also have included slave and poor

14. Ibid., 4.
15. Cleon L. Rogers Jr., "The Dionysian Background of Ephesians 5:18," *BibSac* 136 (1979): 249–57.

wo/men. Most important, the following segment, Ephesians 5:21-33, the so-called household code, speaks not just about households but also about the *ekklēsia* that, as a local *ekklēsia*, meets "in house" (ἐν οἴκῳ) and which, in Ephesians, is also understood in cosmic terms. This is underscored by the concluding sentence, "This is a great mystery, which should be understood with reference to the Messiah and the *ekklēsia*" (5:32-33).

Be Subject: The *Ekklēsia* and Wo/men (5:21-33)

It is debated whether Ephesians 5:21 belongs to the preceding segment or is an introduction to the following one, the so-called household code. Most scholars assume that this section is an elaboration of how the "Christian" household and the relations in it should be governed. While this is correct, insofar as the author works with a traditional household-code pattern taken over from Colossians, the assumption is also misleading because it plays down the emphasis the author places on the *ekklēsia* in 5:21-33.

The same assumption also determines the NRSV translation: "Wives, be subject to your husbands as you are to the Lord." This translation does not indicate that v. 21 is still a part of v. 20. This change in translation is problematic for the understanding of the text, because it does not connect the verse to the preceding phrase in v. 21, "being subject to one another out of reverence for Christ."

Moreover, the NRSV translates γυνή as "wife," rather than "woman," whereas the Greek text speaks of "women submitting to their own men." It is important to read the injunction for wo/men to submit to their own men as a clarification of v. 20. It seeks to specify that freeborn women have only to submit to their own men, that is, that freeborn wives have only to submit to their husbands. According to this reading, the text is clarifying that not all wo/men have to submit to all men in the worship-gathering of the *ekklēsia* but that only married wo/men, freeborn wives, have to do so, and then only to their husbands rather than to all men. A similar injunction is found in 1 Corinthians 14:35, where wo/men (i.e., wives) who want to learn are also told to ask "their own men" (τοὺς ἰδίους ἄνδρας) questions at home. Whether this injunction was known to the author or not, it is clear that not all wo/men are addressed here but only freeborn wives. It seems that the author uses the injunction for wives found in the Colossians source to elaborate the position of the *ekklēsia*. Just as married wo/men are to be subordinated, so also the *ekklēsia* is placed in a subordinate position.

²¹Be subject to one another out of reverence for Christ.

²²Wives, be subject to your husbands as you are to the Lord. ²³For the husband is the head of the wife just as Christ is the head of the church, the body of which he is the Savior. ²⁴Just as the church is subject to Christ, so also wives ought to be, in everything, to their husbands.

²⁵Husbands, love your wives, just as Christ loved the church and gave himself up for her, ²⁶in order to make her holy by cleansing her with the washing of water by the word, ²⁷so as to present the church to himself in

Household Code[16]

The texts classified as "household codes," a label derived from Martin Luther's teaching on social status and roles (*Ständelehre*), are concerned with three sets of relationships: those of the wife, the child, and the slave with the *kyrios* of the house, who is husband, father, and slave master. The partners in each relationship receive reciprocal admonitions. The central interest of these texts lies in the enforcement of the submission of the socially weaker group—freeborn wives, children, and slave wo/men— on the one hand, and the authority of the *paterfamilias*, the freeborn, slave-owning head of the household, on the other.

16. For a review of scholarship on the household codes, see Margaret Y. MacDonald, "Beyond Identification of the *Topos* of Household Management: Reading the Household Codes in Light of Recent Methodologies and Theoretical Perspectives in the Study of the New Testament," *NTS* 57 (2011): 65–90. For feminist work on the household codes, see, for example, Elisabeth Schüssler Fiorenza, "Discipleship and Patriarchy: Towards a Feminist Evaluative Hermeneutics," in *Bread Not Stone: The Challenge of Feminist Biblical Interpretation* (Boston: Beacon, 1985), 65–92, and "Christian Mission and the Patriarchal Household," in *In Memory of Her: A Feminist Theological Reconstruction of Christian Origins* (New York: Crossroad, 1994), 251–84; Angela Standhartinger, "The Epistle to the Congregation in Colossae and the Invention of the 'Household Code,'" in *A Feminist Companion to the Deutero-Pauline Epistles*, ed. Amy-Jill Levine and Marianne Blickenstaff, FCB 7 (New York: T&T Clark, 2003), 88–97; Cynthia Briggs Kittredge, *Community and Authority: The Rhetoric of Obedience in the Pauline Tradition*, HTS 45 (Harrisburg, PA: Trinity Press International, 1998); Antoinette Clarke Wire, "Review Essay on Elliott, *Home for the Homeless*, and Balch, *Let Wives Be Submissive*," *RSR* 10 (1984): 209–16; Clarice Martin, "The *Haustafeln* (Household Codes) in African American Biblical Interpretation: 'Free Slaves' and 'Subordinate Women,'" in *Stony the Road We Trod: African American Biblical Interpretation*, ed. Cain Hope Felder (Minneapolis: Fortress, 1991), 206–31. See also David Schroeder, "Die Haustafeln des

splendor, without a spot or wrinkle or anything of the kind—yes, so that she may be holy and without blemish. [28]In the same way, husbands should love their wives as they do their own bodies. He who loves his wife loves himself. [29]For no one ever hates his own body, but he nourishes and tenderly cares for it, just as Christ does for the church, [30]because we are members of his body. [31]"For this reason a man will leave his father and mother and be joined to his wife, and the two will become one flesh." [32]This is a great mystery, and I am applying it to Christ and the church. [33]Each of you, however, should love his wife as himself, and a wife should respect her husband.

Elements of the household code are also found in 1 Peter 2:18–3:7; 1 Timothy 2:11-15; 5:3-8; 6:1-2; Titus 2:2-10; 3:1-2; 1 Clement 21.6-8; Ignatius, *To Polycarp* 4.1–6.2; *Epistle of Polycarp to the Philippians* 4.2–6.1; Didache 4.9-11; *Barnabas* 19.5-7. However, the complete form of the household code appears only in Colossians 3:18–4:1, which has been taken over, revised, and expanded in Ephesians.

Characteristic of the "household code" pattern is the injunction to submission and obedience. While this pattern functions differently in early Christian documents, the call to submission and obedience for the socially inferior persons remains at its center. Some

---

Neuen Testaments: Ihre Herkunft und ihr theologischer Sinn" (PhD diss., Hamburg, 1959); Karl Weidinger, *Die Haustafeln. Ein Stück Urchristlicher Paränese*, UNT 14 (Leipzig: Hinrichs, 1928); Leonhard Goppelt, "Jesus und die 'Haustafel'-Tradition," in *Orientierung an Jesus: zur Theologie der Synoptiker: für Josef Schmid*, ed. Paul Hoffman (Freiburg: Herder, 1973), 93–106; Dieter Lührmann, "Neutestamentliche Haustafeln und Antike Ökonomie," *NTS* 27 (1980): 83–97, and idem, "Wo man nicht mehr Sklave oder Freier ist. Überlegungen zur Struktur frühchristlicher Gemeinden," *WuD* 13 (1975): 53–83; Klaus Thraede, "Zum historischen Hintergrund der Haustafeln des NT," in *Pietas: Festschrift für Bernhard Kötting*, ed. Ernst Dassmann and Karl Suso Frank, *JAC* 8 (Münster: Aschendorff, 1980), 359–68. Also David Balch, "Household Codes," in *Greco-Roman Literature and the New Testament: Selected Forms and Genres*, ed. David E. Aune (Atlanta: Scholars Press, 1988), 25–50; idem, "Neopythagorean Moralists and the New Testament Household Codes," *ANRW* 2.26.1, ed. Hildegard Temporini and Wolfgang Haase (Berlin: de Gruyter, 1992), 380–411; Carolyn Osiek and David L. Balch, *Families in the New Testament World: Households and House Churches* (Louisville: Westminster John Knox, 1997); John Elliott, "The Jesus Movement Was Not Egalitarian but Family-Oriented," *BibInt* 11 (2003): 173–210. On household codes in Ephesians, see, for example, Martin Dibelius, *An Die Kolosser, Epheser und Philemon*, ed. Huck Greeven (Tübingen: Mohr, 1953); Paul Sampley, *'And the Two Shall Become One Flesh': A*

scholars have argued that this injunction to submission goes back to Jesus, but the majority agree that it is part and parcel of ancient philosophy. Since the mid-1980s the majority scholarly consensus has been that the household code texts are rooted in the Aristotelian philosophical trajectory concerning household management (*oikonomia*) and political ethics.[17] Moreover, scholars also recognize that these texts are prescriptive and not reflective or descriptive of reality. However, the the*logical hermeneutical assessment and evaluation of the household code is divided and often reflects gender bias or conservative social interests that are then couched in the*logical arguments.[18]

In short, the *Haustafel* is best understood as a "pattern of kyriarchal submission" that legitimates the power of the *kyrios*—the free, propertied head of household—over his slaves,

wife, and children, who are subject to his power. That is, they are not "free." The kyriarchal household and *polis*, or city, are the points of reference for the meaning-pattern of kyriarchal submission. The kyriarchal household pattern conceives not only of the family but also of the *ekklēsia* and the state in terms of the kyriarchal household. The messianic community soon comes to be called "the household of G*d," with "G*d" being understood as *Kyrios*, that is, Lord or slave master, and father, in analogy to the great kings of the ancient Near East, as well as to the Roman emperor, who, from the time of Augustus, was understood as "the father of the Fatherland" (*pater patriae*).[19]

Whereas Colossians 3:18–4:1 is clearly interested in the master–slave-wo/man relation, Ephesians focuses not only on the elite husband-wife relation but especially also on the relationship between Messiah/

Study of Traditions in Ephesians 5:21-33, SNTSMS 16 (Cambridge: Cambridge University Press, 1971); Carolyn Osiek, "The Bride of Christ (Ephesians 5:22-33): A Problematic Wedding," *BTB* 32 (2002): 29–39; Lisa Marie Belz, "The Rhetoric of Gender in the Household of God: Ephesians 5:21-33 and Its Place in Pauline Tradition" (PhD diss., Loyola University Chicago, 2013); Ann Holmes Redding, "Together, Not Equal: The Rhetoric of Unity and Headship in the Letter to the Ephesians" (PhD diss., Union Theological Seminary, 1999); Timothy J. Gombis, "A Radically New Humanity: The Function of the *Haustafel* in Ephesians," *JETS* 48 (2005): 317–30.

17. See Schüssler Fiorenza, *Bread Not Stone*, 65–92; MacDonald, "Beyond Identification of the *Topos*," 65–90; see also James P. Hering, *The Colossian and Ephesian Haustafeln in Theological Context* (New York: Lang, 2007).

18. See, e.g., Gombis, "A Radically New Humanity."

19. Ronald Syme, *The Roman Revolution* (Oxford: Oxford University Press, 1939), 509–24. See also my book *The Power of the Word: Scripture and the Rhetoric of Empire* (Minneapolis: Fortress, 2007).

Christ and the *ekklēsia*. In so doing the author combines the traditional household code form with the *ekklēsia*-body the*logy and the bride-bridegroom notion found in 2 Corinthians 11:2. The relationship between Messiah Jesus and the *ekklēsia*, expressed in the metaphor of head and body, as well as in the imagery of bridegroom and bride, becomes the paradigm for the marriage relation, and the marriage relation becomes the paradigm for the relationship between Messiah and *ekklēsia*.

This the*logical paradigm for the messianic marriage relation reinforces the imperial-kyriarchal pattern of subjection and subordination insofar as the relationship between Messiah and *ekklēsia* is not a relationship between equals, since the *ekklēsia*-bride is totally dependent on or subject to her head or bridegroom. What should be understood as a general injunction for all members of the community, "be subject to one another in the fear of Messiah Jesus," is spelled out only for the wife. Submission and inequality are required only from the wife, just as the *ekklēsia* is subordinated to Messiah Jesus.

As the *ekklēsia* is subordinated to Messiah Jesus, so the wife is enjoined to subject herself to her husband "in everything." This phrase "in everything" is connected in the Colossians code with the injunction to children and slave wo/men. In Ephesians it underscores the subordinate position of the wife, which

is equated with the *ekklēsia*'s submission to Messiah Jesus, the *Kyrios*. The instruction to elite wives not only reinforces the kyriarchal marriage relation but also justifies it with reference to Messiah Jesus and the *ekklēsia*.

However, the household code is modified in the exhortation to the husband. The negative demand of Colossians, that men should not be harsh with their wives, is not repeated here. Rather, the freeborn husbands are three times commanded to love (ἀγαπᾶν) their wives, in vv. 25, 28, and 33. Jesus' commandment to "love your neighbor as yourself" (Mark 12:31 // Lev 19:18) is applied here to the husband within the marriage relationship. Moreover, the relationship of Messiah Jesus with the *ekklēsia* in self-giving love becomes the example for the husband to imitate. However, it is not the model for the wife. Kyriarchal domination by the husband is thereby radically questioned but at the same time it remains cemented in the injunction to the wife.

Since Ephesians takes over the household code of Colossians it is important to note that the author changes the Colossians text in order to focus attention on the *ekklēsia*. Ephesians 5:22-33 elaborates the (freeborn) wife-husband relationship with reference to the bond between the Messiah and the *ekklēsia*. These verses emphasize the love relation between Messiah Jesus and the *ekklēsia* as the example for the husband to imitate. The length of the text on Messiah/ Christ and *ekklēsia* indicates that this is the focus of the author and the main point they seek to make. The case is developed as follows:

> Messiah Jesus is the head of the *ekklēsia* and savior of the body (5:23).
>
> The *ekklēsia* submits to Messiah Jesus (5:24).
>
> Hence the *ekklēsia* is the recipient of Messiah Jesus' love, as Jesus gave himself for it (5:25).
>
> The *ekklēsia* is cleansed and sanctified through "the washing" of the water in the word (5:26).
>
> The *ekklēsia* is honored, holy, and unblemished (5:27).
>
> The *ekklēsia* is loved and cherished by the *Kyrios* (5:29).
>
> The members of the *ekklēsia* are members of the Messiah's flesh and bones (5:30).

In short, the *ekklēsia* is figured here in and through the freeborn wife's relation to the husband, who is seen as representing Christ. That this is the main point the author wants to make is expressed in v. 32: "this mystery is great but I speak [λέγω] with reference to the Messiah and to the *ekklēsia*." The reference to Genesis 2:24 is not to husband and wife as such; it is applied here to the relation of the Messiah to the *ekklēsia*. If we assume that the baptismal formula of Galatians 3:28 is shaping the understanding of the "*ekklēsia* of the wise," then the reference to Genesis 2:24 might also be intended as a correction of the baptismal understanding in Galatians 3:28 "no longer male and female" to the effect that membership in the *ekklēsia* is defined by the "husband and wife" relation (Gen 1:27).

If one's reading does not focus on the traditional household code but on the emphasis placed in Ephesians 5:22-33 on Messiah Jesus and the *ekklēsia* one can see that the author uses the traditional code to summarize and spell out the relation between Messiah/Christ and the *ekklēsia*, and does so in kyriarchal terms of subordination. The vocabulary for the transformation of the traditional code taken over from Colossians can be followed throughout the letter and seems to be directed toward freeborn married women. If the community/ies to which the epistle is sent were organized in house assemblies whose members understood themselves as the wise called to proclaim the manifold Sophia-Wisdom of G*d, then the sender of the letter, who writes in the name of Paul, uses the traditional household code teachings, which seek to inculcate the traditional marriage pattern of subordination, to kyriarchally order the life of the *ekklēsia*. To elaborate this *ekklēsial* ethos of "subordination" the author resorts to key *topoi* of the letter: mystery (1:9; 3:3; 5:32; 6:19); love or *agapē/agapan* (1:6; 2:4; 5:2, 25; 6:24); body of Messiah/Christ (1:23; 2:16; 4:4, 12, 16; 5:23); and *ekklēsia* (1:22; 3:10, 21; 5:24, 27, 29, 32). With the help of the traditional household code, the author explicates the relation between Messiah/Christ and the *ekklēsia* of the wise.

Women/wives seem to have been the primary target of these admonitions, since the author not only mentions them first but also uses the same verb, "submit," for them and for the whole community. Thus Ephesians stresses that the love relation between Messiah/Christ and the *ekklēsia* is to be imitated by the husband, but not by the wife, who instead is called to subordination. Like Paul in 1 Corinthians, the author uses the image of the body/corporation of Messiah/Christ but, unlike Paul, kyriarchalizes it by distinguishing between head and body.

The author thereby casts Messiah Jesus in the role of the emperor, using the political language of the time, and at the same time paints the *ekklēsia*, the assembly of the wise, in terms of the democratic citizen assembly, figured as feminine and hence also subordinate. Such democratic citizen assemblies were still very much active in Asia Minor at the time and often stood in tension with the imperial administration.

Without question, Ephesians 5:21-33 is part of the kyriarchal household code trajectory insofar as it appropriates the household code's pattern of submission and uses that pattern for asserting the freeborn wife's submission to the husband as a religious, messianic duty. In the case of the husband, the author modifies the kyriarchal code in terms of the well-known *agapē* (love) commandment, to be lived according to the example of Messiah Jesus. The "gospel of peace" has transformed the kyriarchal relations between Jews and Gentiles, but according to the author it has not changed the status of freeborn and slave wo/men in the *ekklēsia*, the household of G*d. Rather than proclaiming "a radically new humanity,"[20] Ephesians attempts to shift *ekklēsial* identity and the understanding of *ekklēsia* in terms of equality and siblinghood to an understanding shaped by the kyriarchal structures of the household, which are interpreted as those of the "household of G*d."[21]

---

20. Gombis, "A Radically New Humanity."

21. See David Horrell, "From ἀδελφοί to οἶκος θεοῦ: Social Transformation in Pauline Christianity," *JBL* 120 (2001): 293–311.

Catholic and Islamic Talibans
on Woman's Obedience
in the Balkans

Recently I was part of a heated debate on Facebook about the ideal image of "woman" in Christianity and Islam. The first text, "Mary's Obedience and Women Today," was published by a Catholic priest, Dr. Ivica Raguz from Croatia, in the *Voice of Council* magazine. He stated: "If women seek equality, they are disobedient and they do not want to have as their head their husbands or Christ." The second text, by the Muslim Imam Dr. Zijad Ljakic, was a *fatwa* (religious decree) answer to a question from one of his readers about women's sexual availability and obedience to their husbands. The text, titled "My Wife Rejects Sex with Me," was published on his personal website and widely distributed online. He argued that if a woman disobeys her husband he has the right to discipline her.

The rhetoric of both clerics was strikingly similar, with arguments and claims of male authority and leadership in church/religious community and family. If we remove the names of the two clergymen and replace Catholic theological vocabulary with Islamic, or vice versa, we will have the same "kyriarchical" discourse that echoes St. Augustine or Selefi/Wahabi understanding of gender relations framed by obedience to God and man. Of course, today's talibans and puritans always

add that this obedience derives from a woman's love of pleasing her guardian.

Unfortunately, these two clergymen reflect the prevailing mind-set in the Catholic Church and the Islamic Community in the Balkans, which are trapped in ethno-nationalistic and ethno-religious discourses that go against gender equality and women's rights. Many priests and imams still preach about obedience as a woman's greatest virtue that will save her marriage and family and bring her into heaven. Therefore she is often advised to be patient and to suffer, even through violence, to save her marriage and family.

Every discussion regarding women somehow gets back to the creation story about a crooked rib, narrated in the Bible and in the Hadith (the second source of Islam) but not in the Qur'an. Eve is created after Adam, for him, and in order to follow him in everything, and to subject her will to his and consequently to God's will, voluntarily and ideally out of love. According to these two clergymen, and many other scholars and priests, this is the best way to be fully free and saved in the hereafter. A woman thus is not the subject of her own life but an object, and an "other" defined and saved by a man. It seems that she is less capable than a man of guiding her life, let alone of guiding a man. Partnership, equality, and justice are completely overlooked. Male gender is the key prerequisite and a guarantee that the man will be a leader and a guide for a woman who is obviously immature, childish, vulnerable, and needs his protection.

One of the reasons for this is that churches and religious communities in the Balkans have not opened their doors to women theologians who teach feminist theology and bring a female perspective to the process of interpreting the Bible and the Qur'an. Women started studying theology in former Yugoslavia in the 1970s, but only a few women occupy teaching positions at theological institutions and women themselves are still not ready to accept another woman's

authority. Both Catholic and Islamic female theologians are struggling to do their work within these contexts, because their work is not as valued as that of men. Finally, women are terrified of losing the positions they have acquired and would rather stick with "self-sacrificing micro-matriarchy" (wherein a woman sacrifices her time and life for children and family and in return expects respect and control over them) than seek full equality for women and men. It is rather difficult to go against the mainstream, male-dominated world within a male-dominated church or Muslim community.

Zilka Spahić-Šiljak

The Trap of Complementarity: John Paul II on Ephesians 5:22-33

The Gospel Innovation

Pope John Paul II stood against tradition in concluding from Ephesians 5:22-33 that "husband and wife are, in fact, subject to one another, mutually subordinated to one another."[22] He presented his interpretation publicly for the first time in 129 lectures on the theology of the body delivered

in his Wednesday audiences between 1979 and 1984, and then he continued to develop his interpretation of marriage and sexuality inspired by Ephesians 5:22-23 in many of his papal documents. In chapter 7 of his apostolic letter *Mulieris Dignitatem* (1988) he insists: "Whereas in the relationship between Christ and the Church the subjection is only on the part of the Church, in the relationship between husband and wife the

22. John Paul II, *Man and Woman He Created Them: A Theology of the Body* (Boston: Pauline Books & Media, 2006); see idem, *The Theology of the Body: Human Love in the Divine Plan* (Boston: Pauline Books & Media, 1997), 89.3.

'subjection' is not one-sided but mutual." The former pope calls equality in marriage "the gospel innovation."

The Deep Mystery

John Paul II interprets "the deep mystery" mentioned in Ephesians 5:32 as the theological and sacramental significance of a divinely ordained complementarity between husband and wife that extends from the spiritual to the physical. Christ's divine redemptive love expresses the essence of masculinity, that is, the free and loving pouring out of oneself toward "the other" that is life-giving and has a physical correlation in the capacity of the male body to penetrate and impregnate. On the other hand, the church's acceptance of Christ's love expresses the essence of femininity, that is, the free and loving "submission" to "the other" that is equally life-giving and has a physical correlation in the capacity of the female body to be penetrated and to be impregnated. The "deep mystery" of the theological complementarity of the sexes is the ultimate reason why the priest acting *in persona Christi* has to be male and why Mary, the symbol of the church, had to be female. In 2004, a teaching institute (the Theology of the Body Institute, *tobinstitute.org*) was founded in Pennsylvania with the goal of ensuring that the teachings of the now-St. John Paul II are promoted faithfully and effectively in order to bring about a world filled with men and women who freely embrace God's glorious plan for their sexuality.

My Critique

John Paul II's interpretation has the value of radically bringing into unity body and soul and, in so doing, breaking with centuries of a negative vision of sexuality linked to shame and guilt. It also has the value of explicitly defending the mutuality of the spouses and their equal dignity. His model, however, is an ideal construct that does not take into account the real bodies and the actual desires of many people that do not conform to binary heterosexuality. Furthermore, it reinscribes the stereotype of femininity as "being there" for the need of the man, ready to welcome and embrace his expression of "himself" but not to "express herself"; it also reinscribes the stereotype of masculinity as "unable to welcome," unable to be receptive to the desires, the needs, and the woman's unexpected expression of self. John Paul's "deep mystery" turns out to be an old prejudice: it effaces the unique personalities of real women in order to make them welcoming mirrors for the unique personalities of their men.

Teresa Forcades i Vila

Interpretations of Ephesians 5:21-33 in a Korean Protestant Christian Context

I want to focus on how five male pastors from mainstream, evangelically oriented Protestant churches in Korea interpret Ephesians 5:21-33: how they address the text's oppressive/liberative potentialities and the possible impact of their interpretations on Korean wo/men. Taken together, all five readings work to defend against criticisms of the admonition that wives should submit to their husbands. They seek to resolve the contradiction between this text's male-centeredness and the professed egalitarianism of Paul. Among their diverse refutations the most common argument is that the central issue is not male superiority but order.[23] Drawing on other biblical texts, such as Genesis 2; 1 Corinthians 11:3; and 1 Timothy 2:13, they argue that the patriarchal household order, with the husband alone holding authority, is ordained by G*d. Correspondingly, the wife's subjection signifies not inferiority and unconditional obedience but rather her "voluntary" acceptance of this order.[24]

As counterevidence against alleged sexism Ung-Ryul Ryu, Jong-Yun Lee, and Chung-Ryun Park also point to the supposed mutuality of obedience in 5:21.[25] Seong-Soo Nam, Ryu, and Yong-Jo Ha argue that the authority of the husband is redefined as sacrificial love and commitment.[26] Drawing on Genesis 2:18, Nam reinterprets the wives' subjection as a way of helping husbands on G*d's behalf.[27] Park claims that subjection signifies a role that is different but equal in the eyes of G*d.[28]

Despite their endeavors to disprove assertions of sexism, these pastors' interpretations do not escape a patriarchal framework since their theological position entails biblical inerrancy and literalism. Most important, they do not challenge the presumption that male-centered authoritarianism

23. Yong-Jo Ha, *Longing for Unity: An Exposition of Ephesians* (Seoul: Duranno Publishing, 1999), 288; Ung-Ryul Ryu, *Preaching Ephesians According to the Ten-Step Method of Writing* (Seoul: Duranno Academy, 2010), 184–88; Seong-Soo Nam, *An Exposition of Ephesians* (Seoul: Bookstones Publishing, 2014), 295; Chung-Ryun Park, *An Exposition of Ephesians: Abundant Grace and Guidance* (Seoul: Yebon Publishing, 1996), 515; Jong-Yun Lee, *An Exposition of Ephesians* (Seoul: Chung Hyun Publishing, 1991), 271.

24. Ryu, *Preaching Ephesians*, 183–84; Lee, *Exposition*, 271; Nam, *An Exposition*, 295.

25. Ryu, *Preaching Ephesians*, 182; Lee, *Exposition*, 272; Park, *Abundant Grace*, 512–13.

26. Nam, *An Exposition*, 297; Ryu, *Preaching Ephesians*, 188; Ha, *Longing for Unity*, 285–87.

27. Nam, *An Exposition*, 296.

28. Park, *Abundant Grace*, 512.

is a G*d-ordained order. For
wives to hold authority is
deemed a source of trouble.[29]
They do not seriously consider
why authority cannot be shared,
or why Ephesians commends
subjection for wives and love
for husbands despite the call to
mutual submission. Only Lee
addresses the latter, concluding
that such subjection is required
because wives tend to forget
obedience, neglecting their
husbands after bearing children
or becoming mothers-in-law.[30]

Notably, when considering
practical applications of
the text these authors do
not problematize wives'
oppressive experiences in
Korea's patriarchal household
order. Instead they excoriate
problems they see as deriving
from feminism,[31] highlighting
exceptional cases of domestic
abuse against husbands and
problematizing child-centered
household management.[32] In
addressing such problems they
stress that wives should be
subject to their husbands.

Nevertheless, these
interpretations still contain
potential arguments with which
to deconstruct the patriarchal/
oppressive nature of the text.
Significantly, they (1) do not
admit husbands' superiority,
(2) favor wives' equality and
autonomy before G*d, and
(3) emphasize the element
of commitment implicit in
husbands' authority. Yet,
being based on inerrancy and
literalism, these interpretations
serve to solidify the male-
centered authoritarian order of
Korean Christian households.
Therefore, to achieve the
practical goal of equality in
those households it is imperative
that we adopt a critical feminist
interpretative method capable of
analyzing this text's patriarchal
nature and articulating its
oppressive impact.

Young Ra Rhee

29. Ha, *Longing for Unity*, 287; Lee, *Exposition*, 281; Nam, *An Exposition*, 297; Park, *Abundant Grace*, 509.
30. Lee, *Exposition*, 272–73.
31. Ibid.; Park, *Abundant Grace*, 510, 518.
32. Ha, *Longing for Unity*, 284; Lee, *Exposition*, 272; Park, *Abundant Grace*, 516, 520–21.

Reading Ephesians 5 in Africa

In my recent experience of Nigerian world Christianity, one of the conversations revealed the bed-fellowship between heterosexism and patri-kyriachy. It was about Ephesians 5 as a Christian teaching on marital relationships. While the NRSV includes v. 21 in its "Christian Household" section, the wo/men I had this discussion with were using the NIV, which excludes v. 21 from its "Wives and Husbands" section.

The gist of the argument was that Ephesians 5:22-33 sums up G*d's intention for Christian marriage: a relationship of a Christian man and woman involving sex and reproduction. The submission of wife to husband was conceived as divinely ordained: he is head of the household and the husband's love for his wife is modeled on Christ's selfless love for the church (referred to as "she" in NIV). Explicitly, the modeling of marriage on an unbalanced power relationship and construing that as G*d's will could be a not-so-subtle manipulation by the privileged gender, which conceives its relationship to other genders in terms of unaccountable domination.

"So wives should not love their husbands but as a slave to her owner; a wife should obediently submit to him despite the possibility that she inwardly despises him? Meanwhile, the husband insists on getting his own way while ensuring that the wife obeys without question; he should love her as a master loves the slave he owns?"—I inquired.

One of the pastors corrected me: "No, it's not like that. Of course the wife belongs to her husband but submission is based on the fact that G*d has endowed headship and wisdom on husbands as G*d's representatives in Christian marriages. So women's submission is the acknowledgment of such blessing. These husbands are also priests of the family altar."

The women supporting this kind of reading further argued that as long as their husbands cared and provided for them, submitting to them was a natural expression of their love. These ordained women somehow visualized their ministry and marriage as integrated. Their ordained husbands therefore also became heads of their parishes.

"What happens when the husband dies?" I asked. Since the woman's head is her husband, how does she survive headless? In most cases divorce is not an option unless it is the husband's desire; then it becomes biblical (Mark 10:4; Deut 24:1). If the employment hierarchies are evoked as models, then it would be wise for churches to consider how long such a power-imbalanced institution can be sustained.

When a wife's submission is modeled on the church's

total surrender to Christ and the husband's love on Christ's authority, and the church reduced to a submissive slave, several assumptions remain unchallenged. First, the church as the forgiven body of Christ remains sinfully dependent on the sinless Savior's gracious love and forgiveness. Does that mean that wives are intrinsically more sinful than their husbands? Second, the call to husbands to love indicates that, while wives depend on their husbands, the husbands are independently self-sufficient, yet they sacrificially love their wives. Are husbands the sinless liberators of their wives, as Christ is of the church?

This one-sided call to submission instead of being "subject to one another in reverence for Christ" (v. 21) or "[living] in love" (v. 1) means that marriage is like slavery, with wives as bonded slaves. Husbands' call to love their wives could be read through Exodus 21:2-6, which commands slaves to love their masters, but in reverse: as "a legal rather than an emotional concept: it indicates intent as well as consent."[33] What role would sexual "union" play in such "love"? Certainly it would not be mutual love-making climaxing in exciting renewal of reciprocated at-one-ment but rather a submissive sexual hospitality and manipulative self-giving by a sexual slave to her master to ensure her means of livelihood.

How can it be expected that such an experience could be sustained for life? How can such a hierarchal human economic institution be considered a sacrament that embodies and testifies to the encounter with God? How can it be the "sanctuary" that nurtures children who should encounter God through their parents? Unless critically read within the socio-cultural and historical context, this text does not bring out the real image of God as iconed by the Rublev[34] Trinity.

Fulata Moyo

33. Athalya Brenner uses this argument in relation to Ruth and Naomi. Athalya Brenner, "Ruth as the Foreign Worker and the Politics of Exogamy," in *Ruth and Esther*, ed. Athalya Brenner, FCB, 2nd ser. (Sheffield: Sheffield Academic, 1999), 158–62, at 159.

34. The famous Rublev icon depicts three angels embodying the spirituality of unity, peace, harmony, and mutual love and humility. Gabriel Bunge, *The Rublev Trinity: The Icon of the Trinity by the Monk-Painter Andrei Rublev* (Crestwood, NY: St Vladimir's Seminary Press, 2007), 13–14.

If we read the rhetoric of Ephesians 5:21-33 "against its kyriarchal grain" we can assume that the wo/men in the "community of the wise" understood their *ekklēsial* identity differently and that it is this difference, rooted in their baptism, that the author seeks to overcome. Reading the author's text against the grain, we can reconstruct their understanding of the *ekklēsia* as follows (see pp. lxxvi–lxxx above):

> The *ekklēsia* is the body of Messiah Jesus (5:23).
> The *ekklēsia* is beloved by the Messiah (5:24).
> Hence all members of the *ekklēsia* are the recipients of the love of
>   Messiah Jesus, who gave himself for the *ekklēsia* (5:25).
> All members of the *ekklēsia* are cleansed and sanctified through bap-
>   tism, "the washing" of the water by the word (5:26).
> The *ekklēsia* is honored, holy, and unblemished (5:27).
> The *ekklēsia* is loved and cherished by the *Kyrios* (5:29).
> All members of the *ekklēsia* are members of the Messiah's flesh and
>   bones (5:30).

Hence all wo/men, whether married or not, slave or free, fathers or mothers, are full and equal members of the *ekklēsia* of the wise. It must have been especially the freeborn married women, the *matronae*, who insisted: We all have been baptized into the Messiah; there are neither Jewish nor Gentile, slave nor free wo/men, there is neither husband and wife, for we are all one in the Messiah Jesus (Gal 3:28).

We have to remember that *ekklēsia* does not mean church but the decision-making people's assembly of full citizens. Since six of the nine references to *ekklēsia* in Ephesians are found in the admonitions to wives in chapter 5, wo/men must have caused a special problem with respect to the *ekklēsia*. The author's emphasis on "subjection" rather than on "love" indicates that this problem is one of submission. This tells us something about the author's understanding, not only of married wo/men, but also of the *ekklēsia*, the people's assembly. Just as in the Roman political system the decision-making *ekklēsiai* of the city-states in Asia Minor were subjected to the emperor, so also the messianic *ekklēsia* is subjected to Messiah Jesus.[35]

However, the author seems to want to soften this relation of domination and does so by stressing that as the Messiah loves the *ekklēsia*, so also the husband should love his wife. In any case Messiah Jesus becomes

---

35. See Young-Ho Park, *Paul's Ekklesia as a Civic Assembly: Understanding the People of God in Their Politico-Social World* (Tübingen: Mohr Siebeck, 2015), 26–84.

stereotyped as imperial male ruler while the *ekklēsia*, the democratic citizen assembly, becomes stereotyped as subjected female/feminine subaltern. This kyriarchalizing of the relation between the Messiah and the *ekklēsia* is confirmed by the body-image of Messiah Jesus for the community of the wise wo/men. Whereas Paul did not distinguish between the head and body of the Messiah, Ephesians identifies Messiah Jesus with the "head" as distinct from the body.

Children and Slave Wo/men: Obey (6:1-9)

In contrast to the exhortation to freeborn wives, that to children and slave wo/men does not use the Greek verb ὑποτάσσεσθαι, "to be subordinate." Instead, the verb that is used is ὑπακούειν, "to obey." Although Cynthia Briggs Kittredge has shown that there is not much difference between the two verbs, "the verb ὑποτάσσεσθαι is used in a political context to mean 'to be subject.'"[36] Both words have a similar meaning but are differently accentuated. Both exhortations are taken over from Colossians, but the injunction for slave wo/men is greatly abbreviated.

First: As in Colossians, so also in Ephesians (freeborn) children are told to "obey their parents in the Lord, for this is just," but Ephesians omits "in everything" and substitutes "this is pleasing in the Lord" with "for this is just." To underscore this, Ephesians cites Exodus 20:12 and adds a comment: "this is the first commandment with a promise" (v. 2). In v. 4, Ephesians adds to the admonition for fathers, "do not provoke your children to rage, but nourish them with education and knowledge of the Lord."

Two things are remarkable here. On the one hand it is fathers, rather than mothers, who are admonished to educate their children.[37] This is surprising because one would expect the wo/men in the community of the wise to be well versed in the knowledge of G*d and hence also able to teach their children. However, it is not in the interest of the author to draw the hearer's/reader's attention to such an assumption after having just the*logically elaborated the subordinate position of the wife. On the other hand, according to the author, children, both boys and girls (τέκνα), are to be educated. In the community of the wise, *all* children are to be educated. Cecilia Wassen has pointed out that in the Qumran *Rule of the Congregation* (1Q Sa) all children are similarly included "in

36. Briggs Kittredge, *Community and Authority*, 43–44.
37. See the arguments for the translation "fathers," rather than "fathers and mothers," in Andrew T. Lincoln, *Ephesians*, WBC 42 (Dallas: Word, 1990), 406–7.

Ephesians 6:1-9

⁶:¹Children, obey your parents in the Lord, for this is right. ²"Honor your father and mother"—this is the first commandment with a promise: ³"so that it may be well with you and you may live long on the earth."

⁴And fathers, do not provoke your children to anger, but bring them up in the discipline and instruction of the Lord.

⁵Slaves, obey your earthly masters with fear and trembling, in singleness of heart, as you obey Christ; ⁶not only while being watched, and in order to please them, but as slaves of Christ, doing the will of God from the heart. ⁷Render service with enthusiasm, as to the Lord and not to men and women, ⁸knowing that whatever good we do, we will receive the same again from the Lord, whether we are slaves or free.

⁹And, masters, do the same to them. Stop threatening them, for you know that both of you have the same Master in heaven, and with him there is no partiality.

the instruction 'in the statutes of the covenant' and 'their judgements.' The phrase 'from children to women' . . . (1Q Sa I 4) makes it certain that girls are also included. The inclusion of all children, girls and boys, in the instruction in 1 Q Sa I4 thus strengthens the probability that girls are also to be instructed."[38]

It is of course true that well-to-do wo/men are better educated than the average wo/man.[39] (This is also a truism that applies to men.) While we know of more educated men than women in antiquity, it is not necessarily the case that more men were educated, but only that more writings of elite men were preserved than those of educated wo/men about whom we often know only through the writings of elite men that were quoted and preserved.

Second: The exhortation to slave wo/men is also taken over from Colossians 3:22-25, but in a somewhat different form. The greater part of the text is addressed here to slave wo/men in the household. They are commanded to obedience and enthusiastic service in the name of G*d and Messiah Jesus. Commentators underscore and praise the the*logical reasons given, not recognizing that they reinforce and sanction slavery. They stress that whether we are slave wo/men or free wo/men does not matter because we all are rewarded by the Lord/*Kyrios* for the good we do.

38. Cecilia Wassen, *Women in the Damascus Document*, AcBib 21 (Atlanta: SBL Press, 2005), 166.

39. See Craig Keener, "Women's Education and Public Speech in Antiquity," *JETS* 50 (2007): 747–50.

Just as the injunction to freeborn husbands to love (Eph 5:25-33; Col 3:19) does not undermine the traditional kyriarchal structure but reinforces it, so also slave masters are not required to have *agapē* for their slave wo/men. Pointing out that masters are admonished here to stop threatening their slaves underscores the requirement being put on slaves to submit. What is more, why justify such words to slave wo/men in Ephesians by pointing out that masters are admonished here too? "Stop threatening them, for you know that both of you have the same Master in heaven, and with him there is no partiality," masters are told. Why are they told to stop threatening them but not to recognize them as sisters and brothers who must be recognized as free persons? To liken G*d to a slave master is blasphemy and contradicts the emphasis in Ephesians on *agapē*-love. Rather than seeking to "redeem" such a violent text because it is in Scripture, we need to label it: "Caution! Dangerous to your health and survival!"

Finally, in such a kyriarchal structure and mind-set the exhortations of Ephesians to the whole community to love one another would mean something different to freeborn men than to slave wo/men, to freeborn husbands than to freeborn wives who are called not to love but to subordination. Indeed, if *agapē* requires the freedom to love, which is not possible under compulsion and force, then the fulfillment of the much-touted "love ethic" of the letter is not possible for the majority of those "in Messiah Jesus"—it is not imaginable for freeborn or slave wo/men but only for *kyrioi*, or freeborn elite men.

Slavery Still a Problem Today

Although some do recognize the bloody history of slavery that biblical texts such as Ephesians have legitimated, most believe that slavery is in the past and that America is the land of the free. Yet the reality is: slavery not only exists but flourishes throughout the world today. While slavery is no longer legal, it is practiced everywhere in the world. It is estimated that approximately twenty-seven million people are in bondage worldwide; that is more than twice as many people as were taken from Africa in chains during the entire 350 years of the African slave trade. Human trafficking is one of the most profitable criminal enterprises of our time, along with drugs and guns, and it yields tens of billions of dollars in revenues worldwide.[40]

To tell contemporary Christians trafficked as sex-slaves to "obey your earthly masters with fear and trembling, in singleness of heart, as you obey Christ" goes against all sense of justice and decency. To exhort them to "render service with enthusiasm, as to the Lord" is obscene when they are raped and mistreated many times daily. To preach "obey and render service with enthusiasm" in the name of Sacred Scripture is a crime! If we all can agree that slavery is a crime today, why do we justify its existence in the past?

In light of the scholarly consensus on the *Haustafel* as a work of political philosophy, the question whether Paul or only the post-Pauline tradition introduced and advocated this Greco-Roman "pattern of kyriarchal submission" has become even more pressing. Scholars usually address this question by arguing that in his letter to Philemon[41] and in 1 Corinthians 7:21-24[42] Paul advocates that slaves should be made free and be treated as "beloved." However, both texts are so ambiguous that equally as many scholars argue that Paul insists that they remain in slavery. Thus, the opacity of Paul's meaning and the ambiguity of the Pauline texts on slave wo/men's behavior made it possible for the post-Pauline tradition to plausibly claim Paul's teachings on slavery for its own legitimization of slave wo/men's unfreedom.

While it is debated whether Paul advocated the freedom of slave wo/men, there is no doubt that Paul's teaching used the metaphor of slavery to characterize the past and present situation of Christians, the religious realm, and the power

---

40. Ron Soodalter, "A Blight on The Nation: Slavery in Today's America," in *Quests for Freedom: Biblical—Historical—Contemporary*, ed. Michael Welker (Neukirchen Vluyn: Neukirchener Verlag, 2015), 21–31. See also Bernadette Brooten, ed., *Beyond Slavery: Overcoming Its Religious and Sexual Legacies* (New York: Macmillan, 2010).

41. It is debated whether Onesimus was a runaway slave, a slave sent to Paul by Philemon, or no slave at all. See Allen Dwight Callahan, "Paul's Epistle to Philemon: Towards an Alternative Interpretation," *HTR* 86 (1993): 357–76, and idem, *Embassy of Onesimus: The Letter of Paul to Philemon*, The New Testament in Context (Valley Forge, PA: Trinity Press International, 1997); Peter Lampe, "Keine Sklavenflucht des Onesimus," *ZNW* 76 (1985): 135–37; Sarah C. Winter, "Philemon," in *Searching the Scriptures*, vol. 2: *A Feminist Commentary*, ed. Elisabeth Schüssler Fiorenza (New York: Crossroad, 1994), 301–12.

42. The problem of interpreting 1 Corinthians 7:21b is caused by its brachyology, that is, the omission of an object for the phrase μᾶλλον χρῆσαι, meaning "rather use," which one can supplement either with "freedom" or with "slavery."

of sin. Paul's metaphorical use of "slavery" erases the brutal, lived realities of slavery as well as the power differences between slave and free wo/men. It seems that slavery as a socio-political institution and its practices are religiously legitimated, while at the same time the metaphorization of slavery by Paul collapses the differences between slave and free wo/men.

In place of critical analysis and discussion of the replacement of freedom with *agapē* and its consequences, scholars have offered arguments that defend Paul. In a spirited reply to Richard Horsley's claims regarding the egalitarian nature of the *ekklēsia*, Stanley K. Stowers, for example, insists that the understanding of slavery as evil does not come from the Bible but stems from modern Enlightenment thinking that understands the person as "autonomous and self-governing."[43] In Paul's scriptures, Stowers argues, "slavery is pervasive, brutal, and sanctioned by God." The Hebrew Bible not only allows slavery but also speaks of the Israelites as slaves of G*d. Hence, Stowers concludes, "it seems that those who have seen

Paul as an opponent of slavery have not come to terms with the scripture that Paul held as authoritative."[44]

Stowers seems not to recognize, however, that it is he who construes the interpretation of Galatians 3:28 in terms of a modern understanding of the person as autonomous from social roles. Slavery is not a "social role," I would argue, but a kyriarchal institution that robs people of their humanity and personhood. Stowers also falls prey to the same modern fallacy of which he accuses others when he assumes that modern persons, but not ancient Mediterranean people, could envision a life in freedom. This overlooks the information we have on slave wo/men's uprisings in antiquity. Fugitive slave wo/men constituted a serious problem and massive slave revolts took place between 140 and 70 BCE.[45] These uprisings, which "assumed the scale of a war, with thousands of armed men on both sides and pitched battles between armies, sieges, and occupation of cities, were not fought in order to become free of 'slave roles' and find one's 'true self,' but were fought for freedom from

43. Stanley K. Stowers, "Paul and Slavery: A Response," *Semeia* 83/84 (1998): 295–311.
44. Ibid., 306.
45. See also Keith Bradley, *Slavery and Rebellion in the Roman World, 140 BC to 70 BC* (Bloomington: Indiana University Press, 1989).

the dehumanizing bondage of slavery."[46] To suggest that ancient Mediterranean slave wo/men could not envision being free is tantamount to modernist prejudice.

To summarize: the understanding that emerges if one reads Paul, the post-Pauline letters, or the whole Christian Testament in a way that emphasizes the conceptual aspects of teachings about freedom is different from what one derives by reading texts as rhetorical arguments that engage actual problems and opinions. While an analysis in terms of Paul's concepts and thought focuses on the great apostle who teaches with authority and has the power to enforce his teachings, a rhetorical approach sees Paul's as one voice among many within a rhetorical debate.[47]

By defending the teachings of Paul, scholars not only avoid asking whether Paul's teaching was accepted at the time but also fail to explore the consequences of his metaphorical use of slavery in a spiritualizing way. Hence they are unable to address either the violence of unfreedom legitimated by pro-slavery scriptural texts or to ask whether such kyriarchal violence

is intrinsic to Pauline the*logy. Moreover, by identifying Paul's teaching and conceptuality with early Christian beliefs and practices they overlook not only that his "teaching and conceptuality" is argumentative rhetoric but also that there were alternative voices and options that sought to secure and maintain slave wo/men's freedom.

In short, the "defense of Paul and Scripture" tends to resort to a spiritualizing and moralizing approach to freedom in terms of love and to an antiquarian understanding of interpretation that maintains that the desire for freedom and equality is a modern post-Enlightenment projection and that slave wo/men in antiquity were not capable of such desire, although the Roman slave wars and slave resistances document just the opposite. When scholarly arguments neglect the "other" submerged voices in the debate inscribed in the Pauline tradition, or when they neglect to bring slave wo/men and their desires for freedom into view, they re-inscribe familiar prejudices against slave wo/men as "things without voices."

If we assume, instead, that slave wo/men took the

---

46. Allen Dwight Callahan, "Slave Resistance in Classical Antiquity," *Semeia* 83/84 (1998): 133–51, at 143.

47. See my book *Rhetoric and Ethic: The Politics of Biblical Studies* (Minneapolis: Fortress, 1999).

baptismal confession "neither slave nor free wo/men in the messianic corporation" at face value and insisted on their equality, we then must carefully examine the assumptions and methods that allow scholars to rule out such an argument by means of their theoretical framework and to hide behind the apologetic argument that abolition of the institution of slavery was impossible or unthinkable at the time.

Placing slave wo/men at the center of attention requires that one move from a descriptive or apologetic analysis of Ephesians to a rhetorical analysis that pays attention not only to the author and their statements but also to the audience whom the text addresses, the rhetorical problem it seeks to overcome, and the socio-political situation and symbolic universe shared by author and audience. Such a rhetorical approach calls for an ethics of interpretation and a hermeneutics of critical evaluation to be applied to biblical texts such as Ephesians that function as authoritative Scripture in Christian communities today.

A shift of attention from the text of Ephesians to slave wo/men as historical agents requires a shift from a history of ideas to a history of struggles, from text to context. For instance, in his magisterial work *Freedom in the Making of Western Culture*, Orlando Patterson argues that "freedom was socially constructed—not discovered . . . in a specific pair of struggles generated by slavery."[48] Kurt Raaflaub has argued, moreover, that the political notion of freedom was articulated in the context of the Persian wars, when the isonomic Greek *polis* resisted occupation and domination by an authoritarian monarchical empire that had quite different value systems and social-political structures. This confrontation and conflict were then understood in terms of freedom and slavery; the conflict strengthened the *ethos* of the isonomic *polis* as the assembly of free and equal citizens.[49] The explorations of the concept of freedom by both scholars stress that it needs to be understood in terms of struggles against subjection and slavery.

Attention to the democratic language of *ekklēsia* and the subordination discourses of empire in Ephesians and in the Pauline tradition seeks to expand the resources for a feminist discussion of slavery and freedom. It will caution us against understanding freedom too quickly in terms of relationality and self-giving love.

---

48. Orlando Patterson, *Freedom in the Making of Western Culture* (New York: Basic Books, 1991), 3.

49. Kurt Raaflaub, *Die Entdeckung der Freiheit. Zur historischen Semantik und Gesellschaftsgeschichte eines politischen Grundbegriffes der Griechen* (Munich: Beck, 1985), 320–22.

Articulating biblical the*logy
in terms of the tension between
the rhetoric and *ethos* of empire
and *ekklēsia* as the democratic
assembly of full citizens allows
us to trace the interaction of
multiple perspectives and makes
possible a discourse that can
bring those who are historically
silenced and marginalized, such
as slave wo/men, into view.
In the current moment, when
the rhetoric of the "free world"
and the "empires of evil,"
"winners and losers," "good and
evil," "orthodoxy and heresy"
threatens to exclude and to
do violence, such a the*logical
discourse is urgently needed.

If early Christians did not
have the power to abolish the
system of slavery, as many
scholars have pointed out, what
kind of historical-rhetorical
situation does the rhetoric of the
household code in Ephesians
address? Scholars stress that in
contrast to the ancient household
code tradition, slave wo/men
are addressed in Ephesians as
subjects and members of the
community. We have seen that
Philo speaks of such a Jewish
community in his description
of the "contemplative"
or "philosophical" life

of the Therapeutae and
Therapeutrides.[50] Philo stresses
that this ascetic community has
no slaves to wait upon them, as
they consider that the ownership
of servants is entirely against
nature. Nature, they believe,
has created all to be free, but the
wrongful and covetous acts of
some who pursued that source
of inequality have imposed their
yoke and invested the stronger
with power over the weaker.[51]
Instead of slave wo/men, young
freeborn men served at table at
their communal meals.

Philo speaks in a similar
fashion about the Essenes,
a Jewish group that is often
identified with the Qumran
community:

> Not a single slave is found
> among them, but all are
> free, exchanging services
> with each other and they
> denounce the owners of
> slaves, not merely for their
> injustice in outraging the
> law of equality, but also for
> their impiety in annulling
> the stature of Nature, who,
> mother-like, has born and
> reared all alike, and created
> them genuine brothers, not
> in mere names but in very
> reality.[52]

50. See Joan E. Taylor, "The Women 'Priests' of Philo's *De Vita Contemplativa*: Reconstructing the Therapeutae," in *On the Cutting Edge: The Study of Women in Biblical Worlds*, ed. Jane Schaberg, Alice Bach, and Esther Fuchs (New York: Continuum, 2004), 102–22.

51. Philo, *De vita contemplativa*, 70, in *Philo: On the Contemplative Life*, ed. and trans. F. H. Colson (Cambridge: Harvard University Press, 1941).

52. Philo, *Quod omnis probus liber sit*, 7, quoted in Peter Garnsey, *Ideas of Slavery from Aristotle to Augustine* (Cambridge: Cambridge University Press, 1996), 78.

Moreover, Roman slavery condoned manumission by individuals and corporate manumission by communities. Formal manumission reintegrated slave wo/men into society by making them Roman citizens. Although the system of slavery was entrenched in the Roman Empire, the manumission of individual slave wo/men, as well as corporate manumission, was widespread. This willingness to free slaves may not have been for humanitarian reasons, but it indicates that Roman slavery was not automatically a lifelong state.[53]

In light of these two discernible discourses of manumission—the ethical and the legal—two scenarios can be envisioned to have been in play in the messianic *ekklēsia* of Ephesians. One is the *ethos* of equality and freedom in the house-assembly and the attendant manumission of slaves within the community, and the other is the practice of buying the freedom of slave wo/men who belonged to households not yet "in (the sphere of) Messiah Jesus," either by individual patrons or with the funds of the congregation. The fact that this dual possibility existed in the *ekklēsia* at the end of the first and beginning of the second centuries is apparent, for instance, in the injunction

of 1 Timothy 6:1-2, a text that is dated around the same time as Ephesians. The first verse tells slave wo/men to "regard their masters as worthy of all honor, so that the name of G*d and the teaching may not be blasphemed," whereas v. 2 is addressed to those who have "believing masters." In both cases the *ethos* of slavery is rhetorically reinforced. On the one hand, slave wo/men who complain about and call for the repentance of masters who have fallen back into the sin of the kyriarchal practices of slavery are told "not to be disrespectful" to them on the grounds that they are "brothers," or members of the *ekklēsia*. On the other hand, slave wo/men who may have pleaded to be bought free from slave masters outside the community are told to respect them.

Two examples should suffice. The first scenario of slave wo/men asking to be treated as equals in the house-assembly is similar to that of the Therapeutae. This demand would have made sense both in cases in which the whole household was baptized "into Messiah Jesus" and in house-assemblies whose members were from different households. They did not need to undergo a formal manumission because the baptismal affirmation "for freedom Christ has set us free"

---

53. See J. Albert Harrill, *The Manumission of Slaves in Early Christianity*, HUT (Tübingen: Mohr, 1995).

had given them equal standing in the *ekklēsia*. In this case the social-status differences between slave master/mistress and slave wo/men would have been replaced by the notion that all the baptized are "siblings" and "beloved" children of G*d. Hence, on the basis of the *ethos* of equality and freedom, "mutuality and respect among the different members of the household was to be practiced."[54] However, unlike that of Ephesians, 1 Timothy's exhortation admonishes slave wo/men and not masters. It does not rebuke the masters for failing to live the messianic community *ethos* of equality and freedom but rather uses that *ethos* to reinforce the submissive behavior of Christian slave wo/men.

The second scenario is referred to by Ignatius of Antioch (ca. 35–108 CE). Writing to Bishop Polycarp in Smyrna, Asia Minor, he testifies to the early Christian practice of corporate manumission, although he is against it.

> Do not behave arrogantly towards slaves, either male or female. But let them not be puffed up. Rather let them be enslaved all the more to the glory of G*d. Let them not desire to be manumitted out of the money in the common chest, so that they may not be found slaves of desire.[55]

It seems that the messianic Jesus *ekklēsiai* had adopted the Roman practice of manumission to enact the second scenario, which required the formal manumission of slave wo/men who belonged to masters outside the messianic community. Slave wo/men could be and regularly were given their freedom in the Roman Empire. The widespread manumission of slaves was a distinctive feature of the Roman institution of slavery.[56] Archaeological evidence also suggests that corporate manumission would have been practiced by private associations, in cultic places such as Delphi, and by Jewish synagogues. According to J. Albert Harrill, evidence for this practice is found among Jewish communities all over the ancient world, from Egypt to the north shores of the Black Sea. Jewish synagogues had common chests. Harrill writes: "These chests functioned institutionally in ways similar to those in a Roman collegium . . . which one or more officers of the association

---

54. See Reidar Aasgard, *"My Beloved Brothers and Sisters!" Christian Siblingship in Paul*, JSNTSup 265 (London: T&T Clark, 2004); Klaus Schäfer, *Gemeinde als "Bruderschaft": Ein Beitrag zum Kirchenverständnis des Paulus* (Frankfurt am Main: Lang, 1989).

55. Ign. *Poly.* 4.3.

56. Valerie Hope, "Status and Identity in the Roman World," in *Experiencing Rome: Culture, Identity, and Power in the Roman Empire*, ed. Janet Huskinson (New York: Routledge, 2000), 125–52, at 129.

managed. Hellenistic private associations also operated a common fund."[57]

Harrill suggests that Ignatius saw three dangers in the corporate practice of manumission that he seeks to avoid with this exhortation. First, there was the fear that some would join the messianic community only for the sake of money, expecting that the *ekklēsia* would buy their freedom. Second, there was the danger of slander against the messianic *ekklēsia* for subverting slavery. Third, there was the potential problem of rivalry and competition among the different house-assemblies in a metropolitan area that Ignatius sought to unify under the authority of one bishop.[58]

Edwin A. Judge has pointed to a fourth possible reason why such practices of manumission were curtailed or rejected by the writers of the so-called household code tradition:

> With regard to the house-hold obligation, the NT writers are unanimous; its bonds and conventions must at all costs be maintained. . . . There is of course . . . the interest of the patronal class

. . . but the primary reason, no doubt, is that the entrenched rights of the household as a religious and social unit offered the Christians the best possible security for their existence as a group. Any weakening here would thus be a potentially devastating blow to their own cohesion, as well as having revolutionary implications from the point of view of the public authorities.[59]

Judge sees correctly that the rhetoric of the "household code" pays deference to the interest of the "patronal" or, better, the "master" class. Judge's argument presupposes that the house-assembly was governed by the "principles of fraternity" and that it presented a threat only "if enthusiastic members failed to contain their principles within the privacy of the association and thus were led into political indiscretions or offenses against the hierarchy of the household."[60] Such an argument overlooks the fact that the conversion of freeborn wo/men, slave wo/men, and young people who belonged to the household of an unconverted *pater familias* already constituted

57. J. Albert Harrill, "Ignatius, *Ad Polycarp* 4.3 and the Corporate Manumission of Christian Slaves," *JECS* 1 (1993): 103–42, at 122, with references.

58. Ibid., 136.

59. Edwin A. Judge, *The Social Patterns of Christian Groups in the First Century: Some Prolegomena to the Study of New Testament Ideas of Social Organization* (London: Tyndale Press, 1960), 75–77.

60. Ibid., 76.

a potential political offense against the kyriarchal order. This had to have been considered an infringement of the political order, for the kyriarchal order of the house was considered the paradigm for that of the state. Since the kyriarchal *familia* was the nucleus of the state, conversion of the subordinated members of the household, who were expected to share in the religion of the *pater familias,* already constituted a subversive act. Buying them freedom from their masters, however, would not have undermined but would rather have been in line with the established Roman order.

The early Christian assertion "for freedom Christ has set us free" must have engendered a concrete practice of actual freedom from slavery. As I have argued in *In Memory of Her,* slave wo/men who joined the messianic community expected to be treated as free persons.[61] Such expectations were engendered by the Christian proclamation that all members of the community were "set free by Christ/Messiah." Such formulas occur again and again in the Pauline letters: "You were bought with a price; do not become human slaves" (1 Cor 6:20; 7:23). The goal of the call to join the messianic community is freedom: "You were called to freedom" (Gal 5:13), because "where the Spirit of the Lord is, there is freedom" (2 Cor 3:17). To argue that wo/men within messianic communities who insisted on their call to freedom had only "a superficial understanding of the gospel" is to minimize the effects of this the*logical rhetoric of freedom in a Greco-Roman context where both slavery and manumission were commonly accepted institutional practices.[62]

Liberation from slavery to the dehumanizing powers of sin, slave law, and death—from the conditions of the present "evil age"—has "freedom" as its goal and purpose.[63] Therefore slave wo/men who were baptized into Christ must have heard this proclamation of freedom as performative rhetoric asserting that among those baptized "there were neither slave nor freed wo/men" (Gal 3:28).[64] *Agapē*-love without freedom can easily result in continuing slavery.

61. Schüssler Fiorenza, *In Memory of Her,* 251–84.

62. James E. Crouch, *The Origin and Intention of the Colossian Haustafel* (Göttingen: Vandenhoeck & Ruprecht, 1972), 127.

63. Hans Dieter Betz, *Galatians,* Hermeneia (Philadelphia: Fortress, 1979), 255.

64. Elisabeth Schüssler Fiorenza, "Slave Wo/men and Freedom: Some Methodological Reflections," in *Empowering Memory and Movement: Thinking and Working across Borders* (Minneapolis: Fortress, 2014), 447–71.

The *Ekklēsia* in Struggle (6:10-20)

Ephesians 6:10-20 is the concluding argument in the section 5:15–6:20, and it is followed by a short greeting and wish of peace. The martial imagery of 6:10-20 is startling and unique within the argument of the epistle. The only other place it is found is in 4:8, where Messiah/Christ is pictured as a mighty warrior who takes captive the otherworldly forces of darkness.

This passage functions in a twofold way. On the one hand this concluding segment is summing up the whole section on the "*Ekklēsia* of the Wise" (5:15–6:20) by elaborating the spiritual struggles and powers of the *ekklēsia*. On the other hand, the segment Ephesians 6:10-20 also functions in rhetorical terms as a peroration, which sums up the whole letter. In classical rhetoric the final part of a speech/treatise had two main goals: to summarize and remind the audience/recipients of the main points of the speech/message and to appeal to their emotions and solicit their goodwill.

Elaborating the Spiritual Struggles of the Ekklēsia

The Spiritual Armor of the Ekklēsia. Ephesians 6:10-17, which consists of a single sentence in Greek and is followed by a concluding segment, 6:18-20, asserts first the necessity to go into spiritual battle with G*d's weaponry (6:10-13). Second, Ephesians 6:14-17 elaborates the kind of armor the members of the *ekklēsia* should put on as soldiers. Their weapons are the girdle of truth, the breastplate of righteousness. They are called to shoe their feet with the gospel of peace and to take up the shield of faith, the helmet of salvation, and the sword of the Spirit (which is the word of G*d). Finally, in vv. 18-20 the author refers to Colossians 4:3-4, with the call to prayerful persistent vigilance. Their prayer should include the author, who as the ambassador of the gospel is "in bonds." They should pray that "Paul" may continue to "speak boldly to make known the mystery of the gospel" (vv. 19-20).

These metaphorical references to armor, soldiers, and battle probably evoke in the imaginations of readers the image of male soldiers, since the literature of all centuries is replete with depictions of men cultivating and exercising the martial virtues on the battlefield. However, this image and stereotypical assumption of war as an exclusively "masculine" purview must be questioned if we are to be able to understand the text as addressed to all members of the gathering of the wise. Feminist

Ephesians 6:10-20

¹⁰Finally, be strong in the Lord and in the strength of his power. ¹¹Put on the whole armor of God, so that you may be able to stand against the wiles of the devil. ¹²For our struggle is not against enemies of blood and flesh, but against the rulers, against the authorities, against the cosmic powers of this present darkness, against the spiritual forces of evil in the heavenly places. ¹³Therefore take up the whole armor of God, so that you may be able to withstand on that evil day, and having done everything, to stand firm. ¹⁴Stand therefore, and fasten the belt of truth around your waist, and put on the breastplate of righteousness. ¹⁵As shoes for your feet put on whatever will make you ready to proclaim the gospel of peace. ¹⁶With all of these, take the shield of faith, with which you will be able to quench all the flaming arrows of the evil one. ¹⁷Take the helmet of salvation, and the sword of the Spirit, which is the word of God.

¹⁸Pray in the Spirit at all times in every prayer and supplication. To that end keep alert and always persevere in supplication for all the saints. ¹⁹Pray also for me, so that when I speak, a message may be given to me to make known with boldness the mystery of the gospel, ²⁰for which I am an ambassador in chains. Pray that I may declare it boldly, as I must speak.

scholars have reexamined classical sources to uncover the complex but underexplored relationship between wo/men and war in ancient Greece and Rome.⁶⁵ They have documented that wo/men played an active role in battle, displaying martial virtues in both real and mythological combat. Hence we can assume that the wo/men in the *ekklēsia* of the wise could easily connect with this metaphor and imagine themselves as donning such armor.⁶⁶

Tet Li Lau has pointed out that the use of martial imagery is a common practice for describing the life of philosophers as battle and struggle.⁶⁷ But whereas the Stoic philosophers stress self-sufficiency and self-reliance as well as focusing on the solitary individual, Ephesians argues for mutual cooperation and interdependence. To put on the armor of G*d

65. See Jacqueline Fabre-Serris and Alison Keith, eds., *Women and War in Antiquity* (Baltimore: Johns Hopkins University Press, 2015).

66. For the metaphoric communication of the political in Ephesians, see Eckhart Reinmuth, *Neues Testament, Theologie und Gesellschaft* (Stuttgart: Kohlhammer, 2011), 296–311.

67. Tet Li Lau, *The Politics of Peace: Ephesians, Dio Chrysostom and the Confucian Four Books* (Leiden: Brill, 2010), 136–56.

(6:11) recalls the exhortation in 4:24 to "put on the new human" created in the likeness of the Divine.[68] Ephesians thus envisions

> the ultimate conflict between two armies, an army of believers under the headship of Christ and an army of malevolent entities under the leadership of the devil (4:27; 5:16; 6:11-12), locked in a conflict of global and cosmic proportions, a conflict fraught with political implications. Issues at stake here include spheres of power (1:20-22), influence (4:27), authority and allegiance.[69]

This picture of a global cosmic conflict energizes the whole narrative of the epistle.

The Summation of the Letter

Ephesians 6:10-20 not only sums up the hortatory section, 4:1–6:20, in general and 5:20–6:20 in particular; it also functions as peroration for the whole letter. The peroration, according to the rules of classical rhetoric, is the final part of a speech. It has two main purposes: to remind the audience of the arguments in the speech (*recapitulatio*) and especially also those that seek to influence their emotions (*affectus*). Both rhetorical goals are at work in the peroration of Ephesians 6:10-20.

Ephesians on the whole is a mystery story (Eph 1:9; 3:3, 9; 5:32; 6:19). The mystery consists in the information that in the fullness of time Messiah Jesus will become head of the cosmos, according to G*d's pre-determined plan (1:10). This mystery is progressively revealed to the apostles and prophets (3:3-4) and to the nations by the author, "Paul" (1:1; 3:1). It is "Paul" to whom the task to make known the stewardship of the mystery is given, so that the powers in heaven might know the multicolored Sophia-Wisdom of G*d whom Jewish writers understood to have been present at the creation of the cosmos (Prov 8:22-33; Wis 7:21 [LXX]).

This mystery had to become known in ever wider circles: apostles, prophets, the nations, the cosmic principalities and powers. According to this mystery, Messiah/Christ has been given to the *ekklēsia* as ultimate head over the cosmos.

Those who make up the *ekklēsia* are able to confront the cosmic principles and powers with G*d's cosmic wisdom (Eph 3:10), precisely be-

---

68. In Isaiah 59:17-21 and Wisdom 5:17-18a it is G*d who puts on such armor.
69. Lau, *The Politics of Peace*, 148.

cause human beings and the principalities and powers of the cosmos belong to the same lineage (*patria*), which goes back to G*d, their father (*patēr*).[70] However, Messiah Jesus' rule does not yet encompass the whole cosmos, only the *ekklēsia*. A similar limitation is found in the cosmic rulership of the Isis cult. Apuleius Madaurensis (ca. 124–170 CE) points out that "although Isis is the natural parent of all things and the mistress of all Elements, only for those who have been initiated into her mystery does she restrain the harmful course of the stars."[71] The *ekklēsia* is the space in which the power of Messiah Jesus has already been fully installed, whereas the cosmos is still in the process of being "filled" with it.

At Messiah Jesus' ascension the *ekklēsia* has been instituted in its cosmic ministry. The goal and purpose of installing ministers of the *ekklēsia* is the training of all its members so that it can engage in its cosmic task to "fill" the cosmos with the messianic fullness (4:15) and to grow up to its head, Jesus Messiah. "The interest of the author in filling the cosmos is to signify a process rather than an actual status."[72] Whereas Colossians understands the cosmos to be Messiah Jesus' body, according to Ephesians that body is the *ekklēsia*.

The *ekklēsia* is clearly understood in political terms as a commonwealth (*politeia*); its members are co-citizens, not strangers, relations who all belong to the household of G*d.[73] The Messianic fullness that already has "filled" the *ekklēsia* is now extending to the cosmos with the goal of filling it as well. According to the Stoic philosopher Dio Chrysostom (ca. 40 CE–ca. 115 CE) the cosmos is not only a living being but also a city. Yet citizenship does not encompass the whole cosmos but is given only to those who share in "reason and wise judgment." It pertains "to the father of Gods and humans," Zeus, to the city, the whole cosmos, the demons, and to rational human beings who are wise and prohibit ethnic strife.[74]

The armor of the *ekklēsia* consists in truth, peace, and the spoken word of G*d. However, it would be a mistake to see this as a spiritualization of the political. Rather, I would argue that the political language of Ephesians makes the spiritual political. This is an important feminist

70. George H. van Kooten, *Cosmic Christology in Paul and the Pauline School: Colossians and Ephesians in the Context of Graeco-Roman Cosmology, with a New Synopsis of the Greek Texts*, WUNT 2:171 (Tübingen: Mohr Siebeck, 2003), 175.

71. Apuleius, *Metamorphoses* 14.5.

72. van Kooten, *Cosmic Christology*, 189–90.

73. Ibid., 178.

74. Dio Chrysostom, *Oratio* 36.29-38.

insight because the struggle against kyriarchal relations of domination, dehumanization, and exploitation must be understood at one and the same time as both a political and a spiritual struggle if the *ekklēsia*, the democratic assembly of the wise, is to usher in the "new human."

Concluding Greetings (6:21-24)

These final greetings are seen either as part of the peroration concluding the section 5:15–6:20 or as closing words reworking the final greeting of Colossians and concluding the whole epistle.[75] Both letters use similar terminology when speaking of Tychicus. Moreover, since the instructions to the members of the household take up so much space in the preceding chapters, we can assume that the *ekklēsia* of the wise was probably a "house-*ekklēsia*" similar to that of Nympha, mentioned in Colossians 4:15. If the letter was sent to the Laodiceans, as some scholars argue, then this assumption becomes even more persuasive, since we know from Colossians of the house-*ekklēsia* of Nympha there.

The reference to Tychicus as the carrier of the letter in 6:21, which resembles his description in Colossians 4:7, makes this suggestion even more likely. I agree with Cynthia Briggs Kittredge that we do not need to assume that Nympha was a widow, as Margaret MacDonald argues, because no husband is mentioned.[76] Rather, we can assume that the household code's ethic of submission was developed because "the *ekklēsia* of the wise," consisting of wo/men, met in houses and might have been chaired by the *matrona* of the house, who could have been understood as representing G*d, the *matrona* of the universe. The house-*ekklēsia* of Prisca in Ephesus and the one of Nympha in Laodicea were trying to live their baptismal promise (see Gal 3:28) in the house-*ekklēsia*.

The wish of peace is given to the "brethren" (τοῖς ἀδελφοῖς), which the NRSV translates as "the whole community." Since it is clear from the long instruction to wives that the *ekklēsia* of the wise had wo/men in its midst, the greetings sent to the *adelphoi*-brethren can be understood in a twofold way: as generic or as gender specific. If the term "brethren" is used as a generic term it is inclusive of men and wo/men. Moreover,

75. Lincoln, *Ephesians*, 432.

76. Margaret Y. MacDonald, *Colossians and Ephesians*, SP 17 (Collegeville, MN: Liturgical Press, 2000), 188; see Cynthia Briggs Kittredge and Claire Miller Colombo, "Colossians," in *Philippians, Colossians, Philemon*, WCS 51 (Collegeville, MN: Liturgical Press, 2017).

Ephesians 6:21-24

[21]So that you also may know how I am and what I am doing, Tychicus will tell you everything. He is a dear brother and a faithful minister in the Lord. [22]I am sending him to you for this very purpose, to let you know how we are, and to encourage your hearts. [23]Peace be to the whole community, and love with faith, from God the Father and the Lord Jesus Christ. [24]Grace be with all who have an undying love for our Lord Jesus Christ.

the inclusive NRSV translation is preferable, because the letter is also addressed to all those who love "our *Kyrios*" Jesus Messiah in sincerity or incorruptibility (v. 24).

However, the meaning of "brethren," a term used only here in Ephesians, could also have been restricted in the mind of the author to men/males only. If this was the case then the wish of grace is addressed not to the whole community but only to the men in it, the brethren. Moreover, the inclusive translation and interpretation of "brethren" can be further challenged with the observation that the household code admonishes only freeborn men/husbands to love, whereas their wives are told to submit. Hence one wonders whether the sender really meant to address all the members of the community or only the "brethren" with the call to *agape*-love that permeates the whole epistle.[77]

In the introduction I referred to the work of Sarah Tanzer,[78] who, building on the work of Winsome Munro,[79] has argued that "the household code is a later addition to Ephesians, which builds on themes and language found in the text and yet takes them in a different direction."[80] While their proposal has not been widely accepted on historical grounds, I would like to advocate for its acceptance on hermeneutical-the*logical grounds.

If we read Ephesians with the lens of subordination/submission (5:22–6:9) as the "word of G*d," the letter's main theme of *agapē*-love becomes

---

77. For the argument that the theme of love permeates and shapes the whole letter, see the commentary of John Paul Heil, *Ephesians: Empowerment to Walk in Love for the Unity of All in Christ* (Atlanta: SBL Press, 2007).

78. Sarah J. Tanzer, "Ephesians," in Schüssler Fiorenza, ed., *Searching the Scriptures* 2:325–48.

79. Winsome Munro, "Col 3:18–4:1 and Eph 5:21–6:9: Evidence of a Late Literary Stratum?," *NTS* 18 (1972): 434–47.

80. Tanzer, "Ephesians," 340.

oppressive and kyriarchalized. Ephesians 5:22–6:9 thus becomes an outdated kyriarchal cultural text that has been the*logized for cultural-historical reasons with the goal of keeping freeborn and slave wo/men in their subordinate exploitative kyriarchal positions. In the 2016 US presidential election season a woman competed for the highest office in the nation, and we witnessed the negative cultural power this text still has today. If we do not reject the call to submission in Ephesians as a poison-text of kyriarchal culture we are not able to hear the rhetoric of love and equality that also permeates Ephesians. However, if we read Ephesians in terms of Divine Wisdom and *ekklēsia* we can reject the rhetoric of submission and obedience as a kyriarchal oppressive relic of imperial culture and domination and recover the letter's rhetoric of love and "divine fullness" as the central the*logical theme of Ephesians.

The feminist reader of Ephesians is left with this open question: Is the main call of Ephesians a call to love and peace, or is it a call for domination and subordination? Is it addressed to all of us, or only to the "brothers"? To read this letter's message of love, peace, and grace inclusively and to make it our own requires that we vehemently reject the author's call to subordination addressed to freeborn married and slave wo/men in the community of the wise. In the process we will re-discover G*d-*Matrona*, Divine Wisdom, whose love cares for the world and everyone in it.

Works Cited

Aasgaard, Reidar. *"My Beloved Brothers and Sisters!" Christian Siblingship in Paul.* JSNTSup 265. London: T&T Clark, 2004.

Atsuko, Usui. "Women's 'Experience' in New Religious Movements: The Case of Shinnyoen." *JJRS* 30 (2003): 217–42.

Bain, Katherine. *Women's Socioeconomic Status and Religious Leadership in Asia Minor: In the First Two Centuries CE.* Minneapolis: Fortress, 2014.

Balch, David. "Household Codes." In *Greco-Roman Literature and the New Testament: Selected Forms and Genres,* edited by David E. Aune, 25–50. Atlanta: Scholars Press, 1988.

———. "Neopythagorean Moralists and the New Testament Household Codes." In *ANRW* 2.26.1, edited by Hildegard Temporini and Wolfgang Haase, 380–411. Berlin: de Gruyter, 1992.

Barrett, Michelle. *The Politics of Truth: From Marx to Foucault.* Stanford: Stanford University Press, 1991.

Barth, Markus. *Ephesians 1–3.* AB 34. Garden City, NY: Doubleday, 1974.

———. *Ephesians 4–6.* AB 34A. Garden City, NY: Doubleday, 1974.

———. *The People of God.* Sheffield: JSOT Press, 1983.

Beattie, James. *The Theory of Language in Two Parts.* London: A. Strahan, T. Cadell, and W. Creech, 1788.

Belz, Lisa Marie. "The Rhetoric of Gender in the Household of God: Ephesians 5:21-33 and Its Place in Pauline Tradition." PhD diss., Loyola University Chicago, 2013.

Berger, Peter L., and Thomas Luckmann. *The Social Construction of Reality: A Treatise in the Sociology of Knowledge.* Garden City, NY: Doubleday, 1966.

Bernstein, Richard. "What Is the Difference That Makes a Difference? Gadamer, Habermas, and Rorty." In *Hermeneutics and Modern Philosophy,* edited by Brice R. Wachterhauser, 343–76. Albany: State University of New York Press, 1986.

Best, Ernest. *Ephesians: A Critical and Exegetical Commentary*. ICC. New York: T&T Clark, 1998.

Betz, Hans Dieter. *Galatians*. Hermeneia. Philadelphia: Fortress, 1979.

Boyarin, Daniel. *Border Lines: The Partition of Judaeo-Christianity*. Divinations. Philadelphia: University of Pennsylvania Press, 2004.

———. *The Jewish Gospels: The Story of the Jewish Christ*. New York: New Press, 2012.

Bradley, Keith. *Slavery and Rebellion in the Roman World, 140 BC to 70 BC*. Bloomington: Indiana University Press, 1989.

Brenner, Athalya. "Ruth as the Foreign Worker and the Politics of Exogamy." In *Ruth and Esther*, edited by Athalya Brenner. FCB, 2nd ser., 158–62. Sheffield: Sheffield Academic, 1999.

Briggs Kittredge, Cynthia. *Colossians*. WCS 51. Collegeville, MN: Liturgical Press, 2016.

———. *Community and Authority: The Rhetoric of Obedience in the Pauline Tradition*. HTS 45. Harrisburg, PA: Trinity Press International, 1998.

Brooten, Bernadette, ed. *Beyond Slavery: Overcoming Its Religious and Sexual Legacies*. New York: Macmillan, 2010.

Brooten, Bernadette. "Early Christian Enslaved Families: First to Fourth Century." In *Children and Family in Late Antiquity: Life, Death and Interaction*, edited by Christian Laes, Katariina Mustakallio, and Ville Vuolanto, 111–34. Leuven: Peeters, 2015.

———. "Junia . . . Outstanding among the Apostles." In *Women Priests: A Catholic Commentary on the Vatican Declaration*, edited by Leonard Swidler and Arlene Swidler, 141–44. New York: Paulist, 1977.

———. *Women Leaders in the Ancient Synagogue: Inscriptional Evidence and Background Issues*. BJS 36. Chico, CA: Scholars Press, 1982.

Brown, Raymond E. *The Semitic Background of the Term "Mystery" in the New Testament*. Philadelphia: Fortress, 1968.

Buckland, W. W. *The Roman Law of Slavery: The Condition of the Slave in Private Law from Augustus to Justinian*. Cambridge: Cambridge University Press, 1908.

Bunge, Gabriel. *The Rublev Trinity: The Icon of the Trinity by the Monk-Painter Andrei Rublev*. Crestwood, NY: St Vladimir's Seminary Press, 2007.

Caird, G. B. *Paul's Letters from Prison: Ephesians, Philippians, Colossians, Philemon*. Oxford: Oxford University Press, 1976.

Callahan, Allen Dwight. *Embassy of Onesimus: The Letter of Paul to Philemon*. The New Testament in Context. Valley Forge, PA: Trinity Press International, 1997.

———. "Paul's Epistle to Philemon: Towards an Alternative Interpretation." HTR 86 (1993): 357–76.

———. "Slave Resistance in Classical Antiquity." *Semeia* 83/84 (1998): 133–51.

Camp, Claudia V. *Wisdom and the Feminine in the Book of Proverbs*. BLS 14. Sheffield: Almond Press, 1985.

———. "Woman Wisdom: Bible." *The Jewish Women's Archive*. http://jwa.org /encyclopedia/article/woman-wisdom-bible. Accessed September 2016.

Carillo, Roxana. *Battered Dreams: Violence against Women as an Obstacle to Development*. New York: United Nations Development Fund for Women, 1992.

Christ, Carol P. "A Servant of All or a Lover of Life." Feminism and Religion, June 27, 2016. https://feminismandreligion.com/2016/06/27/shall-i-be-a-servant-to-all-or-shall-i-love-the-world-ever-more-deeply-by-carol-p-christ. Accessed September 2016.

Christ, Carol P., and Plaskow, Judith, eds. *Goddess and God in the World: Conversations in Embodied Theology*. Minneapolis: Fortress, 2017.

Chung, Hyun Kyung. *Struggle to Be the Sun Again: Introducing Asian Women's Theology*. Maryknoll, NY: Orbis Books, 1990.

Clarke, Thomas B. "What Is a Chiasm (or Chiasmus)? Definition and Explanation of the Chiastic Structure." http://bible-discernments.com/joshua/whatisachiasm.html. Accessed June 17, 2016.

Cohen, Shaye J. D. "Crossing the Boundaries and Becoming a Jew." *HTR* 82 (1989): 13–33.

———. "The Origins of the Matrilineal Principle in Rabbinic Law." *AJSR* 10 (1985): 19–53.

———. "The Rabbinic Conversion Ceremony." *JJS* 41 (1990): 177–203.

Cohick, Lynn H. *Ephesians*. Eugene, OR: Cascade Books, 2010.

Colson, Francis H., trans. *Philo: On the Contemplative Life*. Cambridge: Harvard University Press, 1941.

Crouch, James E. *The Origin and Intention of the Colossian Haustafel*. Göttingen: Vandenhoeck & Ruprecht, 1972.

Darko, Daniel D. *No Longer Living as the Gentiles: Differentiation and Shared Ethical Values in Ephesians 4.17–6.9*. London: T&T Clark, 2008.

de Beauvoir, Simone. "Woman as Other." In *The Second Sex*. https://www.marxists.org/reference/subject/ethics/de-beauvoir/2nd-sex/introduction.htm. Accessed September 2016.

Dibelius, Martin. *An Die Kolosser, Epheser und Philemon*. Edited by Huck Greeven. Tübingen: Mohr, 1953.

DuBois, Page. *Centaurs and Amazons: Women and the Pre-History of the Great Chain of Being*. Ann Arbor: University of Michigan Press, 1982.

Dunn, James D. G. "Anti-Semitism in the Deutero-Pauline Literature." In *Anti-Semitism and Early Christianity: Issues of Polemic and Faith*, edited by Craig A. Evans and Donald A. Hagner, 151–65. Minneapolis: Fortress, 1993.

Dunning, Benjamin H. "Strangers and Aliens No Longer: Negotiating Identity and Difference in Ephesians 2." *HTR* 99 (2006): 1–16.

Eisen, Ute. *Women Officeholders in Early Christianity: Epigraphical and Literary Studies*. Translated by Linda M. Maloney. Collegeville, MN: Liturgical Press, 2000.

Elliott, John. "The Jesus Movement Was Not Egalitarian but Family-Oriented." *BibInt* 11 (2003): 173–210.

Ellis, E. Earle. "Paul and His Co-Workers." *NTS* 17 (1971): 437–52.

Epp, Eldon J. *Junia: The First Woman Apostle*. Minneapolis: Fortress, 2005.

————. "Textual Criticism." In *The New Testament and Its Modern Interpreters*, edited by Eldon J. Epp and George W. MacRae, 75–126. Atlanta: Scholars Press, 1989.

Fabre-Serris, Jacqueline, and Alison Keith, eds. *Women and War in Antiquity*. Baltimore: Johns Hopkins University Press, 2015.

Faust, Eberhard. *Pax Christi et Pax Caesaris: Religionsgeschichtliche, Traditionsgeschichtliche und Sozialgeschichtliche Studien zum Epheserbrief*. Fribourg: Universitätsverlag, 1993.

Filson, Floyd V. "The Significance of the Early House Churches." *JBL* 58 (1939): 105–12.

Flannery, Austin, ed. *Vatican Council II: The Basic Sixteen Documents*. Northport, NY: Costello, 1996.

Fowl, Stephen E. *Ephesians: Being a Christian at Home and in the Cosmos*. Sheffield: Sheffield Phoenix, 2014.

Furstenberg, Yair. "The Shared Dimensions of Jewish and Christian Communal Identities." In *Jewish and Christian Communal Identities in the Roman World*, edited by Yair Furstenberg, 1–21. Boston: Brill, 2016.

Gadamer, Hans Georg. *Truth and Method* and *Philosophical Hermeneutics*. Berkeley: University of California Press, 1976.

Gamble, Harry Y. *The Textual History of the Letter to the Romans: A Study in Textual and Literary Criticism*. SD 42. Grand Rapids: Eerdmans, 1977.

Garnsey, Peter. *Ideas of Slavery from Aristotle to Augustine*. Cambridge: Cambridge University Press, 1996.

Getty, Mary Ann. "God's Fellow Worker and Apostleship." In *Women Priests: A Catholic Commentary on the Vatican Declaration*, edited by Leonard Swidler and Arlene Swidler, 176–82. New York: Paulist, 1977.

Gimbutas, Marija. *The Language of the Goddess: Unearthing the Hidden Symbols of Western Civilization*. San Francisco: Harper & Row, 1989.

Gnilka, Joachim. *Der Epheserbrief*. Freiburg: Herder, 1971.

Goettner-Abendroth, Heidi, ed. *Societies of Peace: Matriarchies Past, Present and Future; Selected Papers, First World Congress on Matriarchal Studies, 2003; Second World Congress on Matriarchal Studies, 2005*. Toronto: Inanna Publications, 2009.

Gombis, Timothy G. *The Drama of Ephesians: Participating in the Triumph of God*. Downers Grove, IL: InterVarsity Press, 2010.

————. "A Radically New Humanity: The Function of the *Haustafel* in Ephesians." *JETS* 48 (2005): 317–30.

Goppelt, Leonhard. "Jesus und die 'Haustafel'-Tradition." In *Orientierung an Jesus: zur Theologie der Synoptiker: für Josef Schmid*, edited by Paul Hoffman, 93–106. Freiburg: Herder, 1973.

Graham, R. W. "Women in the Pauline Churches: A Review Article." *LTQ* 11 (1976): 25–33.

Grant, Colin. "For the Love of God: Agape." *JRE* 24 (1996): 3–21.

Greene, Brian. *The Hidden Reality: Parallel Universes and the Deep Laws of the Cosmos*. New York: Knopf, 2011.

Ha, Yong-Jo. *Longing for Unity: An Exposition of Ephesians*. Seoul: Duranno Publishing, 1999.

Hanmer, Jalna, and Mary Maynard, eds. *Women, Violence, and Social Control*. London: Macmillan, 1987.

von Harnack, Adolf. "Probabilia über die Addresse und den Verfasser des Hebräerbriefes." *ZNW* 1 (1900): 16–41.

Harrill, J. Albert. "Ignatius, *Ad Polycarp* 4.3 and the Corporate Manumission of Christian Slaves." *JECS* 1 (1993): 103–42.

———. *The Manumission of Slaves in Early Christianity*. HUT. Tübingen: Mohr, 1995.

Heil, John Paul. *Ephesians: Empowerment to Walk in Love for the Unity of All in Christ*. Atlanta: SBL Press, 2007.

Heine, Ronald. *The Commentaries of Origen and Jerome on St Paul's Epistle to the Ephesians*. Oxford: Oxford University Press, 2002.

Hering, James P. *The Colossian and Ephesian Haustafeln in Theological Context*. New York: Lang, 2007.

Heyward, Carter. "Lamenting the Loss of Love: A Response to Colin Grant." *JRE* 24 (1996): 23–28.

Hinkelammert, Franz. *The Ideological Weapons of Death: A Theological Critique of Capitalism*. Maryknoll, NY: Orbis Books, 1986.

Hirsch, Emil G. "SHEOL (שאול)." http://www.jewishencyclopedia.com/articles/13563-sheol. Accessed June 17, 2016.

Hoehner, Harold W. *Ephesians: An Exegetical Commentary*. Grand Rapids: Baker Academic, 2002.

Hope, Valerie. "Status and Identity in the Roman World." In *Experiencing Rome: Culture, Identity, and Power in the Roman Empire*, edited by Janet Huskinson, 125–52. New York: Routledge, 2000.

Hoppe, Rudolf. "Ekklesiologie und Paränese im Epheserbrief (Eph 4:17–5:20)." In *Ethik als angewandte Ekklesiologie. Der Brief an die Epheser*, edited by Michael Wolter, 139–62. Rome: Benedictina, 2005.

Horrell, David. "From ἀδελφοί to οἶκος θεοῦ: Social Transformation in Pauline Christianity." *JBL* 120 (2001): 293–311.

———. "The Label Χριστιανός: 1 Peter 4:16 and the Formation of Christian Identity." *JBL* 126 (2007): 361–81.

Ichykoo. "Four Kinds of Love; Eros, Agape, Phileo & Storge." *Eros to Agape*, October 31, 2015. https://fromerostoagape.wordpress.com/2012/08/09/eros-romantic-love-and-agape-unconditional-love. Accessed June 17, 2016.

Isherwood, Lisa. "The Violence of Gender: Christian Marriage as a Test Case." In *Weep Not for Your Children: Essays on Religion and Violence*, edited by Lisa Isherwood and Rosemary Radford Ruether, 54–64. London: Equinox, 2008.

Jensen, Anne. *God's Self-Confident Daughters: Early Christianity and the Liberation of Women*. Translated by O. C. Dean. Louisville: Westminster John Knox, 1996.

John Paul II. *Man and Woman He Created Them: A Theology of the Body*. Boston: Pauline Books & Media, 2006.

————. *The Theology of the Body: Human Love in the Divine Plan.* Boston: Pauline Books & Media, 1997.

Jones, Ann. *Next Time She Will Be Dead.* Boston: Beacon, 1993.

Jones, Horace Leonard, trans. *The Geography of Strabo.* Vols. 1–7. LCL. Cambridge: Harvard University Press, 1917–1932.

Judge, Edwin A. *The Social Patterns of Christian Groups in the First Century: Some Prolegomena to the Study of New Testament Ideas of Social Organization.* London: Tyndale Press, 1960.

Käsemann, Ernst. *An die Römer.* HNT 8a. Göttingen: Vandenhoeck & Ruprecht, 1973.

Katafuchi, Miyoko. "Children's Bodies and Women's Bodies: Viewing Their Lives from the Discourse of Personal Health Care in the Edo Era" [in Japanese]. *Journal of Wakayama University* 63 (2013): 49–56.

Kee, Howard Clark. "Aretalogy and Gospel." *JBL* 92 (1973): 402–22.

Keener, Craig. "Women's Education and Public Speech in Antiquity." *JETS* 50 (2007): 747–50.

Kienast, Dietmar. "*Corpus Imperii.* Überlegungen zum Reichsgedanken der Römer." In *Romanitas, Christianitas: Untersuchungen zur Geschichte und Literatur der Römischen Kaiserzeit,* edited by Gerhard Wirth, et al., 1–17. Berlin: de Gruyter, 1982.

Kraemer, Ross S. "The Book of Aseneth." In *Searching the Scriptures.* Vol. 2: *A Feminist Commentary,* edited by Elisabeth Schüssler Fiorenza, 859–88. New York: Crossroad, 1994.

Lampe, Peter. "Keine Sklavenflucht des Onesimus." *ZNW* 76 (1985): 135–37.

Lau, Tet Li. *The Politics of Peace: Ephesians, Dio Chrysostom and the Confucian Four Books.* Leiden: Brill, 2010.

Lee, Jong-Yun. *An Exposition of Ephesians.* Seoul: Chung Hyun Publishing, 1991.

Lemaire, André. "From Services to Ministries: '*Diakoniai*' in the First Two Centuries." *Concilium* 14 (1972): 35–49.

————. "The Ministries in the New Testament: Recent Research." *BTB* 3 (1973): 133–66.

Leshem, Dotan. "What Did the Ancient Greeks Mean by Oikonomia?" *Journal of Economic Perspectives* 30 (2016): 225–31.

Liddell, Henry George, Robert Scott, Henry Stuart Jones, and Roderick McKenzie. *A Greek-English Lexicon.* Oxford: Oxford University Press, 1996.

Lieu, Judith. "Circumcision, Women, and Salvation." *NTS* 40 (1994): 358–70.

Lincoln, Andrew T. "The Church and Israel in Ephesians 2." *CBQ* 49 (1987): 605–24.

————. *Ephesians.* WBC 42. Dallas: Word, 1990.

Lohse, Eduard. *Colossians and Philemon.* Translated by William R. Poehlmann and Robert J. Karris. Hermeneia. Philadelphia: Fortress, 1971.

Lovejoy, Arthur A. *The Great Chain of Being: A Study of the History of an Idea.* Cambridge: Harvard University Press, 1936.

Lüdemann, Susannne. *Metaphern der Gesellschaft*. Munich: Fink, 2004.

Lührmann, Dieter. "Neutestamentliche Haustafeln und antike Ökonomie." *NTS* 27 (1980): 83–97.

———. "Wo man nicht mehr Sklave oder Freier ist. Überlegungen zur Struktur frühchristlicher Gemeinden." *WuD* 13 (1975): 53–83.

MacDonald, Margaret Y. "Beyond Identification of the *Topos* of Household Management: Reading the Household Codes in Light of Recent Methodologies and Theoretical Perspectives in the Study of the New Testament." *NTS* 57 (2011): 65–90.

———. "Can Nympha Rule This House? The Rhetoric of Domesticity in Colossians." In *Rhetoric and Reality in Early Christianity*, edited by Willi Braun, 99–120. Waterloo, ON: Wilfrid Laurier University Press, 2005.

———. *Colossians and Ephesians*. SP 17. Collegeville, MN: Liturgical Press, 2000.

———. "The Politics of Identity in Ephesians." *JSNT* 26 (2004): 419–44.

Maier, Harry O. *Picturing Paul in Empire: Imperial Image, Text and Persuasion in Colossians, Ephesians and the Pastoral Epistles*. London: Bloomsbury, 2013.

Malherbe, Abraham. "Hellenistic Moralists in the New Testament." In *ANRW* 2.26.1, edited by Hildegard Temporini and Wolfgang Haase, 267–333. Berlin: de Gruyter, 1992.

Markus, Robert A. "The Problem of Self-Definition: From Sect to Church." In *Jewish and Christian Self-Definition*. Vol. 1: *The Shaping of Christianity in the Second and Third Centuries*, edited by E. P. Sanders, 1–15. Philadelphia: Fortress, 1980.

Martin, Clarice J. "The *Haustafeln* (Household Codes) in African American Biblical Interpretation: 'Free Slaves' and 'Subordinate Women.'" In *Stony the Road We Trod: African American Biblical Interpretation*, edited by Cain Hope Felder, 206–31. Minneapolis: Fortress, 1991.

Martin, Dale B. *The Corinthian Body*. New Haven: Yale University Press, 1995.

———. "Slave Families and Slaves in Families." In *Early Christian Families in Context: An Interdisciplinary Dialogue*, edited by David L. Balch and Carolyn Osiek, 207–30. Grand Rapids: Eerdmans, 2003.

McKelvey, Robert J. *The New Temple: The Church in the New Testament*. Oxford: Oxford University Press, 1969.

Mellaart, James. *The Neolithic of the Near East*. New York: Scribners, 1975.

Miller, Anna C. *Corinthian Democracy: Democratic Discourse in 1 Corinthians*. Eugene, OR: Pickwick Publications, 2015.

Miller, Casey, and Kate Swift. *The Handbook of Nonsexist Writing for Writers, Editors, and Speakers*. New York: Barnes & Noble Books, 1980.

———. *Words and Women: New Language in New Times*. New York: Doubleday, 1977.

Miller, J. Mitchell. "Otherness." In *The SAGE Encyclopedia of Qualitative Research Methods*, edited by Lisa Given, 588–91. Thousand Oaks, CA: SAGE Publications, 2008.

Mitton, C. Leslie. *The Epistle to the Ephesians: Its Authorship, Origin and Purpose*. Oxford: Clarendon, 1951.

Moore, Michael S. " 'Wise Women' or Wisdom Woman? A Biblical Study of Women's Roles." *RQ* 35 (1993): 147–58.

Morton, Nelle. *The Journey Is Home*. Boston: Beacon, 1985.

Muddiman, John. *The Epistle to the Ephesians*. BNTC. London: Continuum, 2001.

Munro, Winsome. "Col 3:18–4:1 and Eph 5:21–6:9: Evidence of a Late Literary Stratum?" *NTS* 18 (1972): 434–47.

Nakashima Brock, Rita. "And a Little Child Will Lead Us: Christology and Child Abuse." In *Christianity, Patriarchy, and Abuse: A Feminist Critique*, edited by Joanne Carlson Brown and Carole R. Bohn, 42–61. New York: Pilgrim Press, 1989.

———. *Journeys by Heart: A Christology of Erotic Power*. New York: Crossroad, 1988.

Nakashima Brock, Rita, and Rebecca Ann Parker. *Proverbs of Ashes: Violence, Redemptive Suffering, and the Search for What Saves Us*. Boston: Beacon, 2001.

Nam, Seong-Soo. *An Exposition of Ephesians*. Seoul: Bookstone Publishing, 2014.

Nayak, Jessie Tellis. "Institutional Violence against Women in Different Cultures." *In God's Image* 8 (1989): 4–14.

The New Schaff-Herzog Encyclopedia of Religious Knowledge. Vol. 2. New York: Funk & Wagnalls, 1908–1912. http://www.bible-researcher.com/chapter-verse.html. Accessed June 17, 2016.

Novak, David. "The Covenant in Rabbinic Thought." In *Two Faiths, One Covenant? Jewish and Christian Identity in the Presence of the Other*, edited by Eugene B. Korn, 65–80. Lanham, MD: Rowman & Littlefield, 2004.

Nunberg, Geoff. "Everyone Uses Singular 'They,' Whether They Realize It or Not." NPR, January 13, 2016. http://www.npr.org/2016/01/13/462906419/everyone-uses-singular-they-whether-they-realize-it-or-not. Accessed June 07, 2016.

Nygren, Andres. *Agape and Eros: The Christian Idea of Love*. Translated by Philip S. Watson. Chicago: University of Chicago Press, 1953.

Öcalan, Abdullah. *Liberating Life: Woman's Revolution*. Translated by International Initiative. Cologne: International Initiative Edition; Neuss: Mesopotamian Publishers, 2013.

Okono, Haruko. "Weiblichkeitssymbolik und Sexismus in alten und neuen Religionen Japans." In *Japan: Ein Land der Frauen?*, edited by Elisabeth Gössmann, 217–42. Munich: Iudicium, 1991.

Olson, Kelly. "Matrona and Whore: The Clothing of Women in Roman Antiquity." *Fashion Theory: The Journal of Dress, Body and Culture* 6 (2002): 387–420.

Osiek, Carolyn. "The Bride of Christ (Ephesians 5:22-33): A Problematic Wedding." *BTB* 32 (2002): 29–39.

Osiek, Carolyn, and David L. Balch, eds. *Families in the New Testament World: Households and House Churches*. Louisville: Westminster John Knox, 1997.

Park, Chung-Ryun. *An Exposition of Ephesians: Abundant Grace and Guidance*. Seoul: Yebon Publishing, 1996.

Park, Young-Ho. *Paul's Ekklesia as a Civic Assembly: Understanding the People of God in Their Politico-Social World*. WUNT 2.393. Tübingen: Mohr Siebeck, 2015.

Patterson, Orlando. *Freedom in the Making of Western Culture*. New York: Basic
    Books, 1991.

Perkins, Pheme. *Ephesians*. ANTC. Nashville: Abingdon, 1997.

Peterson, Erik. "Christianus." In *Frühkirche, Judentum und Gnosis. Studien und
    Untersuchungen*, 64–87. Freiburg: Herder, 1959.

"Philosophy, Jewish." *Encyclopaedia Judaica*. https://www.jewishvirtuallibrary
    .org/jsource/judaica/ejud_0002_0016_0_15718.html. Accessed September
    2016.

Plaskow, Judith. "Anti-Judaism in Feminist Christian Interpretation." In *Searching
    the Scriptures*. Vol. 1: *A Feminist Introduction*, edited by Elisabeth Schüssler
    Fiorenza, 117–29. New York: Crossroad, 1993.

———. "Christian Feminism and Anti-Judaism." *Cross Currents* 33 (1978): 306–9.

Pomeroy, Sarah B., trans. *Xenophon, Oeconomicus: A Social and Historical Com-
    mentary*. Oxford: Clarendon, 1994.

Priests for Equality. *The Inclusive New Testament*. Hyattsville, MD: Quixote Cen-
    ter, 1994.

Raaflaub, Kurt. *Die Entdeckung der Freiheit. Zur historischen Semantik und Gesell-
    schaftsgeschichte eines politischen Grundbegriffes der Griechen*. Munich: Beck,
    1985.

Radford, Jill, and Diana E. H. Russell. *Femicide: The Politics of Woman Killing*. New
    York: Twayne Publishers, 1992.

Redding, Ann Holmes. "Together, Not Equal: The Rhetoric of Unity and Head-
    ship in the Letter to the Ephesians." PhD diss., Union Theological Semi-
    nary, 1999.

Redmond, Sheila. "Christian 'Virtues' and Recovery from Child Sexual Abuse."
    In *Christianity, Patriarchy, and Abuse: A Feminist Critique*, edited by Joanne
    Carlson Brown and Carole R. Bohn, 70–88. New York: Pilgrim Press, 1989.

Reicke, Bo. "*Prohistemi*." TDNT 6:703.

Reinmuth, Eckhart. *Neues Testament, Theologie und Gesellschaft*. Stuttgart: Kohl-
    hammer, 2011.

Ricoeur, Paul. *Hermeneutics and the Human Sciences: Essays on Language, Action,
    and Interpretation*. Translated by John B. Thompson. Cambridge: Cambridge
    University Press, 1981.

Rogers, Cleon L., Jr. "The Dionysian Background of Ephesians 5:18." *BibSac* 136
    (1979): 249–57.

Roitto, Rikard. *Behaving as a Christ Believer: A Cognitive Perspective on Identity and
    Behavior Norms in Ephesians*. ConBNT 46. Winona Lake, IN: Eisenbrauns,
    2011.

Roose, Hannah. "Die Hierarchisierung der Leib-Metapher im Kolosser- und
    Epheserbrief als 'Paulinisierung': Ein Beitrag zur Rezeption Paulinischer
    Tradition in Pseudo-Paulinischen Briefen." *NovT* 47 (2005): 117–41.

Rudolph, David, and Joel Willetts, eds. *Introduction to Messianic Judaism: Its
    Ecclesial Context and Biblical Foundations*. Grand Rapids: Zondervan, 2013.

Ryu, Ung-Ryul. *Preaching Ephesians According to the Ten-Step Method of Writing*. Seoul: Duranno Academy, 2010.

Sampley, Paul. *"And the Two Shall Become One Flesh": A Study of Traditions in Ephesians 5:21-33*. SNTSMS 16. Cambridge: Cambridge University Press, 1971.

Schäfer, Klaus. *Gemeinde als "Bruderschaft": Ein Beitrag zum Kirchenverständnis des Paulus*. Frankfurt am Main: Lang, 1989.

Schelkle, Karl Hermann. "Ministry and Ministers in the New Testament Church." *Concilium* 11 (1969): 5–11.

Schlesinger, Louis B. *Sexual Murder: Catathymic and Compulsive Homicides*. Boca Raton, FL: CRC Press, 2004.

Schlier, Heinrich. *Der Brief an die Epheser*. Düsseldorf: Patmos, 1957.

———. *"Kephalē."* TDNT 3:673–82.

Schnackenburg, Rudolf. *Ephesians: A Commentary*. Translated by Helen Heron. Edinburgh: T&T Clark, 1991.

Schroeder, David. "Die Haustafeln des Neuen Testaments: Ihre Herkunft und ihr theologischer Sinn." PhD diss., Hamburg, 1959.

Schuler, Margaret, ed. *Freedom from Violence: Women's Strategies from Around the World*. New York: United Nations Development Fund for Women, 1992.

Schüssler Fiorenza, Elisabeth. *1 Peter: Reading against the Grain*. Sheffield: Sheffield Phoenix, 2015.

———. *Bread Not Stone: The Challenge of Feminist Biblical Interpretation*. Boston: Beacon, 1984.

———. *But She Said: Feminist Practices of Biblical Interpretation*. Boston: Beacon, 1992.

———. *Changing Horizons: Explorations in Feminist Interpretation*. Minneapolis: Fortress, 2013.

———. *Congress of Wo/men: Religion, Gender and Kyriarchal Power*. Cambridge: FSR Books, 2016.

———. "Cultic Language in Qumran and in the New Testament." *CBQ* 38 (1976): 159–79.

———. *Empowering Memory and Movement: Thinking and Working across Borders*. Minneapolis: Fortress, 2014.

———.*"En la senda de Sofía": Hermenéutica feminista crítica para la liberación*. Translated by Severino Croatto and Cristina Conti. Buenos Aires: Lumen-Isedet, 2003.

———. *In Memory of Her: A Feminist Theological Reconstruction of Christian Origins*. New York: Crossroad, 1994.

———. *Jesus: Miriam's Child, Sophia's Prophet; Critical Issues in Feminist Christology*. New York: Continuum, 1994.

———. *Los Caminos de la Sabiduría. Una Introducción a la Interpretación feminista de la Biblia*. Translated by José Manuel Lozano Gotor. Santander: Sal Terrae, 2004.

———. *The Power of the Word: Scripture and the Rhetoric of Empire*. Minneapolis: Fortress, 2007.

———. *Rhetoric and Ethic: The Politics of Biblical Studies*. Minneapolis: Fortress, 1999.

———. "Slave Wo/men and Freedom: Some Methodological Reflections." In *Empowering Memory and Movement: Thinking and Working across Borders*, 447–70. Minneapolis: Fortress, 2014.

———. *Transforming Vision: Explorations in Feminist The*logy*. Minneapolis: Fortress, 2011.

———. *Wisdom Ways: Introducing Feminist Biblical Interpretation*. Maryknoll, NY: Orbis Books, 2001.

Seaford, R. A. S. "The Mysteries of Dionysos at Pompeii." http://www.stoa.org/diotima/essays/seaford.shtml. Accessed August 2016.

Shange, Ntozake. "With No Immediate Cause." In *Nappy Edges*, 114–17. New York: St. Martin's Press, 1972.

Smith, Jonathan Z. "Good News Is No News: Aretalogy and Gospel." In *Christianity, Judaism and other Greco-Roman Cults: Studies for Morton Smith at Sixty*, 4 vols., edited by Jacob Neusner, 21–38. SJLA 12. Leiden: Brill, 1975.

Smith, Morton. "Prolegomena to a Discussion of Aretalogies, Divine Men, the Gospels, and Jesus." *JBL* 90 (1971): 174–99.

Soodalter, Ron. "A Blight on the Nation: Slavery in Today's America." In *Quests for Freedom: Biblical—Historical—Contemporary*, edited by Michael Welker, 21–31. Neukirchen Vluyn: Neukirchener Verlag, 2015.

Spicq, Ceslas. *Theological Lexicon of the New Testament*. Translated and edited by James D. Ernest. Peabody, MA: Hendrickson, 1994.

Standhartinger, Angela. "The Epistle to the Congregation in Colossae and the Invention of the 'Household Code.'" In *A Feminist Companion to the Deutero-Pauline Epistles*, edited by Amy-Jill Levine and Marianne Blickenstaff, 88–97. FCB 7. New York: T&T Clark, 2003.

Stowers, Stanley K. "Paul and Slavery: A Response." *Semeia* 83/84 (1998): 295–311.

Strelan, Rick. *Paul, Artemis, and the Jews in Ephesus*. BZNW 80. Berlin: de Gruyter, 1996.

Strobel, Regula. "Der Beihilfe beschuldigt. Christliche Theologie auf der Anklagebank." *Fama. Feministisch Theologische Zeitschrift* 9 (1993): 3–6.

———. "New Ways of Speaking about the Cross: A New Basis for Christian Identity." In *Toward a New Heaven and a New Earth: Essays in Honor of Elisabeth Schüssler Fiorenza*, edited by Fernando F. Segovia, 351–68. Maryknoll, NY: Orbis Books, 2003.

Syme, Ronald. *The Roman Revolution*. Oxford: Oxford University Press, 1939.

Tannen, Deborah. "The Self-Fulfilling Prophecy of Disliking Hillary Clinton." *Time*. March 15, 2016.

Tanzer, Sarah J. "Ephesians." In *Searching the Scriptures*. Vol. 2: *A Feminist Commentary*, edited by Elisabeth Schüssler Fiorenza, 328–32. New York: Crossroad, 1994.

Taylor, Joan E. *Jewish Women Philosophers of First-Century Alexandria: Philo's "Therapeutae" Reconsidered*. Oxford: Oxford University Press, 2003.

————. "The Women 'Priests' of Philo's *De Vita Contemplativa*: Reconstructing the Therapeutae." In *On the Cutting Edge: The Study of Women in Biblical Worlds*, edited by Jane Schaberg, Alice Bach, and Esther Fuchs, 102–22. New York: Continuum, 2004.

Taylor, Joan E., and Philip R. Davies. "The So-Called Therapeutae of *De Vita Contemplativa*: Identity and Character." *HTR* 91 (1998): 3–24.

Thistlethwaite, Susan Brooks. "Every Two Minutes: Battered Women and Feminist Interpretation." In *Weaving the Visions: New Patterns in Feminist Spirituality*, edited by Judith Plaskow and Carol P. Christ, 302–13. San Francisco: Harper & Row, 1989.

Thomas, W. Derek. "The Place of Women in the Church at Philippi." *ExpTim* 83 (1972): 117–20.

Thomason, Steve. "Thketch of *Democratizing Biblical Studies* by Elizabeth [*sic*] Schüssler Fiorenza." YouTube, 2012. https://www.youtube.com/watch?v=AEwyT21tAG8. Accessed September 4, 2016.

Thraede, Klaus. "Zum historischen Hintergrund der Haustafeln des NT." In *Pietas: Festschrift Für Bernhard Kötting*, edited by Ernst Dassmann and Karl Suso Frank, 359–68. *JAC* 8. Münster: Aschendorff, 1980.

Trevett, Christina. *Christian Women and the Time of the Apostolic Fathers: AD c.80–160; Corinth, Rome and Asia Minor*. Cardiff: University of Wales Press, 2006.

Vacek, Edward Collins. "Love, Christian and Diverse: A Response to Colin Grant." *JRE* 24 (1996): 29–34.

van Kooten, George H. *Cosmic Christology in Paul and the Pauline School: Colossians and Ephesians in the Context of Graeco-Roman Cosmology, with a New Synopsis of the Greek Texts*. WUNT 2:171. Tübingen: Mohr Siebeck, 2003.

Walzer, Michael. "On the Role of Symbolism in Political Thought." *PSQ* 82 (1967): 191–204.

Wassen, Cecilia. *Women in the Damascus Document*. AcBib 21. Atlanta: SBL Press, 2005.

Weidinger, Karl. *Die Haustafeln. Ein Stück urchristlicher Paränese*. UNT 14. Leipzig: Hinrichs, 1928.

Wink, Walter. *Engaging the Powers: Discernment and Resistance in a World of Domination*. Minneapolis: Fortress, 1992.

————. *Naming the Powers: The Language of Power in the New Testament*. Philadelphia: Fortress, 1984.

Winter, Sarah C. "Philemon." In *Searching the Scriptures*. Vol. 2: *A Feminist Commentary*, edited by Elisabeth Schüssler Fiorenza, 301–12. New York: Crossroad, 1994.

Wire, Antoinette Clark. "Review Essay on Elliott, *Home for the Homeless*, and Balch, *Let Wives Be Submissive*." *RSR* 10 (1984): 209–16.

Witt, R. E. *Isis in the Ancient World*. Baltimore: Johns Hopkins University Press, 1997.

"Word of the Year Is Singular 'They.'" *American Dialect Society*, January 8, 2015. http://www.americandialect.org/2015-word-of-the-year-is-singular-they. Accessed June 7, 2016.

Yamaguchi, Satoko. "Father Image of G*d and Inclusive Language: A Reflection in Japan." In *Toward a New Heaven and a New Earth: Essays in Honor of Elisabeth Schüssler Fiorenza*, edited by Fernando F. Segovia, 199–224. Maryknoll, NY: Orbis Books, 2003.

Yee, Tet-Lim N. *Jews, Gentiles and Ethnic Reconciliation: Paul's Jewish Identity and Ephesians*. SNTSMS 130. Cambridge: Cambridge University Press, 2005.

Young, Kate, Carol Wolkowitz, and Roslyn McGullagh. *Of Marriage and the Market: Women's Subordination in International Perspective*. London: CSE Books, 1981.

Index of Scripture References and Other Ancient Writings

Index of Subjects

General Editor

Barbara E. Reid, OP, is a Dominican Sister of Grand Rapids, Michigan. She holds a PhD in biblical studies from The Catholic University of America and is vice president and academic dean and professor of New Testament studies at Catholic Theological Union, Chicago. Her most recent publications are *Wisdom's Feast: An Invitation to Feminist Interpretation of the Scriptures* (2016) and *Abiding Word: Sunday Reflections on Year A, B, C* (3 vols.; 2011, 2012, 2013). She served as president of the Catholic Biblical Association in 2014–2015.

Volume Editor

Linda M. Maloney, PhD, ThD, is a native of Houston, Texas. She studied at St. Louis University (BA, MA, PhD), the University of South Carolina (MIBS), and Eberhard-Karls-Universität Tübingen, where she earned her ThD in New Testament in 1990 under the direction of Prof. Gerhard Lohfink. She has taught at public and private colleges, universities, and seminaries in the United States and was academic editor at Liturgical Press from 1995 to 2005. She is a priest of the Episcopal Church (USA) and lives in Vermont and California.

Author

Elisabeth Schüssler Fiorenza, Krister Stendahl Professor at Harvard University Divinity School, is an internationally known biblical scholar and path-breaking feminist intellectual. She has done pioneering work in biblical interpretation and feminist theology. Dr. Schüssler Fiorenza's teaching and research focus on questions of biblical and theological hermeneutics, ethics, rhetoric, and the politics of interpretation, and on issues of the*logical education, diversity, and democracy. She is the co-founding senior editor of the *Journal of Feminist Studies in Religion*, was the first woman president of the Society of Biblical Literature, and was elected a member to the American Academy of Arts and Sciences in 2001. Her landmark work, *In Memory of Her*, has become a classic in biblical studies.